Exploring the Lives of Women 1558–1837

Exploring the Lives of Women 1558–1837

Principal Editors:

Louise Duckling
Sara Read
Felicity Roberts
Carolyn D. Williams

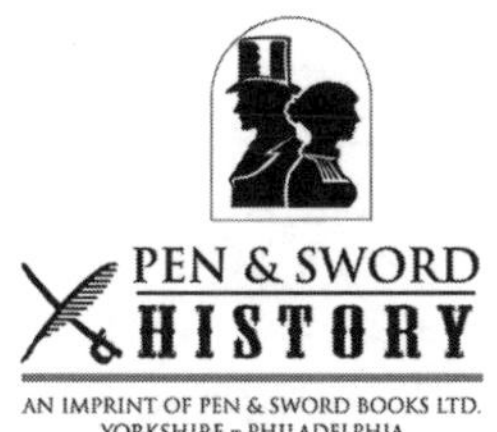

AN IMPRINT OF PEN & SWORD BOOKS LTD.
YORKSHIRE – PHILADELPHIA

First published in Great Britain in 2018 by
Pen & Sword History
An imprint of
Pen & Sword Books Ltd
Yorkshire - Philadelphia

Hardback ISBN 978 1 52674 497 5
Paperback ISBN 978 1 52675 139 3

A CIP catalogue record for this book is available from the British Library.

Printed and bound in England by TJ International Ltd.

Pen & Sword Books Ltd incorporates the Imprints of Pen & Sword Books Archaeology, Atlas, Aviation, Battleground, Discovery, Family History, History, Maritime, Military, Naval, Politics, Railways, Select, Transport, True Crime, Fiction, Frontline Books, Leo Cooper, Praetorian Press, Seaforth Publishing, Wharncliffe and White Owl.

For a complete list of Pen & Sword titles please contact

PEN & SWORD BOOKS LIMITED
47 Church Street, Barnsley, South Yorkshire, S70 2AS, England
E-mail: enquiries@pen-and-sword.co.uk
Website: www.pen-and-sword.co.uk

or

PEN AND SWORD BOOKS
1950 Lawrence Rd, Havertown, PA 19083, USA
E-mail: uspen-and-sword@casematepublishers.com
Website: www.penandswordbooks.com

Contents

List of Contributors

Louise Duckling is an independent scholar working on eighteenth-century women writers and their posthumous reputations. She has previously co-edited *Woman to Woman: Female Negotiations in the Long Eighteenth Century*, with Carolyn D. Williams and Angela Escott (University of Delaware Press, 2010).

Marion Durnin is an editor and author whose focus is the work of Anglo-Irish women writers. She edited a critical edition of *Sketches of Irish Character by Mrs S. C. Hall (1800-1881)* in the Chawton House Library Series (Pickering and Chatto, 2014) and contributed (with Jarlath Killeen) to *Children's Literature Collections: Approaches to Research* (Palgrave, 2017).

Jennifer Evans is a Senior Lecturer in History at the University of Hertfordshire. Her first monograph, *Aphrodisiacs, Fertility and Medicine*, was published in 2014. She has published articles on the history of infertility and miscarriage. She is currently working on a project exploring men's sexual health in the seventeenth century. She has also co-authored a popular history book, *Maladies and Medicine* (Pen and Sword, 2017).

Tabitha Kenlon is an Assistant Professor of English at the American University in Dubai. Her work focuses on eighteenth-century English novels, plays, and conduct manuals, with a particular emphasis on women writers and characters. Her forthcoming book, *Woman As She Should Be: A History of Conduct Books*, will be published next year by Anthem Press.

Jacqueline Mulhallen is an actor, playwright, poet and author of *The Theatre of Shelley* (Openbooks, 2010) and *Percy Bysshe Shelley: Poet and Revolutionary* (Pluto Press, 2015). She contributed to the *Oxford Handbook of the Georgian Theatre* (2014). She is currently touring in her play *Sylvia* for Lynx Theatre and Poetry.

Marie Mulvey-Roberts is Professor of English Literature at the University of the West of England, Bristol. She is editor and co-founder of the quarterly journal *Women's Writing*. Her publications include *Global Frankenstein* (ed. with Carol Margaret Davison, 2018), *Dangerous Bodies: Historicising the Gothic Corporeal* (2016), winner of the Alan Lloyd Smith Memorial Prize, and *Literary Bristol: Writers and the City* (2015).

Yvonne Noble is a scholar in eighteenth-century studies and has published articles on John Gay and Anne Finch, Countess of Winchilsea. She has taught at the University of Pennsylvania and New York University and has been tenured at the University of Illinois in Urbana-Champaign. She is a founder member of the Women's Studies Group, 1558-1837.

Sarah Oliver is an independent scholar living in Exeter, UK. She worked as an Associate Lecturer with the Open University, and is now retired. Sarah's interests are eighteenth-century women's writing, particularly rape themes, Mary Hays and radical writers. She is currently co-writing a novel set in the eighteenth century.

Julie Peakman is a Fellow of the Royal Historical Society and Honorary Fellow at Birkbeck College, University of London. Her books include *Amatory Pleasures: Explorations in Eighteenth-Century Sexual Culture* (Bloomsbury, 2016); *The Pleasure's All Mine: A History of Perverse Sex* (Reaktion, 2013), and *Lascivious Bodies: A Sexual History of the Eighteenth Century* (London, Atlantic Books, 2004). She is the author of *Peg Plunkett: Memoirs of A Whore* (Quercus, 2015), and contributor of numerous articles to various books and academic journals.

Peter Radford was Titular Professor at Glasgow University, and Professor of Sport Sciences at Brunel University. He has a particular interest in seventeenth and eighteenth-century sport and the sporting performances and physical capabilities of women in the long eighteenth century. As an athlete he set world records and won Olympic medals in the sprint events.

Sara Read is a Lecturer in English at Loughborough University. She specialises in literary and cultural representations of women's lives and reproductive health in the early modern era. Her publications include *Menstruation and the Female Body in Early Modern England* (Palgrave, 2013). She has produced two previous volumes for Pen and Sword: *Maids, Wives, Widows* (2015) and *Maladies and Medicine* (with Jennifer Evans, 2017).

Felicity Roberts is a member of the Women's Studies Group, 1558-1837, organising committee. She has a particular interest in the connections between natural history, literature, gender and material culture and has published on Mary Delany's botanical collages and manuscript novella.

Brianna E. Robertson-Kirkland is a Lecturer of Historical Musicology at the Royal Conservatoire of Scotland and is the music research associate for the AHRC-funded project 'The Collected Works of Allan Ramsay'. She has a keen interest in eighteenth-century female musicians, and co-organised the 'Women and Education in the Long Eighteenth Century' workshop, which inspired a special issue of *Women's History: Journal of the Women's History Network* (Spring, 2018).

Valerie Schutte is author of *Mary I and the Art of Book Dedications: Royal Women, Power, and Persuasion* (Palgrave, 2015). She has published several essays and has edited four collections on royal women, including *The Birth of a Queen: Essays on the Quincentenary of Mary I* (Palgrave, 2016), the Tudor dynasty, books, and Shakespeare.

Carolyn D. Williams is an Honorary Fellow at the Early Modern Research Centre, University of Reading. Her publications include *Pope, Homer and Manliness: Some Aspects of Eighteenth-Century Classical Learning* (Routledge, reprinted 2014) and *Boudica and Her Stories: Narrative Transformations of a Warrior Queen* (University of Delaware Press, 2009).

Gillian Williamson is currently an Honorary Research Fellow at Birkbeck College, University of London. She read Classics as an undergraduate at Cambridge at the conventional age and received an MA and PhD in History from Birkbeck, as a mature student, resulting in her first monograph, *British Masculinity in the Gentleman's Magazine, 1731-1815* (Palgrave, 2016).

List of Illustrations

A poster for the Prince of Wales' birthday celebrations in Brighton in 1789. (*Photograph (c) Peter Radford, poster in his personal collection*)

Detail from the poster showing the age classes and prizes for the ladies' foot-race. (*Photograph (c) Peter Radford*)

A detail from 'A Village Scene with Girls Spinning', by Thomas Rowlandson (1756-1827). (*Yale Center for British Art, Paul Mellon Collection*)

'Women coal bearers.' (*Wellcome Collection*)

'It is very dangerous to be under a load.' Report of the Children's Employment Commission, 1842. (*British Library, Shelfmark 1509/353*)

Frontisplate to *A Cyclopaedia of Female Biography* edited by H.G. Adams (1866).

Mrs S.C. Hall. Drawn by Daniel Maclise R.A. in 1830 and engraved by Lumb Stocks R.A. (*Open Library, OL5652855W*)

'A Change for the Better' by Sir Joseph Swain, after Sir John Tenniel. (*Punch, 31 July 1869*)

Preface

Women's Studies Group, 1558–1837: Exploring the Lives of Women Since 1987

The purpose of this book is to celebrate the thirtieth anniversary of the Women's Studies Group, 1558–1837, an informal, multidisciplinary organization formed to promote women's studies in the early modern period and long eighteenth century. The Women's Studies Group, commonly known as WSG, was founded by academics; however, membership of the group has always been open to anyone with an interest in women and gender studies. The inclusive, supportive and friendly environment nurtured by WSG has enabled the group and its members to creatively explore women's lives in history and expand knowledge in the field. The fact that the group has survived and thrived for thirty years is testament to the intellectual generosity and enthusiasm of its members.

Neither the group's remit nor its membership is restricted to women. Our regular seminars and annual workshop, held in London, welcome discussion of anything that affects or is affected by women in this period, and the wider histories of gender and sexuality are embraced. While some scholars have begun to redress centuries of historical and critical neglect by concentrating on women, others have directed their attention to the interplay of masculine and feminine influences in the world where these women lived. Those attending WSG's events will therefore discover a wide variety of material and approaches; one constant, however, is the sense of community and companionship.

Women's Studies Group, 1558–1837: A Brief History

WSG was founded by Yvonne Noble to create a collegial environment for those who found themselves isolated or working outside mainstream academia. At a gathering of the British Society for Eighteenth-Century Studies (BSECS), Yvonne called for a pilot meeting to explore the possibility of a group for women's studies. Nineteen women attended the inaugural meeting on 7 January 1987, including our editor Carolyn D. Williams, and Jean Bloch, who interceded to arrange meeting rooms at the University of London's

Senate House. Initially, the group held bi-monthly meetings and organized several Day Schools on different themes. For example, Marilyn Brooks, with Yvonne's encouragement and administrative help, held a regional Day School in Cambridge entitled 'Appropriations of Power'. Of these early meetings, Yvonne's favourite was a two-day event on 'Liminality', featuring Shakespearean boy actors, the coming of actresses to the Restoration stage, hermaphrodites and castrati.

Under Yvonne's management, the group enjoyed rapid growth. It became actively involved in the annual conferences, beginning in 1988, of BSECS. The group's own events featured pioneering work by many renowned scholars, including Dame Olwen Hufton, and Professors Elaine Hobby and Janet Todd. As Isobel Grundy explains, WSG was created 'at a time of great intellectual excitement, with a gathering of extraordinarily able scholars', when the process of exploring women's historical lives was in its infancy. To illustrate this point, when Olwen Hufton delivered a BSECS-linked talk on women in the French Revolution, the WSG newsletter sharply observed that it seemed to be about a different revolution from the one mentioned elsewhere at the conference, which had clearly 'taken place in a country and century in which no woman seemed to have been alive!' Isobel describes how 'those were heady times, because we stood on the brink of exploring and coming to know a whole field of … women's history and writing.'

By 1989 WSG had members in nineteen countries. In August of that year, Yvonne was offered a year's teaching at New York University and, in her absence, WSG collapsed. Yet the importance of the group to its individual members was already deeply entrenched and it would experience two major reincarnations. The first revival was instigated by Lois Chaber, who valued 'the friendly, non-competitive atmosphere of the group'. Lois recalls how she convened a meeting at her home to re-launch WSG in a more sustainable format, with an organizing committee. As Yvonne has noted, WSG's continued existence has been 'sustained by the improvisatory efforts of members without institutional support'. According to Marie Mulvey-Roberts, it was the 'energy and drive of members' that 'created the right sort of climate' for her to co-found the journal *Women's Writing* with Janet Todd. In Janet's estimation, WSG member Mary Waldron served *Women's Writing* as an 'excellent' Reviews Editor and 'also edited one of our best ever issues' on Jane Austen. WSG has continued its association with the journal and, fittingly, guest-edited a special issue in memory of Mary Waldron in 2010.[1]

The second major revival of the group came in the early 2000s with a revised programme of activities and the introduction of an online presence. Sarah Oliver and Victoria Joule were key committee members during this time, simultaneously organizing the annual workshops and serving as treasurers. They described taking on these roles as a 'privilege', despite a low point in which they struggled to 'convince the bank … we were bona fide members of the WSG!' The group continues to evolve. Bursaries are now offered annually to early career researchers and independent scholars. Angela Escott has found a new and extremely congenial meeting venue for the group at the Foundling Museum, London. WSG has re-established its presence at the BSECS annual conference, thanks to Yvonne Noble's energy and Carolyn D. Williams' ability to recruit speakers. Carolyn has also been instrumental in guiding WSG towards publication, as she conceived the original idea for our previous book celebrating female collaboration, *Woman to Woman: Female Negotiations During the Long Eighteenth Century*, and again took a leading role in the present edition when Sara Read initially proposed a volume to mark this important anniversary.[2]

In the words of Marie Mulvey-Roberts, the founding of WSG was both 'timely and inspirational'. In the early days, Marie had introduced Marilyn Brooks to the 'welcoming and encouraging atmosphere' of the group. Many years later, on her retirement to France in 2000, Marilyn describes how she felt 'geographically and psychologically isolated' and returned to WSG for 'nurturing support'. The Women's Studies Group will no doubt experience further change in the years to come but, with the dedication and loyalty of its members, it will continue to offer valued opportunities for collaboration and conviviality. To quote Marilyn Brooks once again: 'Thank you Yvonne for the vision and thank you all for fulfilling it.'

About this Book

A key editorial objective of this book has been to capture in print the essential qualities of the Women's Studies Group, 1558–1837. Each chapter is therefore intellectually rigorous, but accessible. The book is arranged in chronological order, but the chapters are designed to stand alone so the reader can choose to approach them in any sequence. While the topics covered are wide-ranging in terms of chronology and theme, there is also cohesiveness and synergy – ever present in the group's activities – and readers will quickly spot the connections and interactions within the volume. One significant connection is of particular relevance to the editorial team: within this book you will encounter a number of Elizas, ranging from 'Good Queen Bess' to the novelist Eliza Haywood and actress Eliza O'Neill. While we worked on this volume, their ranks were swelled by another, Eliza Read, born on 9 March 2018. As WSG enters its fourth decade, we hope this book may inspire its present readers – and, in the future, inspire the latest Eliza's generation – to continue exploring the lives of women in history. Indeed, proceeds from this book will be used towards the funding of our bursary scheme to help this ambition become a reality. Beyond this book's pages, there is still much to be discovered in the archives. For those wishing to join WSG on the journey, come and find out more at www.womensstudiesgroup.org.

Acknowledgements

We would like to thank Heather Williams and the team at Pen & Sword Books for accepting our proposal and enabling us to celebrate our thirtieth anniversary in print. We are grateful to all our contributors for their diverse and fascinating chapters. The book has benefited from the insights provided by our excellent readers who generously volunteered their time and energy to review the work in progress. We applaud the following scholars for their expert advice and support: Susan Civale, Li-ching Chen, Angela Escott, Loraine Fletcher and Gina Luria Walker. We owe a great deal to the many institutions that have made part or all of their digital image collections freely available online. Our plates section has been further enriched by Chloe Victoria Howard, who hunted down and photographed a monument in York Minster, and Rachel Adcock, who created the wonderful illustration depicting the Witch of Newbury. Louise Duckling, Angela Escott and Peter Radford kindly gave their permission for us to reproduce print material from their personal collections. The co-editors would also like to take this opportunity to record their thanks to one another for bringing this volume together with the collegiality and good humour that exemplifies the best traditions of the WSG, and to express in particular our gratitude to Carolyn for her expertise, diligence and patience.

We would also like to thank our members for sharing their memories of the Women's Studies Group, which combine to form the historical account in this preface. Reminiscences and factual details were supplied by Marilyn L. Brooks, Lois Chaber, Isobel Grundy, Yvonne Noble, Victoria Joule and Sarah Oliver. Recollections also emerged from Marie Mulvey-Roberts' conversation with Janet Todd, and Sara Read's with Elaine Hobby. These memoirs and interviews have been published in full on our website. They are worth consulting, not only for their entertaining accounts of the group, but also for the light they shed on the careers of individual women scholars and the wider history of the field of women's studies.

Finally, we are indebted to everyone who has supported the Women's Studies Group during its thirty-year history and helped to shape the group's spirit and ethos. This spirit is exemplified by long-term member Marion Durnin in her generosity, humour and intelligence: this volume is dedicated to Marion, with our gratitude.

Introduction

by Carolyn D. Williams

The celebration of a thirtieth anniversary is self-explanatory. The attainment of any round number is an achievement, but the thirtieth year has a particularly organic appeal, because it measures a generation. Members of the Women's Studies Group, 1558-1837, are justified in applauding the survival, not to say the expansion, of an organization that has achieved this measure of permanence: our group's membership includes successful scholars who had not even been born when it was founded, but whose talents and enthusiasm instil hope for an extended future. The date range of the period we study, however, is not so self-explanatory. In a general way, it serves the useful purpose of combining two notoriously indefinable entities: the early modern period and the long eighteenth century. Its 279-year extent, however, reflects the arbitrary untidiness of specific historical events. It inevitably draws attention to Britain and Ireland, since the first year saw the death of Mary I (1516–58), the first woman to be crowned as reigning Queen of England and Ireland, and the accession of her half-sister Elizabeth I (1533–1603). The centre is flanked by the reigns of two more sovereign sisters: Mary II (1662–94) ruled jointly, from 1689 until her death, with her husband, William III (1650–1702); Anne (1665–1714) succeeded to the throne in 1702. The final year is indelibly associated with the accession of Queen Victoria (1819–1901). These temporal parameters do not, however, restrict our attention to British and Irish affairs, and even when they are under discussion, we are constantly reminded that these years witnessed an expansion of trade, exploration and exchange of ideas that forged connections between this queendom and nearly every part of the planet. We are also happy to discuss earlier and later material, if it casts light on women within our period. Furthermore, if representations of women from earlier in history occur within our date range, then they are also considered legitimate subjects for investigation. For example, our first chapter, Valerie Schutte's discussion of Lady Jane Grey (1537–54), also considers the early lives of Mary I and Elizabeth I, and although Lady Jane Grey did not live to see the beginning of our period, much of the material cited was published after Elizabeth's accession.

To focus on women in this period is to be concerned with victims of sexual discrimination, sometimes deliberately resisted, sometimes internalized (with various degrees of intellectual and psychic discomfort), but often stimulating some attempt at negotiation or compromise. Their experiences yield abundant examples of the workings of a phenomenon known today as patriarchy, not a legally defined system in itself (though upheld by many laws), but rather a very broad spectrum of social organizations, whose key features are that men have more authority than women and younger men, all things being equal, defer to their male elders. There were, of course, many occasions on which men deferred to women, but usually because the women concerned derived superior status from their husbands or male relatives. Queens are a special case: their power and high visibility draw attention to contrasts and commonalities with other women, and their often anomalous position provides an excellent starting-point for the explorations in this book.

It is not fashionable to present history as a succession of dates and monarchs, but a few facts about 'queens and things' might provide a useful context for the book as a whole. Some of the resulting perspectives, considered from the viewpoint of a sovereign queen or her subjects, are alarming. The first fact to consider might have occurred to many auditors when Lady Jane Grey was proclaimed queen in 1553: she was breaking new, and dangerous, ground. The last woman to attempt to rule England had been Matilda (1102–67), the heir and only legitimate child of Henry I (1068–1135). The result was a prolonged civil war. In 1141 Matilda finally managed to get to London for her Westminster coronation, but the people rose against her: far from being crowned, she was not even proclaimed. It is, of course, clear to us that, after a lapse of 412 years, this medieval episode was totally irrelevant to conditions in Tudor England, but some would have argued that those years had elapsed for a reason. John Knox (c.1513–72) argued that to serve a ruling queen was 'nothing els, but continuallie to rebell against God', who had made women subservient to men.[1] Theology apart, there was an immediate practical concern: marriage transferred power over the wife and (in the absence of contracts to the contrary) ownership of her property to her husband. So a reigning queen had two choices of marriage partner: a subject, whom she would then, paradoxically, have to obey, or a foreigner, which could lead to the 'translation of realmes and nations' to alien control.[2] Yet remaining single was not a popular option, because every monarch was expected to secure the succession by producing an heir. All except Elizabeth took the plunge, thereby aligning themselves not only with queens consort and with women who passed on royal blood without becoming queens in any capacity, but with all potential mothers.

Although sovereign queens were in power for only sixty-two years, a mere two-ninths of our period, the role of women as links in the succession was crucial throughout. Elizabeth I came to the throne after her half-brother, Edward VI (1537–53), and half-sister, Mary I, had died without issue. After Elizabeth herself died childless, the crown went to James I of England and Ireland and VI of Scotland (1566–1625), who was descended from the elder sister of Henry VIII (1491–1547): in the circumstances, this is exactly what should have happened, according to common law.[3] Henry's will had given priority to his younger sister's line but, either way, so long as women were accepted as links in the chain, it would take more than a few episodes of childlessness to disrupt the succession.[4] Only the abolition of the monarchy did that, and not for long. In the reign of James's son, Charles I (1600–49), disputes between king and parliament ignited a series of civil wars that raged from 1642 to 1651. Religion was deeply involved. The royalists tended to be members of the Church of England (Protestants who regarded the monarch as supreme head of the church), or Roman Catholics, who owed a measure of obedience to the pope. Many parliamentarians, on the other hand, were Protestant Dissenters, who often regarded the Church of England, as well as the Church of Rome, as a hotbed of superstitious idolatry. Charles I was beheaded, and his sons, Charles Prince of Wales (1630–85) and James Duke of York (1633–1701), took refuge in Europe during the resulting interregnum.

In 1660, the Restoration came as a happy deliverance to many. Charles II (who had become king on the death of his father) returned to his kingdoms; although he failed to father legitimate heirs and James was a Roman Catholic, most Protestants were reassured by the fact that the Princesses Mary and Anne, James's daughters by his first wife, were brought up in their faith and married to Protestant princes. James's second wife, Mary of Modena (1658–1718), though a devout Catholic, presented no obvious threat to the Protestant succession: she bore children but they never lived long. When James came to the throne in 1685, many of his loyal subjects were grimly resigned to waiting for him to die a natural death and be succeeded by a Protestant daughter. Then on 10 June 1688, the queen bore a healthy son, James Francis Edward (d. 1766), later known as the Old Pretender. This apparent dynastic success was a political disaster. As a male, he took precedence over his half-sisters, and he would certainly be brought up a Catholic: Protestants who had reconciled themselves to the rule of a single Catholic king now faced the prospect of a Catholic dynasty.[5] What followed has become known as the 'Glorious' or 'bloodless' Revolution.[6] The latter term was inaccurate, especially in Scotland and Ireland.[7] James's son-in-law, William of Orange, arrived with his troops on 5 November; by February 1689 James had fled, which William's supporters interpreted as abdication, and William III and Mary II began their joint reign.

After Mary's death without issue in 1694, the reproductive burden fell heavily upon her younger sister Anne. She was pregnant at least seventeen times, bearing five living babies; only one of them, William, Duke of Gloucester (1689–1700), survived infancy. Her ill-fated ventures into motherhood still resonate in our culture: they are the subject of the opening of Helen Edmundson's play *Queen Anne* (2015). After Gloucester's death, King William realized that urgent steps must be taken to keep the crown in Protestant hands: a suitable line was traced back to James I's daughter, Elizabeth, Queen of Bohemia (1596–1662). An Act of Parliament duly declared that, 'in Default of Issue', the succession must pass to 'the most Excellent Princess Sophia Electress and Dutchess Dowager of Hannover Daughter of the most Excellent Princess Elizabeth late Queen of Bohemia', and 'the Heirs of Her Body being Protestants'.[8] In fact, Princess Sophia (1630–1714) predeceased Queen Anne, so the crown went to her son, George I (1660–1727), whose direct descendants have occupied the throne ever since. Dynastic warfare did not end overnight: many Jacobites, as they were called, remained loyal to James II and his descendants, and there were several risings, culminating in the battle at Culloden Moor in 1746 when the supporters of the Young Pretender, Charles Edward Stuart (1720–88), were defeated by William ('Butcher'), Duke of Cumberland (1721–65). In other words, Mary of Modena's grandson was beaten by the great-grandson of Princess Sophia. The quintessentially patriarchal institution of monarchy was behaving in a remarkably matrilineal manner.

Yet the women involved paid a heavy price: their struggle to produce the necessary offspring was painful, dangerous and often accompanied by bitter failure. A hard fact, not fully apparent until the end of our period, is that no sovereign queen before Victoria left a surviving child. To this dismal tally we can add a potential sovereign: Princess Charlotte of Wales (1796–1817), at that point the only legitimate grandchild of George III (1738–1820), died after bearing a stillborn son. This was a tragedy which 'the whole nation felt as one man'.[9] The reproductive problems faced by many of the royal women sadly exemplify topics raised in this book. They often experienced the desirability and difficulty of conception, discussed by Jennifer Evans in Chapter 3. Others, like Queen Anne, who simply could not keep their children alive, are more relevant to Sara Read's chapter, highlighting views on childcare as a religious duty.

Queens can become conveniently conspicuous exemplars of many beliefs about women, including their physical and mental inferiority to men. Elizabeth I is famously recorded as having said that she had 'the bodie, but of a weak and feeble woman'.[10] As for their minds, Knox asserts that women are not qualified to reign, since God has deprived them of 'wisdome to consider, and providence to forsee the thinges, that be profitable to the common welth'.[11] It was probably more than a man's head was worth to agree openly with Knox's statement, at least during the reign of a female sovereign, but his contempt of female intellect in general would have rung true to many. Most women were trapped in vicious circles where limited education, training and employment opportunities left them unable to compete on equal terms with men. As this book will show, this often had a disastrous effect, as an accumulation of misfortunes could reduce them to destitution; others, however, found ways to survive, prosper and express themselves.

Many women took up the pen, though there were risks attached. Louise Duckling's 'Conclusion', citing various attacks on learned ladies, including a mock-condemnation of Jane Grey by Jane Austen (1775–1817), suggests that, even at the end of our period, a woman who displayed her literary talents might be condemned for a lack of proper femininity. Yvonne Noble's account of Anne Finch, Countess of Winchilsea (1661–1720), shows how cautious she was about publishing: she was eventually persuaded to print a collection of her poems in 1713, but left twice as many in manuscript to be discovered, published and enjoyed long after her death. In contrast, Marie Mulvey-Roberts focuses on women writers at the end of the eighteenth century, including Mary Hays (1759–1843), Mary Wollstonecraft (1759–97) and Mary Robinson (1757–1800), whose fictional and polemical works argued that treating women as men's inferiors was unreasonable and immoral. As female authorship became increasingly conspicuous, however, it could be argued that, even when not openly protesting against their treatment, women were revealing its injustice by demonstrating their intellectual potential. Gillian Williamson's research on the *Gentleman's Magazine* in the eighteenth and nineteenth century indicates that the obituaries for women were less numerous and detailed than those for men, but that great respect was paid to women writers, especially those who contributed to its pages.

Publishing became increasingly hospitable to women: in Marion Durnin's study, we find Mrs S.C. Hall, née Anna Maria Fielding (1800–81), editing nineteenth-century annuals both in collaboration with her husband and independently, as well as using them to bring her own fiction to the notice of the public. With such a wealth of literature to investigate, it is not surprising that our group has enjoyed a close and fruitful relationship with *Women's Writing*, a journal that has flourished since 1994.

Authorship was not the only area of endeavour where women's skills overlapped with those considered appropriate to men. Jacqueline Mulhallen's study evokes the combination of theatrical talent and emotional energy, often hailed as genius, that enabled the actress Eliza O'Neill (1791–1872) not only to interpret but to inspire great drama. Concentrating on the world of opera, Brianna E. Robertson-Kirkland has shown how Elizabeth Billington, née Weichsel (c.1768–1818), and Gertrude Mara, née Schmeling (1749–1833), utilized their technical ability and flair for publicity to profit from their well-advertised stage rivalry. Today, we may be surprised that these women achieved so much, but would acknowledge that the quality of their intellectual and artistic achievements would have been equally remarkable in either sex. If we are still inclined, however, to concede physical superiority to the men, Peter Radford's account of the agility, strength, speed and endurance displayed by women of all ages, from coal mine to cricket pitch, should make us think again.

On the other hand, women had one monopoly on which men could never intrude: motherhood. Texts composed from the time of Aristotle (c.384–322 BC) onwards bear witness to male attempts to enhance the status of paternity by arguing that fathers played a more important part than mothers in the composition of the child, but the situation continued to engender much masculine anxiety.[12] The more completely power and property were reserved for men, the more important it was that their wives' children, especially the boys born to inherit the titles and estates of elite males, were their own offspring. Yet how could anybody be sure? On 14 September 1773, Dr Samuel Johnson (1709–84), with his customary trenchancy, summed up patriarchy's awkward predicament: 'Consider, of what importance to society the chastity of women is. Upon that all the property in the world depends. We hang a thief for stealing a sheep: but the unchastity of a woman transfers sheep, and farm and all, from the right owner.'[13]

Men tried to limit risk factors by controlling female sexual activity, but unfortunately failed to control their own, so the high value set on female chastity often resulted in girls who had lost their virginity through seduction, rape or child abuse being cast out of respectable homes and forced to choose between prostitution and starvation.[14] Three chapters in our book investigate contrasting representations of victims of sexual exploitation. Julie Peakman examines the cooperative networks that enabled eighteenth-century prostitutes, including the glamorous courtesan Peg Plunkett (c.1740–97), to support each other through their alternately hilarious and heart-rending adventures. Using an anonymous pamphlet, Tabitha Kenlon shows working-class unmarried mothers being rebuked for lust and vanity: the possibility that they might have been forced to have intercourse is never mentioned. Sarah Oliver's study of novels of the long eighteenth century reveals a growing tendency for female characters to refuse to be defined by unwanted sexual experiences.

It is interesting, even reassuring, to note that our members' perceptions of the contradictions and difficulties affecting women in our period were shared by some contemporary observers. They might not always have used our critical terminology, and we might not want to adopt their solutions, but they saw the same problems. Martin Madan (1726–90), who had been chaplain at the Lock Hospital where poor women, often prostitutes, were treated for venereal disease, was overcome with pity for their plight and indignation at a society that allowed them to be abandoned to poverty and despair while the men who exploited them went scot free. He proposed a return to a lifestyle that was literally patriarchal, in that it involved what he believed to be the marital practices ordained in the Old Testament. He argued that God had never revoked polygamy, and that any man who deflowered a virgin became her husband by that act, thus ensuring that every fallen woman would enjoy protection and support.[15] This rule applied only to men: he had heard of 'the tribe of the *Naires*, on the coast of *Malabar*, where the women have many husbands' but considered their customs 'contrary to nature'.[16] On closer examination, 'nature' appears to be a combination of biological and social imperatives:

> As the *woman* had the business of *parturition* allotted to her, she must necessarily be looked upon as the *repository* of those bonds and cements of human society, without which it cannot subsist; such as family descents, pedigrees, genealogies, inheritances, and all communications and distinctions of relationship. Therefore the *Creator* did, in his infinite wisdom, set bounds to the *commerce of the sexes*, on the part of the *woman*, which could not be passed under pain of death.[17]

James Henry Lawrence (1773–1840), on the other hand, turned to the Malabar coast for a logical solution to these dilemmas. It became the setting for a 'Utopian Romance' in which women choose and change their sexual partners as they please, mothers only have 'charge of the children', men have 'no other heirs than the children of their sisters', and a child 'speaks of the lovers of his mother, and of his uncles, but never of his father'.[18] It is a welcoming paradise for the mother of a baby born out of wedlock: 'The child, which she bore in her arms, would in England have shut every door against her; here it was a recommendation, a passport from the hands of nature.'[19] The common element in Madan's patriarchal manifesto and Lawrence's matriarchal aspirations is a conviction that some change in women's status is urgently needed. As citizens of a very different world, though one in which work still needs to be done, the members of the Women's Studies Group can honour both of them, along with many of the women whose lives we have been exploring, for their refusal to leave the world as they found it.

Chapter One

Michelangelo Florio and Lady Jane Grey: A Case Study of a Book Dedication to a Royal Tudor Lady

by Valerie Schutte

One aspect of the tightly-interwoven relationships connecting Mary I, Elizabeth I and Jane Grey has only recently become the focus of scholarly attention: book dedications.[1] For centuries, authors in hope of patronage maintained the tradition of dedicating their works to royalty and nobility, a practice enabling clients and patrons to make connections, increase their prestige, and promote and give authority to books.[2] Although the Tudor monarchs received numerous dedications, in manuscript and print, only one extant dedication survives for Lady Jane Grey. It was an undated manuscript entitled *Regole et Institutioni della Lingua Thoscana* (*Rules and Precepts of the Tuscan Language*) by Michelangelo Florio (1515–72), her tutor in Latin and Italian.[3] Discussion of this text will be preceded by a brief survey of the events that led to Jane's death, and of relevant features in the culture of creating and giving books of which dedications formed a part; it will be followed by an account of its relationship with another manuscript by Florio, *Regole de la Lingua Thoscana*, dated 21 August 1553, dedicated to Jane's brother-in-law Henry Herbert (after 1538–1601).[4] Two points of interest emerge from this study: a tendency for the dedications to refer to influential male relatives, especially fathers, and the ways in which the authors' choice of dedicatee, the books' contents, and the texts of the dedications themselves reflect the religious and dynastic turmoil involving all three royal ladies.

The fates and reigns of the two queens regnant were closely intertwined with that of their cousin, Jane, who was proclaimed queen between the death of Edward VI and the coup that enabled Mary to take the throne. Jane derived her royal blood from her mother, Frances (1517–59), daughter of Mary (1496–1533), the younger sister of Henry VIII. Jane's father, Henry Grey (1517–54), became Marquis of Dorset in 1530 and Duke of Suffolk in 1551. However, Jane's prospects of succession were remote, since Henry VIII married six times and had three living children. One outcome of Henry's marriages, besides his declaring himself head of the Church of England, was that Mary and Elizabeth were both bastardized. The 1536 Act of Succession made them both illegitimate and excluded them from the succession, thereby elevating the position of Frances.[5] Henry VIII composed another Act of Succession in 1543, as he prepared for war with France. This particular act reinstated Mary and Elizabeth into the line of succession, after Edward and his heirs, although it did not change their bastardized status.[6] When Henry VIII expressed his final intentions for the succession in his will, he made no mention of his elder sister and her descendants, and also excluded Frances but included the heirs of her body: in the event, these comprised three daughters, Jane, Katherine (1540–68) and Mary Grey (1545–78).[7] Consequently, when Edward VI succeeded Henry VIII in 1547, Jane was third in line, preceded only by Henry VIII's daughters, Mary and Elizabeth Tudor.

As Frances and Henry Grey had no son, they strongly supported their eldest daughter's marriage potential, going so far as attempting to match her with Prince Edward, which required giving her an education befitting her potentially royal status.[8] His failing health, however, precluded the possibility of any marriage. On 25 May 1553, Jane was married to Guildford Dudley (c.1535–54), fourth son of John, Duke of Northumberland (1504–53), Lord President of the Council, who worked closely with Jane's father. On the same day, her sister Katherine married Henry Herbert, son of William, Earl of Pembroke (c.1501–70), another powerful politician. Exactly six weeks later, on 6 July, Edward died. These events might have ended Jane's royal destiny, were it not for a document drawn up by Edward entitled 'My devise for the succession': first in line came Lady Frances' 'heires masles', followed by 'L' Jane and her heires masles'.[9] Edward's main concern appears in the statement that his chosen successors had all been 'exercised in good and godly learninge': in other words, they were reformists or, as we would say today, Protestants.[10] Edward was determined to use any means he could find to prevent the Catholic Mary from inheriting the crown, even if Elizabeth was excluded in the process. At Edward's death, this made Jane queen in her own right. Northumberland initially concealed Edward's death, hoping to capture Mary before she realized what had happened and tried to claim the throne.[11] On 10 July, Edward's death was finally announced, and Jane proclaimed queen.[12] Mary, however, outmanoeuvred Northumberland, strategically and politically, and was proclaimed queen in London on

19 July.[13] She was initially inclined to mercy, but after the Wyatt Rebellion Jane was considered a dangerous focus of unrest and was beheaded on 12 February 1554.[14]

High-ranking parents of all religious views considered learning vitally important in preparing children for the exercise of power; daughters unlikely to become rulers in their own right might attract powerful husbands by their intellectual attainments. Carefully-chosen texts in a variety of ancient and modern languages were intended to inculcate virtue, provide examples of good and bad rule, and enable pupils to understand and defend their respective religious principles. As befitted the offspring of Henry VIII, Mary and Elizabeth received exceptional humanist educations at the hands of famous scholars: Mary's tutors included Giles Duwes (d. 1535), while Elizabeth was taught by Roger Ascham (1515–68).[15] Yet Jane was at least as well educated: Aysha Pollnitz suggests that Jane's parents arranged her upbringing with an even more 'focused ambition' than that devoted to her cousins.[16] Her father, a staunch reformist and patron of humanism, fostered a rich learning environment within his household, which included Ascham's friend John Aylmer (1521–94), a future Bishop of London, who gave Jane tuition in Greek.[17] The result was the emergence of 'an intelligent, highly educated, evangelical princess'.[18] She was a leading light among an assemblage of learned ladies who commanded respect at an international level. In a letter to Johannes Sturm (1507–89), the well-known educator from Strasbourg, Ascham conferred much praise on Elizabeth, but even more on Jane, whom he had once found reading Plato's *Phaedo* with a degree of understanding and enjoyment that '*mihi ipsi summam admirationem injiceret*' ('inspired me with the greatest wonder').[19] He coupled her with the phenomenally-learned Mildred Cecil, née Cooke (c.1526–89), '*quae haud aliter Graece intelligit et loquitur quam Anglice*' ('who understands and speaks Greek almost as well as English').[20]

Mildred Cecil may have even been the anonymous translator who sent Jane a gift of a translation of a book by Basil the Great (330–79), Bishop of Caesaria, accompanied by a letter in Greek.[21] The book has disappeared but the letter, whose language indicates female composition, survives.[22] The donor compares Jane to Basil in holiness and wisdom, noting that Jane should find this volume more valuable to her than gold or precious stones.[23] Henry Parker, Lord Morley (1533–77), made a similar remark in a pre-accession manuscript dedication to Mary accompanying Richard Rolle of Hampole's Latin Psalter, saying Mary would find it more valuable than precious stones or pearls.[24] The ardently reformist John Bale (1495–1563) refers to Elizabeth's book, 'The Glasse of the Synnefull Soule' (1545), originally a richly-bound manuscript presented to Catherine Parr (1512–48), as a 'treasure' when he dedicates a printed edition to her.[25] Jane elaborates further on this trope in a letter written to her 13-year-old sister Katherine at the end of her Greek Testament, the night before her execution. She begins, 'I Have heere sent you (good Sister Katherine) a booke, which although it be not outwardly trimmed with gold, yet inwardly it is more worth then precious stones', then refers, appropriately, to the New Testament itself: 'if you apply diligently this booke, seeking to direct your lyfe after it, you shall be an inheritour of such riches, as neither the covetous shall withdrawe from you, neither theefe shall steale, neyther yet the mothes corrupt.'[26] This recalls Matthew 6, 20: 'geather ye treasures to gether in heven where nether rust nor moulthes corrupte, & where theves nether breake up nor yet steale.'[27] Katherine must, if necessary, prepare herself to 'dye in the true Christian fayth', from which she must 'never swarve, neither for hope of life, nor for feare of death'.[28] The journey from precious objects to spiritually valuable ideas has reached a point where all worldly goods, including life itself, have become expendable. Jane's message cannot be called a dedication: it is, rather, an exceptionally stern gift tag. The appearance of the idea of text as treasure in such a variety of bibliographical contexts serves today as a reminder of the close relationships between the manuscripts, printed books, original texts, translations, copies, gifts of books written by others and dedications of books written by the donors that interacted with the lives of Mary, Elizabeth and Jane.

The giving and receiving of books, printed and in manuscript, with their attendant covering letters and dedications, was a mainstay of elite learned networks at this period; before their accessions, at least nineteen printed books and manuscripts were dedicated to Mary, while Elizabeth received at least seven. Although Jane makes a poor showing in comparison with only one dedication, it was not for lack of effort. In the course of her education, she was, like Mary and Elizabeth, closely connected to the English and foreign literary scene. She was represented not only as a learned and appreciative reader, but as a well-connected aristocrat with rich and influential male relatives and the best possible marriage prospects. The young Swiss student Conrad ab Ulmis, a protégé of Jane's father, told the German Hebraist Konrad Pellican (1478–1556) that Jane, 'a lady who is well versed both in Greek and Latin', now wished to learn Hebrew; he made two requests on her behalf: 'Write therefore a letter to her as soon as possible, in which you will briefly point out a method of learning the sacred language, and then honourably consecrate to her name your Latin translation of the Jewish

Talmud.'[29] He added strong inducements: 'The young lady is the daughter of the marquis, and is to be married, as I hear, to the king.'[30] Meanwhile, Ascham set his sights on Sturm, whose *De Periodis* (1550), a book on the composition of Latin oratory, had been dedicated to Elizabeth.[31] He had been '*cupidus*' ('passionately desirous') that Sturm should dedicate his edition of speeches by Aeschines and Demosthenes to Jane, and although this had not happened, possibly through a breakdown of communications, he still hoped that Sturm would dedicate something to this '*lectissimae virgini*' ('excellent virgin').[32] Ascham failed, but could not be accused of losing his point through excessive restraint: not only did he mention that Jane's mind was cultivated by Plato's doctrine and Demosthenes' eloquence, but he invoked her royal descent, and added that the death of a rich uncle had made her personal wealth greater than ever.[33]

What is clear is Jane's connection to a circle of prominent reformers who expected that eventually she would be a useful source of patronage. They were no different from the men who dedicated to Elizabeth and Mary, expecting that, as the king's daughters, they had patronage to dispense and might even recommend their works to their father, creating possible opportunities for further patronage and reward. However, Jane was not so well placed as Mary and Elizabeth; she was not so obviously in the direct line of succession and she was not so prominent at court. Furthermore, once she did become a prominent figure, her days were numbered. Edward's 1553 'devise' was not made public in time for authors or translators to present dedications to her, and she was not 'queen' long enough to receive dedications. Richard Grafton (c.1507–73), King's Printer under Henry VIII and Edward VI, would have been the man to print books dedicated to Jane, as he immediately styled himself 'Printer to the Queen', but upon Mary's accession he was removed from the position.[34] This left Michelangelo Florio as the sole dedicator: his subsequent actions suggest that he found this an uncomfortably precarious distinction.

Probably best-known today as the father of John Florio (1553–1625), Michelangelo was an interesting character in his own right: descended from Tuscan Jews who converted to Christianity, he took orders as a Franciscan friar and engaged in itinerant preaching, but became a reformist, was 'tortured by the Inquisition and imprisoned in Rome', escaped, and arrived in England in 1550.[35] After further troubles, some of his own making, he eventually became tutor in Italian, French and Latin to Lady Jane Grey, who was moved to tears by his account of his sufferings.[36] The dedication resembles others addressed to royal ladies in its promptness to focus on a powerful male relative. It begins '*ALLA ILLUSTRISSIMA ET DOTTA SIGNORA GIOVANNA GRAIA*' ('To the most Illustrious and Learned Lady Jane Grey'), a phrase commonly used to describe female patrons, after which Florio turns his focus to her father's clemency, generosity and courtesy, which oblige him to love, reverence and respect not only him, but the lowest-ranking servants of his well-nurtured and well-conducted ('*ben*' *nudrita et costumata*') household.[37] Since '*nudrita*' literally means 'fed', and '*costumata*' can mean either 'clad' or 'well-bred', the ambiguity at this point might reflect the dedicator's need for material support as well as his approval of the high moral and spiritual standards of a worthy reforming household: he resolves the matter soon after with a reference to '*costumi santi*' ('sanctified ways').[38] Florio tries to preclude any suspicion that his praise is excessive by declaring that he would say a great deal more, if he were not unwilling to be '*tenuto adulatore*' ('taken for a flatterer'): a useful ploy for any dedicator.[39] The sympathetic Jane would have understood his priorities, since Florio states that compiling his *Regole* for her is the only way he can express his gratitude to the noble house by which '*ne tempi delle mie maggior' bisogne sono stato aiutato*' ('I was helped in the time of my greatest need').[40] Florio was to confirm this view in his *Historia*, giving high praise to Jane's father as '*Mecenate vero di tutti i virtuosi, e padre amorevolissimo de poveri*' ('a true Maecenas to all men of talent, and a most affectionate father to the poor').[41] Jane herself, however, receives praise for her faith and intellect: she accepts '*tutti i veri dogmati della Christiana, et non Papistica, religione*' ('all the true doctrines of the Christian, and not Papistical, religion'), and understands them so thoroughly that she can '*renderne ragione à tutto il monde*' ('give reasons for them to all the world').[42] The behaviour he attributes to her is a model of reformist virtues: it includes prudence in counsel, sobriety in eating and drinking, a modest appearance, devotion to God, and compassion to everybody; these are the '*doti e gratie*' ('gifts and graces') that declare her status as a true member of Jesus Christ.[43] He tells her to give the honour to God if anything in his book pleases her: if otherwise, she must blame his poor ability.[44] He ends by bidding her '*State sana, et vivete (come solati fare) à Christo*' ('Keep well, and live [as is your custom] to Christ').[45]

The textbook is thorough and systematic, with an array of rules and examples, written in two different colours. A pale colour, probably once red, now faded to the verge of illegibility, is generally used for headings, single words and passages in Italian that exemplify the rules under discussion. Black ink is usually reserved for explanations and translations of Italian into Latin, a language with which Jane was more familiar. The work's most distinctive feature is a 'confluence of linguistic usage and politics' connecting 'language practice to the realities of the world'.[46] It is created by Florio's use of statements about religion to illustrate grammatical principles. At first the situation is both stable and predictable: '*che il papa sia Antichristo, è gran tempo che io lo ho sospito*' ('I have suspected for a long time that the Pope is Antichrist').[47] It is not surprising that, being a tyrant, the Pope persecutes pious Christians, and is the Vicar of Satan.[48] However, he eventually sees the error of his ways, though it is too late for him to do anything about it: '*Dicesi ch'il papa è disperato*' ('They say the Pope is in despair').[49] Then comes the reformist happy ending: '*Non è guari ch'il papa è morto*' ('It is not long since the Pope died').[50]

Florio's dedication served several purposes. First, he praised Jane and her family, as they were his employers and gave him the ability to stay in England and escape disgrace. Florio claimed that he did not write so much about his admiration of the Grey household to flatter Jane, but because it was true; it was very typical for dedicators to use modesty as a means to appear compliant to the needs and wants of their patrons. Secondly, Florio's dedication attempts to demonstrate why he was the best Italian tutor for Jane, as Henry Grey could have employed any tutor for his daughters. Not only did Florio compile his text from the Tuscan writers, but he was also devoted to teaching her Italian to strengthen her relationship with God, something that might not have been so important to other Italian tutors. Thirdly, Florio structured his dedication similarly to pre-accession dedications directed to Mary and Elizabeth. Dedications to the royal ladies tended to begin with praise, explain the goals of the text or translation, describe how the text made the dedicator think of the dedicatee, and end with prayers and supplication.

One interesting connection between the pre-accession dedications given to Mary, Elizabeth and Jane is that the majority mention at least one of their male relatives. Where Mary and Elizabeth are concerned, dedications frequently mentioned their father, their brother, or both. For example, Henry Parker, Lord Morley, even went so far as to conclude one of his dedications to Mary by asking God to honour King Henry, Prince Edward and 'the children of hys Grace to cum'.[51] Florio's dedication to Jane mentioned her father and the learning environment he created within his home. A male relative would have been included for several reasons. First and foremost, a dedication to a royal lady with a living and powerful father would honour that father in the hopes that he would also look favourably upon the dedicator and patronize or reward him.[52] By appealing to both the royal lady and her powerful male relative, a dedicator would have the greatest chance of being rewarded for his efforts. Secondly, a male relative was mentioned to remind a royal lady of her role as an intermediary.[53] Mary, Elizabeth and Jane may not have had much patronage to dispense, but they could recommend a book or its author/translator to their father or brother for reward and perhaps even future employment. Third, dedicators probably also included male relatives in order to remind their readers that the ladies they were dedicating to came from powerful families. Mary and Elizabeth, even though bastardized and demoted from princesses to ladies, were still daughters of the king and had access to him. As for Jane, her father was the Duke of Suffolk and a known patron of humanist scholars, so he was a potentially useful contact. Some of the dedications that mention Henry VIII show a close correlation between the amount of attention he receives and his performance or potential as a patron. After his death, Henry served as a guarantor of his offspring's royal blood: John Bale accords him very perfunctory treatment in his dedication of *A Godly Medytacyon* (1548), which addresses Elizabeth as 'the noble doughter of our late soverayne kynge Henry the viii' and pays no further attention to him.[54] In 1570, twenty-three years after his death, Henry figures very briefly at the end of a dedication, in a pious wish that Elizabeth's reign will be as long as her father's.[55]

Sadly for Florio, and even more sadly for Jane, events in the real world did not unfold like those in the *Regole*. The Greys could no longer offer him support, and he needed a new patron. The evidence suggests that at this point he wrote a new version of his textbook, entitled *Regole de la Lingua Thoscana*, dedicated to Henry Herbert, son of William Herbert, Earl of Pembroke (1501?–70). Pellegrini argues that Florio's book dedicated to Jane is the first version, being more carelessly written, while the Herbert version is a little more full and accurate, and seems to have been prepared with a view to publication.[56] The date, 21 August 1553, supports this view, since by then Jane was a prisoner in the Tower.[57]

Differences between the two dedications reflect not only the changes in Florio's circumstances, but the complex interactions between gender, rank and power generally referred to as patriarchy. Henry is addressed in a grand style that places him on Jane's level: '*All'illustrissimo, et Eccellentissimo signore, il signore Arrigo Harbart*' ('To the most illustrious, and most Excellent Lord, Lord Henry Herbert').[58] This time, though, Florio is not in such haste to start praising the dedicatee's father: first, he mentions the privations that have made him unable to present a better gift, describing himself as a '*povero forestiero, privo di tutti quegli aiuti, favori, e soccorsi che dalla patria e dagl' amici sperar' si possano*' ('poor foreigner, deprived of all the assistance, favour, and succour that could be looked for from one's fatherland and friends').[59] In his dedication to Jane, Florio celebrated the generosity with which her father had rescued him from great calamities; now, however, his troubles are a matter for present concern. Florio might be considering his young dedicatee as a direct source of help. His language seems calculated to encourage an ambitious teenager to start considering independent action: he says Henry Herbert's nobility and virtues are accompanied by '*si fatti santi costumi, che in questo regno, e in qualunque altro dove vi troverrete, vi fanno parere vecchio d'anni, e isperimentato ne governi*' ('such well-established sanctified ways, that in this kingdom, and in any other where you find yourself, they make you appear old in years, and experienced in government').[60] He makes an explicit bid for future patronage, saying that he has a great desire to serve Henry '*in maggior' cosa*' ('in some greater matter').[61] Even when he mentions the great qualities of the Earl of Pembroke, he does so in terms likely to arouse emulation in his son: '*si vede in ogni vostro affare la vera stampa del grande spirito de l'illmo vostro padre*' ('in everything you undertake, there appears the true imprint of the great spirit of your most illustrious father').[62] Despite his attribution of '*santi costumi*' to both of them, Florio treats his dedicatees very differently, emphasizing Jane's private, domestic virtues, which would have been seen as more feminine, while Henry Herbert, although still lacking the power, wealth and independence appropriate for an adult, is already displaying the skills he would need to deploy them in a manner befitting the heir of a powerful aristocrat. Florio gives Jane and her father complementary roles, while Henry and William Herbert appear as almost equals, maybe even potential rivals. In one respect, however, both versions of *Regole* agree: neither offers any quarter to the pope. As Florio says in Henry Herbert's copy, '*Il papa dice d'essere vicario di Christo, ma all' incontra lo spirit santo ci mostra che egli è antichristo*' ('The Pope says he is the Vicar of Christ, but on the contrary the Holy Ghost says he is Antichrist').[63]

If Florio was trying to find another patron, he failed. Lord Pembroke initially supported Jane's claim to the throne, but switched sides when it became clear that Mary was going to be queen; he had his son's marriage annulled, not just to separate himself from the Grey family but to ensure that Katherine did not conceive a child who might, at that critical juncture, be regarded as a potential rival to Mary.[64] Henry Herbert did indeed demonstrate maturity beyond his years, but employed it in gaining favour with the new regime at home rather than displaying his abilities abroad. He was made a Knight of the Bath at Mary's coronation on 29 September

1553 and later became a gentleman of the bedchamber to her husband, King Philip (1527–98). Like many of their contemporaries, the Herberts were too concerned with protecting their own position to shelter wandering reformers. Florio eventually fled to the continent and settled in Switzerland.[65]

This chapter has made it clear that, through book dedications, Mary, Elizabeth and Jane were all closely involved with book history, often in ways that emphasized the most painful complications in their tangled relationships with each other. This comparison is important because it shows how Lady Jane Grey was considered and treated as a possible alternative to inherit the throne. In his dedication, Florio mentioned the merits of Jane's household and how her father established and supported a house with a great learning environment that was a safe haven for reform, merits that any noble house should strive to have. As for Mary and Elizabeth, dedicators also praised their learning and assumed that their households had all the merits that Florio mentioned as uniquely characteristic of the Greys' (except with the expectation that Mary's household was a safe haven for Catholics instead of reformers). Yet what is important is not just that these women all received book dedications, but that Florio, and other reformers in his network, treated Jane as a princess. Florio's emphasis in his dedication was not actually on learning Italian, but on piety and religion, characteristics that Jane would need as Edward's wife and future queen. Similarly, both Mary and Elizabeth received several dedications that attempted to encourage the pursuit of religion in various directions, as religion was one aspect of queenship that dedicators were willing to concede was under the purview of women, much more so than statecraft.[66] Authors used dedications to seek their patronage or, through them, that of their male relatives: a sensible strategy, since most of the women who actually had money were accountable for it to husbands or fathers. Yet authors might make a passing reference to a dedicatee's dead father and ignore a living (and reigning) brother, as Bale did when he published *A Godly Medytacyon* in 1548. Florio promoted Jane's piety and steered her towards reformed religion, rather than using his dedication to ask Jane to promote his text for other readers, as many dedicators did who desired patronage. Rather, he wrote to Jane in anticipation that the men around her would reward him for his loyalty, be it her father or her future husband. The one certainty at present is that the study of dedications to these ladies has much to reveal about the workings of early modern book production.

Chapter Two

'*The* Wine *much better then the* Bush': Thomas Lodge's Address to the Reader in *The Countesse of Lincolnes Nurserie*

by Sara Read

The Countesse of Lincolnes Nurserie (1622), written by Elizabeth Clinton, née Knevitt (1574?–1630?), dowager Countess of Lincoln, is most normally read in the context of either the 'mother's legacy' genre or as part of the Puritan revival of maternal nursing, or a mixture of both.[1] The overlooked presence in Clinton's treatise of a two-page address 'To the Courteous, chiefly most Christian, Reader' by Thomas Lodge (c.1558–1625), literary author turned physician, complicates this position: not only was Lodge a well-known convert to Catholicism, but his writings, which were remarkably diverse in subject and genre, often adopted an aggressively satirical tone. The coupling of these authors, initially rather surprising, requires further investigation. In fact, a brief survey of Lodge's achievements and social connections, viewed in the light of Clinton's situation, suggests that this was an apt and efficient pairing. This is borne out by comparisons between Lodge's address and other addresses to the reader, and detailed examination of its relationship with Clinton's text. A broader investigation, placing Clinton's religious views in their contemporary context, suggests that not only moderate Protestants but even Puritans had stronger affinities with Catholics than some of their contemporaries cared to acknowledge. Finally, some brief remarks on the occurrence and authorship of addresses to the reader in works by Lodge and other writers, both male and female, will, it is hoped, encourage scholars to find further links between women's studies and the history of the printed book.

Lodge was an almost textbook example of the Renaissance man. Graduating with a BA from Trinity College, Oxford in 1577, he proceeded to study law at Lincoln's Inn. Much later, in 1598, he took a medical degree in Avignon, passing in just two years instead of the usual three.[2] He was also an original, versatile and influential writer, whose literary publications began in 1579 with the first response to Stephen Gosson's *Shoole* [sic] *of Abuse, Conteining a plesaunt invective against Poets, Pipers, Plaiers, Jesters and such like Caterpillers of a Commonwelth* (1579); he countered the densely-packed classical learning supporting Gosson's argument with plenty of his own, but was also devastatingly direct on occasion: 'No mervel though you disprayse poetrye, when you know not what it meanes.'[3] He was also prolific: his original works fill four volumes, in addition to three substantial translations.[4] His literary interests, however, did not preclude other activities. He took part in adventuring on the high seas: on a voyage to the Canaries he occupied his spare time by writing *Rosalynde* (1590), the romance that inspired Shakespeare's *As You Like It* (1599). Unfortunately, the preliminaries to *A Margarite of America* (1596) reveal that seafaring was not always conducive to writing. In his dedication to Lady Elizabeth Russell, née Cooke (1528–1609), he recalls his sufferings '*in those straits christened by* Magelan', which included '*bitter and extreme frosts*', '*scantie fare*' and '*mightie discouragements*'.[5] His subsequent epistle 'To the Gentlemen Readers' evokes, even more vividly, the incompatibility of shipboard life with literary inspiration: 'it can not but stand with your discretions to pardon an undiscreete and unstaied penne, for hands may vary where stomacks miscary.'[6]

Lodge's medical knowledge interacted more comfortably, though not exactly predictably, with his literary talents. The title of his verse miscellany, *A fig for Momus* (1595), reflects a defiant mood: Momus, 'the god of reprehencion', represents any foolish and hostile critic.[7] It duly contains some fierce attacks on society's ills, including a pioneering adaptation of Juvenal's Satire XIV.[8] The less confrontational poems, however, include an epistle 'To his Mistres A.L.', in answer to the lady's request for guidance on her weight problem: 'You pray me to advise, and tell you what / Will take away your pursines and fat.'[9] After a great deal of advice based on contemporary medical theories, he concludes in a manner that would win him favour today by urging her to love her curves: she should

count her fatnes no deformitie,
But as it is the guise in *Italie*,
To nourish that: for fat, slicke, faire, and full,
Is better lik't, then leane, lancke, spare, and dull.[10]

His most important medical publication was *A Treatise of the Plague* (1603), published during an epidemic that probably caused 'the destruction of one-quarter of the population that was forced to stay in London.'[11] As C.D. O'Malley has argued, this was a text 'which sought to display his newly acquired ability', incidentally demonstrating his skill in using the press to advance his reputation.[12] Lodge exhibits a strong sense of righteous indignation on behalf of people unable to afford medical aid: '*For where the infestion most rageth there povertie raigneth among the Commons, which having no supplies to satisfie the greedie desire of those that should attend them, are for the most part left desolate & die without reliefe.*'[13] Moved by 'a great desire to doe good', he has written 'a true Methode how to knowe and cure the Plague', which he offers 'freely and charitably', preferring 'a common good' to 'all the gaping desires of gaine and profit in this world'.[14] Fortunately, nobody noticed that it was a translation of *Traicté de la Peste* (1556) by François Vallériole (1504–80).[15] However, Lodge's combination of medicine with morality would lend weight to his endorsement of Clinton's advocacy of maternal breastfeeding among the upper classes.

Although Lodge's Catholicism apparently raised problems, it did not ultimately prevent his development of a successful professional career, or a network of congenial social contacts. He had his medical degree incorporated by the University of Oxford on 25 October 1602, but 'his application for a licence from the College of Physicians was denied. Between 1598 and 1610 Lodge practised medicine, at times in London and at times in the Low Countries and France.'[16] He was finally admitted to the College of Physicians in 1610. It may be that his Catholic faith was the reason for his initial rejection from this body: indeed, it is believed that as early as 1584 Lodge's MA was withdrawn by Oxford on the same basis. However, in 1611, Lodge signed an oath of allegiance and was granted immunity from prosecution for his Catholicism from this point. So, although his name appears on a list of recusants as late as 1618, Alexandra Halasz contends that his faith did not cause him any difficulties after he was granted the protection of the Privy Council. Instead, 'the biographical assumption is that he established a viable medical practice in London in part because he attracted Catholic patients.'[17] As Halasz has noted, 'Lodge's dedications and direct or indirect autobiographical statements suggest personal friendships, some of long standing', including 'The aristocratic Howard, Carey, and Strange families, the poets Spenser, Daniel, and Drayton' and 'the professional writers Robert Greene and Barnabe Riche'.[18] The nature of his original contact with Clinton remains obscure: it may have come through acting as her physician, sharing family ties, or even seeing her manuscript; in any case, he was probably appointed to see it through the press at Oxford University where he had studied. The most likely link, though, is through the Howards, one of the most prominent Catholic families in the country: although Clinton was a firm Protestant, she had close Catholic connections.

Lady Katherine Howard (c.1564–1638), Countess of Suffolk, was Elizabeth Clinton's elder sister: she was ten years older than Clinton and little is known of their relationship, but it may be significant that both women gave the name Theophilus to their sons. Thomas Howard, Earl of Suffolk (1561–1626), held roles in the courts of both Elizabeth I and James I, being sworn of the privy chamber on 12 September 1599; Katherine was a lady of the bedchamber for Elizabeth and for James's consort, the Catholic convert Queen Anna (1574–1619); for the latter, she also became keeper of the jewels. Like many courtiers, Katherine performed in court entertainments and danced in two of Queen Anna's six masques: Samuel Daniel's *The Vision of the Twelve Goddesses* (8 January 1604) and Ben Jonson's *The Masque of Blackness* (6 January 1605). These performances provided spectacular connections between the aristocracy and literary leading lights. Howard's substantial influence at court, however, was not to last. First, in 1615–16 she was caught up in the trial of her daughter Frances (1590–1632), whose reputation was already damaged by aspersions arising from the annulment of her first marriage, for the murder of Sir Thomas Overbury (1581–1613).[19] Then, in 1619, Katherine suffered from the revelation of her own involvement in corruption, an attack of smallpox that ruined her famous beauty, and the death of her patron, Queen Anna. If the Howards, with whom Lodge was acquainted, had lost influence, then his own connections with the court would have been depleted. Viewed in this light, the address provided an opportunity to curry favour with new aristocratic contacts, perhaps including a younger generation of nobles such as Theophilus (c.1600–67) and Bridget Clinton (c.1604–d. before 1644), the new Earl and Countess of Lincoln. He could also join the dowager countess in a move towards the high moral ground, away from the decadence and scandal that tainted the atmosphere of the last years of the reign of James I.

While dedications have been singled out for study as a topic in their own right, addresses to the reader (many of which can also be classified as epistles or prefaces) have usually been considered alongside other kinds of paratext: this is probably why Lodge's address has received so little attention.[20] Examination of this example reveals that, whatever the reason, Lodge was on his best behaviour. To start with, he follows his usual custom of adhering to typographical conventions: dedicatee and reader 'are usually addressed in two different typefaces', and in this case Clinton's dedication to her daughter-in-law is in Roman type, while Lodge's prose address is in smaller italic type, followed by six lines of verse in even smaller Roman type.[21] Less typical of Lodge's approach are the direction of the address 'To the Courteous, chiefly most Christian, Reader', and the absence of insults.[22] It was a common strategy for authors to divide readers into two camps: discerning (therefore favourable) and foolish (therefore hostile); this was designed to encourage readers to seek merit in the book, or at least claim they had found it. Lodge's most blatant use of this method appears at the end of the address prefixed to his translation of Seneca: 'Gentle Reader for thee I laboured, for thy good have I made this admirable Roman speake English, if it profit thee I have my wish, if it displease thee, it is thy want of judgment. *Farewel.*'[23] The conclusion of an address in which he adopts the persona of the Cynic philosopher Diogenes (404/410 BC–323 BC) is uncomfortably true to his assumed character: '*If any of you read and like, why then it likes me: if read and dislike, yet it likes me: for Philosophie hath taught me to set as light by envie, as flatterie.*'[24] On another occasion he is divisive throughout, starting 'To the Reader of either sort', and concluding, '*Farewell and thanke him that hath studied thee so much profit; if thou doest not I pardon thee because thou doest as the world teacheth thee.*'[25] Comparison with a book in whose publication Lodge takes no part, published a year after the *Nurserie*, serves to show that Lodge conforms to normal practice: the editors address it '*To the great Variety of Readers.* From the most able, to him that can but spell', and conclude by advising them to read the author's works repeatedly: 'if then you doe not like him, surely you are in some manifest danger, not to understand him.'[26]

It is true that Lodge divides the readers of the *Nurserie* into two categories, but not according to any moral or intellectual quality whose imputed absence might give offence; his sole criterion, too objective to admit dispute, is rank: '*If* Noble *who readest*, (likenesse is Mother & Nurse of liking) *this comes from* Nobility; Approve *the rather, and* practise. *If* meaner; *blush to deny, what* Honour *becomes* speaker *to perswade to*, president *to lead the way to. And so I either* humbly *take my leave; or bid farewell.*'[27] In early modern England, everybody knew their own and everybody else's place. Lodge himself sets an example of cheerful acceptance, behaving 'humbly' towards his honourable (i.e. noble) readers, and reserving a friendlier greeting for his 'meaner' equals. He conscripts the class system to support Clinton's arguments in favour of maternal breastfeeding, by leaving nobles and commoners equally obliged to accept them. He also manages to involve not one countess but two in the process: the dowager Elizabeth Clinton, as author, is the 'speaker *to perswade*', but since she did not nurse her own children, cannot be the 'president [precedent] *to lead the way*'.[28] This is her daughter-in-law, Bridget Clinton, née Fiennes, the present Countess of Lincoln,[29] praised in the dedication for performing this 'lovely action'.[30] Lodge also utilizes the permeability of this kind of division between readers: the 'meaner' sort would enjoy eavesdropping on his reminder to a noble reader that if their ancestry goes back far enough, they must already be the author's friend, and probably her relative: '*The Author so* Eminent *in* Honour; *thou canst hardly be anciently* Honourable; *and not be interested in her* Honours acquaintance; *scarcely not* Alliance.'[31]

This is not the only instance where Clinton's high standing is exploited. In his opening sentence, Lodge adds snobbery to an already potent brew of sensationalism and sex appeal: '*The Generall Consent of too many mothers in an unnaturall practise, (most Christian Reader) hath caused one of the* Noblest *and* Fairest *hands in this land to set pen to paper*.'[32] The lady's nobility would give an extra thrill to readers who, having skipped the dedication, are already wondering what unspeakable horrors are about to be revealed. Lodge, however, is not flaunting aristocratic connections for their own sake: he sees an author's 'Eminency' as an inducement to read the text.[33] In the treatise, Clinton, too, displays a strongly practical awareness that rank has its uses; she argues that it can give maternal breastfeeding a higher public profile, while making it more convenient:

> were it not better for *Us greater persons* to keepe Gods ordinance, & to shew the meaner their dutie in our good example? I am sure wee have more helpes to performe it, and have fewer probable reasons to alleage against it, then women that live by hard labour, & painfull toile.[34]

In her eyes, the privileges of aristocratic mothers confer weighty obligations.

Lodge and Clinton, then, both seem determined to emphasize the aristocracy's natural position as role models. This in itself suggests a certain humility on the part of the aristocrats involved, since there would be no point in setting examples that the lower orders were unable to follow: suckling babies is a very different activity from dancing in masques. The brevity of Clinton's work and her direct style create an impression of accessible simplicity. Lodge accordingly claims that the effort of reading this short treatise has much more to offer than its unpretentious appearance suggests: '*The* pay, *assure thy selfe, will bee larger than the* promise. *The* Wine *much better then the* Bush.'[35] He is invoking a familiar proverb, based on established custom: in an era of low literacy, when visual signs were used outside shops, an ivy bush on the end of a pole, looking like a witch's broomstick, was displayed outside vintners and taverns to denote their trade. The proverb is best known today in the form that appears in the epilogue of *As You Like It*: 'If it be true, that good wine needs no bush, 'tis true, that a good play needes no Epilogue.'[36] Or, in other words, just as a good vintner's reputation will spread by word of mouth, rendering a sign redundant, so a good play does not require the embellishment of an epilogue. It can also be found in some commendatory verses Lodge had contributed over thirty years previously to another useful work, a textbook on calligraphy and shorthand by Peter Bales (1547–1610?):

> There needes no Ivie, where the wine is good:
> Nor queint discourse, where judgement leads the pen (lines 1-2).[37]

In the address, this argument continues in Lodge's concluding poem, as clearly as its crabbed couplets will permit, that the nation's rulers have a sacred duty to be its teachers and exemplars:

> Blest is the land where Sons of Nobles raigne.
> Blest is the land where Nobles teach their traine.
> To Church for blisse Kings, Queenes, should Nurses be.
> To state its blisse great Dames Babes nurse to see.
> Go then Great booke of Nursing plead the Cause.
> Teach High'st, low'st, all, it's Gods and Natures lawes.[38]

The lines have at least the merit of containing Lodge's first direct reference to the subject of Clinton's treatise.

Most of the poem's language is designed to be taken literally, apart from personifications involving the 'state' deriving joy from the spectacle of high-ranking ladies suckling their babies and, on a more abstract level, the 'Church' being nursed by kings and queens. The latter image is derived from Isaiah 49:23: 'And kings shall be thy nursing fathers, and their queenes thy nursing mothers.'[39] The translators of the King James Bible clearly found 'nursing fathers' a puzzling concept: a marginal note removes potential contradictions by explaining that the term means '*nourishers*' in the original

Hebrew. Milk here represents whatever support or protection is needed by God's chosen people. In the New Testament, it comes to represent Christian doctrine, especially those elements suitable for new converts; a typical text is 1 Peter 2:2: 'As new borne babes desire the sincere milke of the word, that yee may grow thereby.' Both texts are combined in the preliminaries to the Bible, where the 'noursing fathers and mothers' are the designated providers of material support to the clergy, who in turn provide spiritual sustenance, and the translators advise the powers that be not to disrupt the cycle of mutual suckling by unilateral weaning:

> that the Church be sufficiently provided for, is so agreeable to good reason and conscience, that those mothers are held to be lesse cruell, that kill their children assoone as they are borne, then those noursing fathers and mothers (wheresoever they be) that withdraw from them who hang upon their breasts (and upon whose breasts againe themselves doe hang to receive the Spirituall and sincere milke of the Word) livelyhood and support fit for their estates.[40]

Clinton, too, combines these texts in a passage condemning taking steps to dry up a mother's breasts 'in which your owne child (and perhaps one of Gods very elect, to whom to be a noursing father, is a Kings honour; and to whom to be a noursing mother, is a Queen's honour) might finde food of syncere milke.'[41] At this point, milk flows through the barriers between literal and metaphorical, acquiring spiritual power in the process, with a symbolic energy that leaves Lodge's verse looking prosaically literal in comparison.

Clinton's reference here to the 'elect' raises questions about her beliefs. The concepts of election and predestination were crucial to Calvinist Protestantism, so the idea that a child might be among the elect made the maternal duty of breastfeeding all the more urgent. They also raised puzzling questions about the efficacy of good works. Nobody would expect a Catholic like Lodge to doubt that encouraging people to obey 'Gods and Natures lawes' increased their chances of salvation.[42] For Clinton, the matter might be less certain. Doubts might be countered by the belief that the elect would receive the ability to behave more virtuously than the reprobate; this appears in Clinton's dedication to her daughter-in-law, whom God has adorned with 'the practise of true Christian religion; dedicating your selfe to Gods service; answerablenesse to all holy commands of the holy God, which are Testimonies of Gods love.'[43] Yet Clinton is not content to let matters rest there: her treatise is the result of her determination to persuade less virtuous women to improve their conduct. She brings the Bible to her support, citing 1 Timothy 5, 10-14, to show that bringing up children, which includes nursing them, 'is numbred as the first of the good workes, for which godly women should be well reported of'.[44] Another aspect of her treatise that might strike some readers as unusual in a Protestant is the amount of respect she pays to the Virgin Mary. Has Clinton absorbed Catholic doctrine, perhaps through her connection with Lodge? It seems unlikely. Clinton's son Theophilus, the 4th Earl of Lincoln, was a strict Puritan: his chief steward was Thomas Dudley (1576–1653), father of Puritan poet Anne Bradstreet (1612–72), and two of her daughters accompanied their husbands to the New World as part of the Puritan migration. If there are passages in her treatise where she does not seem to align herself exclusively with any single confessional position, the reader should consider whether some aspects of her faith have been misunderstood, and perhaps wilfully misrepresented, in the early modern period.

In the first place, it is true that Protestants in general, and Puritans in particular, were accused of neglecting good works, since they considered them unnecessary to salvation. At the sixth session of the Council of Trent, convened on13 January 1547, Pope Paul III (1468–1549) anathematized thirty-three variations of the doctrine that salvation was possible by faith alone.[45] Yet doctrine did not directly affect conduct. Searchers for a clear path through the theological maze can find one clearly mapped out in Jane Grey's words to the monk John Feckenham (c.1515–84), shortly before her execution on 12 February 1554:

> *Jane*: To love our neighbor is to feede the hungry, to cloth the naked, and geve drinke to the thirsty, and to doe to him, as we would doe to our selves.
>
> *Feck*: Why? then it is necessary unto salvation, to doe good workes also, and it is not sufficient only to beleeve.
>
> *Jane*: I denye that, and I affirme that faith onely saveth: but it is meete for a Christian, in token that hee followeth his Maister Christe, to doe good workes: yet may wee not say that they profit to our salvation. For when we have done all, yet we be unprofitable servants, and faith only in Christes bloud saveth us.[46]

Clinton's comparison of nursing mothers to the 'blessed Virgin' also seems free from specifically Catholic sympathies: as Rachel Trubowitz has observed, Puritan writers tended to portray Mary as 'but one of a long scriptural line of exemplary, natural nursing mothers', as Clinton does, rather than as a divine mediator between believers and God whose breast milk had 'special mystical meaning accorded to it by Roman Catholic tradition'.[47] It is the case, though, that in Clinton's list of biblical mothers Mary is given the most acclaim: '*Eve* the mother of al the living; *Sarah* the mother of al the faithfull; *Hannah* so gratiously heard of God; *Mary* blessed among women, and called blessed of all ages.'[48] When it comes to breastfeeding, passing Protestant references to Mary are not very different from her detailed portrayal in Lodge's own *Prosopopeia, Containing the Tears of the holy, blessed, and sanctified Marie, the Mother of God* (1596). Lodge is following precedents set by 'five & twenty ancient, holy, and Catholique Fathers of the Church'.[49] Nevertheless, his Mary says nothing contrary to Protestant belief when she reminisces on the practicalities of motherhood: 'Ah that the adversitie of an houre shoulde make mee thus forget the pleasures I had in lyfe; when I lulled thee in my lap my son, fostered thee at these teates, followed thee in travels, fedde with thee in Ægypt.'[50] John Bale, a reformist whom one would never suspect of excessive devotion to Mary, compares her to the future Queen Elizabeth I in his dedication of *A Godly Medytacyon* (1548): 'Your penne hath here plenteouslye uttered the habundaunce of a Godly occupyed harte, lyke as ded the vyrgynall lyppes of Christes most blessed mother, whan she sayd with heavenly rejoice, My sowle magnyfyeth the lorde.'[51]

People who still believe that ardent reformists were incapable of advocating good works, or showing respect for the Virgin Mary, might consult the *Short Catechisme* (1553) composed by John Ponet (1514–56). This document prescribes the belief and conduct of ordinary people. Edward VI's prefatory 'Injunction' stresses the importance of teaching young children 'howe they maye please God, wherin we oughte, wyth all the doynges and dutyes of oure lyfe, to travayle'.[52] Action was thus vitally important to the development of a Christian. As for Mary, the scholar memorizing his answers to the master's questions is taught to say that Jesus was 'conceaved of the holy Gost: engendred of the wombe and substaunce of Marie, the blessed pure & undefiled maide: and was so borne & fostred by her as other babes be, savinge that he was most far from all infection of synne.'[53] Sadly, the image and perhaps even the occasional reality of Puritans as narrow-minded extremists persisted. John Earle (1601?–65), who was to become Bishop of Salisbury in 1643, published, in 1628, a brief pen-portrait of 'A Shee precise Hypocrite' (i.e. female Puritan):

> She doubts of the Virgin Marie's Salvation, and dare not Saint her, but knows her owne place in heaven as perfectly, as the Pew shee ha's a key to. Shee is so taken up with Faith, shee ha's no roome for Charity, and understands no good Workes, but what are wrought on the Sampler.[54]

Clinton, however, was a very different woman. In using scripture to promote maternal breastfeeding, she follows a tradition that can be traced to 'Puerpera' ('The woman who has just given birth') (1526), a dialogue by the humanist Catholic priest Desiderius Erasmus (1469–1536).[55] We find a young mother being told, on the basis of some rather dubious ancient Greek etymology, that 'to take altogither a hired Nurse for a poore tender Infant, as yet warme from the mother, is a kinde of exposing, or casting it foorth to hazarde', while 1 Timothy 2:15 is cited to support the statement that 'you have not yet done the part of a mother, unlesse you first frame aright his tender bodie, and then his mind as tender as that with good education.'[56] Although some humanist views, including the idea that marriage was superior to virginity, had since been rejected by the Catholic Church, Erasmus's ideas on the crucial importance of motherhood and its duties were drawn from scriptural and classical authorities that still provided Christians with common ground.[57] This would explain the harmonious relationship between Lodge's address and Clinton's text. Lodge's biographer, Edward Andrews Tenney, describes his contribution to the *Nurserie* in no uncertain terms as 'fulsome and bombastic', considering it 'no credit to his declining years', but when considered in its historical, generic and religious context, it becomes clear that the address serves its purpose well.[58]

The presence of the address raises further issues, however, which cannot be resolved within the scope of this chapter. Heidi Brayman Hackel observes: 'By the early seventeenth century, many conventions were firmly established for both the dedicatory epistle and the address to the reader, the most basic of which was the expectation of their presence in most printed books.'[59] It became customary for printers to start the book's main text on the second gathering, usually B1 (recto), reserving the A gathering for the preliminaries: this is the case with Clinton's text. It was also customary for authors to provide dedications and addresses to the reader themselves. Since such a robust tradition was established, irregularities in the process may repay investigation. Examination of Lodge's complete works, supplemented by the other texts mentioned in this chapter – admittedly a small sample – reveals several cases, each involving loss of authorial control. Distance could be a crucial factor: when Lodge departed 'to sea upon a long voyage', he entrusted a manuscript to his friend Robert Greene (1558–92), who duly provided the proper preliminaries.[60] The situation involving the Lady Elizabeth's *Godly Medytacyon* was reversed: she was in England, but John Bale, who published the volume, contributing the dedication and address to the reader, and possibly working without her knowledge or consent, was out of the country. Shakespeare died seven years before the 1623 Folio was published; Edward Blount writes a letter 'To the Reader' explaining that John Earle's *Micro-cosmographie* was being published in haste as a precaution against the publication of 'imperfect and surreptitious' copies of his carelessly-circulated manuscripts; John Ponet's *Catechisme*, a work too important to be the property of a private man, is introduced by Edward VI's 'Injunction'.[61] The three 'mother's legacy' books bear testimony to their authors' determination to perform their bibliographical duties: the only obstacle they faced was death, and even that might be circumvented. Richardson published her *Ladies Legacie* in perfect order, six years before she died; Leigh's *The Mothers Blessing* appeared posthumously, complete with her dedication to Elizabeth of Bohemia and a letter '*To my beloved Sonnes*', the only readers she wanted.[62] Even Elizabeth Jocelin, whose *Mothers Legacie* was 'found in her Deske unfinished' after her death, left a letter 'To my truly loving, and most dearly loved Husband', that was published as an 'Epistle Dedicatorie'.[63] The address to the reader, however, entitled 'The Approbation', was provided by a family friend, the clergyman Thomas Goad (1576–1638), who 'undertooke the care of the publication'.[64]

Although this evidence shows that it was not unprecedented for a man to provide preliminaries for a woman's work, or even for another man, it does not fully explain Clinton's case, since there is no evidence, biographical or bibliographical, that she lacked control of the situation. It is highly probable that she chose Lodge for this service. She may have felt the need for an extra layer of protection for herself and her treatise; although she expressed indifference, the fact that she bothered to do so indicates a fear of ridicule:

> I speake of so much as I reade, and know in my owne experience, which if any of my sexe, and condition do receave good by, I am glad: if they scorne it, they shall have the reward of scorners. I write in modestie, and can reape no disgrace by their immodest folly.[65]

The reference to her 'condition' is a reminder that, as well as being a woman seeking to protect her modesty, she was an aristocrat wishing to preserve her dignity. If so, she had excellent precedents: not just the Lady Elizabeth but Catherine Parr, the first Englishwoman to put her name on the cover of an original book, *The Lamentacion of a Sinner* (1547), which contains a preface addressed to the readers by William Cecil (1520–98).[66] Whatever the motives of Clinton or Lodge may have been, examination of their brief collaboration has raised questions about the interactions of gender, rank and class with early modern book production that resemble those arising at the end of Chapter 1. Whether future investigation will find answers or just more questions, it will be interesting.

Chapter Three

God-Given Pleasure: Aphrodisiacs, Fertility and Sexual Pleasure in Early Modern England

by Jennifer Evans

In his famous diary, Samuel Pepys (1633–1703) noted that on 26 July 1664 he had been at a dinner celebrating the birth of Anthony Joyce's child. While everyone was merry, Pepys took the opportunity to ask a group of women for their opinions and advice about his own 'not getting of children'.[1] Pepys and his wife Elisabeth (1640–69) had been married for eight years and, as his diary reveals, he was full of fears about their infertility. Pepys was not alone. The antiquarian and diarist Sir Simonds D'Ewes (1602–50) recorded that infertility had afflicted several of his family members. He stated that he was born in 1602 which 'brought great joy to both' his parents as his mother had 'remained barren about six years after her marriage' before producing a daughter, and now, two years further on, he was 'their first-born son, and so the hope of continuing both their names and families'.[2] Likewise he explained that

> My wife's aunt had remained barren for some six or seven years after her marriage, and would often say, when we sojourned with her, that I might have many children by my wife, but that she was out of hope of any; and therefore this child, though a daughter, was very welcome both to her and her husband, because it gave them hope of further issue.[3]

D'Ewes had first-hand experience of infertility. In 1629 he recorded that his wife had suffered from 'sterility and barrenness' but thankfully his 'doubts and sad apprehensions' had been 'abundantly eased', now that he was 'certainly assured' that his wife had conceived.[4] Indeed, infertility was such a common experience that the barren wife became a trope in popular and ephemeral literature. In the *Ten Pleasures of Marriage* (1682), a satirical account of married life, the new bride, mere months after her marriage, complained to her neighbours that she was yet to get pregnant.[5] In return, the author wryly noted, 'Whosoever she speaks with every one pities her, and gives her their advice' on the best means to augment the sexual prowess and fertility of her husband.[6]

Early modern medical writers devoted substantial attention to the question of fertility. It was evident to them that many men and women did not easily conceive and bear children once they were married. This was an issue of importance because of the well-known biblical injunction from Genesis, 9:1 that Noah and his sons should 'Be fruitfull and multiply, and replenish the earth.'[7] These authors paint a vivid picture of the frustrations, anxiety and despair childless women, and men, experienced by drawing comparisons with the biblical tale of Rachel who was unable to conceive. Jane Sharp, for example, included in her midwifery manual Rachel's cry to Jacob, '*Give me Children or else I die*' (Genesis 30:1).[8] In his treatise *The Practice of Physick*, Robert Johnson (b. 1640?) includes Rachel's lament alongside the observation that 'Very few Women in a Marriage state but desire Children, yea some would give all they have in the world for a Child, and are very impatient if they do not Conceive.'[9] In using such examples, medical men implicitly configured barrenness as a female illness. Drawing on the language of the Bible where barrenness was used to describe women's wombs or infertile land reinforced the cultural bias that viewed infertility as a female disorder.[10] This, however, was at odds with their other discussions of barrenness which, particularly in the sixteenth and early seventeenth century, maintained that barrenness was both a male and a female condition. *The Expert Midwife* (1637), an anonymous translation of *De Conceptu et generatione hominis* (1554) by Jakob Rueff (1500–58), explained that 'We say, that sterility or barrennesse … is not onely a disability and unaptnesse of bringing forth children in women, contracted and caused by some cause that may be corrected and remedied: but in men also of ingendering and sending forth fruitfull seede.'[11] For Rueff, barrenness was a term designating a complete inability to produce children, whether this came from a deficiency in the man's ability to eject seed or in the woman's ability to carry a child to term.

It was universally acknowledged that fertility was a gift given by God. He could bless people with children or cause them to be infertile. Throughout the early modern period marriage was understood to be the proper institution for the regulation of unbridled lusts. The marriage bed was the only site for the legitimate expression of sexuality and was thought to reduce the temptation towards fornication and adultery.[12] Prior to the Reformation, celibacy had been exalted as the ideal religious and spiritual state that allowed the avoidance of sin. By contrast, Protestants such as Martin Luther (1483–1546) criticized celibacy because it was unattainable and also prevented procreation. Instead, marriage was elevated as the natural and ideal state for everyone.[13] These ideas were taken up by English Protestants who praised marital sexuality and the outlet it provided for natural desires.[14] According to Patricia Crawford, Protestant ministers considered it 'not just allowable', but 'good in itself'.[15] Both William Perkins (1558–1602) and William Gouge (1575–1653) expounded the conceptive and sexually pleasing nature of marital sexuality and the benefits it brought to couples.[16]

Within this understanding, children were, potentially, an expression of the godliness and happiness of a marriage. Yet scholars have debated the importance of fertility and children to married life. Alan Macfarlane has argued that early modern parents were not always swayed by religious motivations to have children, but became parents for their own psychological gratification.[17] He also highlighted parents' concern with the potential for multiple children to become an economic burden.[18] Mary Rich, married to the younger son of an English earl, noted her husband's concern when she fell pregnant for a third time: though he was 'fond of his children .... He would often say he feared he would have so many as would undo a younger brother.'[19] Despite evident economic concerns, most scholars agree that children were prized as a sign of God's blessing.[20] One problem with Macfarlane's interpretation was that he viewed the desire for children and anxiety about children as conflicting extremes, but of course it is also possible for people to want to have children and, simultaneously, to be concerned that having too many children would be financially overwhelming.

Viewing the matter from the perspective of those who were infertile (rather than those who were fertile) provides further evidence that men and women interpreted the birth of children as a sign of God's favour, and that in many cases they were generally welcomed. Infertility was intimately bound to religious and moral ideas and being infertile could damage social status.[21] Ballads and ephemeral literature from the era reveal that a wife who did not bear children could be subjected to the 'taunts and jeers of my Neighbours, who call me *Barren-Doe*'.[22] In some cases the ability to conceive was also tied to professional identity. Many midwives derived part of their authority from their own experience of childbirth. One broadside ballad told the story of a barren midwife who used a 'little Pillow' (line 17) to deceive her husband and her community into thinking she was pregnant.[23] Realizing that her due date was fast approaching, the midwife had to escalate her deception and recovered the body of a new-born infant recently buried; 'pretending suddain pains' (line 54), she claimed that she had given birth to the child. According to the ballad the midwife was arrested and languished in jail. The ballad framed this story as one about nature: 'Thus did she strive for to obtain, / what nature did deny' (lines 89-90); in its final lines, however, it hinted that all childbirth was viewed within a religious framework by acknowledging, with a certain wry admiration, that the midwife performed a 'cunning slight, / as ever did befall' (lines 93-4) in trying 'To bring a Child into the World, / and feel no pain at all' (lines 95-6).

As is still acknowledged by some, and was well-known in the early modern period, the pain of childbirth was Eve's punishment for eating the forbidden fruit in the Garden of Eden. Jane Sharp explained in her midwifery manual of 1671 that 'hard labour attends most of them [women], it was that curse that *God* laid upon our sex to bring forth in sorrow, that is the general cause and common to all as we descended from the same great Mother *Eve*, who first tasted the forbidden fruit.'[24] The mistaken midwife was an object of pity, revulsion and grudging respect because, as the ballad's prefatory summary says, she was driven to these drastic measures in an attempt to remove 'the scandal of [her] Barreness', and because she tried to circumvent God's will by producing a child without experiencing the pain of a natural childbirth.[25]

Medical literature from the early modern period clearly framed infertility as governed by God's will. The anonymously-authored *The English Midwife Enlarged* (1682) told its readers that 'All rational men know, that the generation of mankind … is the most perfect, excellent and exquisite work of God's Vicegerent *Nature*.'[26] The author thus made clear to his audience that fertility, although working through natural actions, was instigated, created and regulated by God: 'exquisite' in this context is best understood as 'ingeniously devised'.[27] Robert Barret's midwifery treatise also reminded readers that fertility was a blessing when introducing his thoughts on the causes of barrenness and its cure. He wrote: 'there is no Necessity of amassing Arguments for the encouragement of Fertility, or aggravating the curse of Barrenness; I could appeal to every Womans thoughts what a blessing it is to have Children, tho' with inexpressible Pain and Labour, and how uneasie and bitter it is to be depriv'd of 'em by the shutting up of their Womb.'[28] Similarly, Robert Pierce observed, in a record of his practice as a doctor in Bath, that many women attended the baths for the '*common Cause*', barrenness.[29] He included several observations of such women and noted that the wife of Lord Blessington drank and bathed in the waters for her health and to have children and 'by the Blessing of God upon the Means, she not only recover'd a better State of Health, but afterwads [*sic*] became a Mother of Children.'[30] Jane Sharp was even more forthright, saying plainly that God was sometimes the cause of barrenness and, consequently, prayer was a chief part of any treatment regime undertaken.[31]

Medical writers throughout the period offered a plethora of remedies and treatments for barrenness. As mentioned above, women with the means visited the baths to seek a cure for their infertility. Remedies were tailored to the specific ailments of the patient that were inhibiting their reproductive functions, including treatments for the whites (an abundance of vaginal discharge), prolapse of the womb, dryness and heat of the womb, ulceration and menstrual disorders. In addition to treating underlying conditions, medical writers also advocated that men and women eat a range of foods known to act as aphrodisiacs. A 1658 English edition of *The Secret Miracles of Nature* by Levinus Lemnius (1505–68) explained that infertile couples should amend their diets to improve their reproductive organs. He suggested ingredients that would 'make them fruitful for propagation', defined as 'such things as stir up venery, and breed seed for generation'.[32] He thus conflated aphrodisiacs and fertility remedies, demonstrating clearly the way in which the boundary between these two foods was at least blurred, at most not relevant at all. In many historical studies of sex and reproduction sexual pleasure has figured as an ahistorical constant whose experience is considered the same for all people at all times. Concurrently aphrodisiacs are dehistoricized: they are described as provoking lust in the same way in all time periods. This limits our understanding of these substances. In early modern England sexual pleasure was inextricably connected to conception and aphrodisiacs were overwhelmingly understood to promote both sexual desire and fertility.

Not all scholars have fallen into this 'trap'. In *Consuming Passions* (1970), Philippa Pullar noted that aphrodisiacs in the past were inextricably connected with fertility and sexual potency.[33] Likewise, Angus McLaren explained in 1984 that early modern perceptions of close links between procreation and sexual pleasure provided a means of interpreting and understanding attitudes to aphrodisiacs.[34] McLaren's analysis, however, positioned this as a predominantly male concern, claiming that female barrenness was treated with remedies that warmed and invigorated the body but did not necessarily increase libido.[35] Again, evidence from the period suggests that many remedies and actions were designed to stimulate a woman's fertility by enhancing her libido. In thinking about sex and sexual pleasure with a modern mindset, scholars have obscured the intriguing and nuanced history of substances like aphrodisiacs. These titillating foods were not simply sexual curiosities for early modern men and women: they were a crucial medical tool in the fight for fertility. Framing these discussions and understandings was the belief that sexual pleasure, fertility and medicinal substances were all provided by God for the benefit of mankind. Thus both sexual pleasure and the means to enhance it were God-given.

Aphrodisiac foods and substances were thought to act in a range of ways.[36] By heating the body, they fuelled the flames of desire (like rocket and ginger).[37] Capons, parsnips and eryngo nourished the body and encouraged it to produce seed by tickling and irritating the reproductive organs as it moved through them.[38] Borax and salt meats added salt to men and women's seminal matter, increasing its titillating qualities.[39] What unified the diverse categories of aphrodisiacs was the fact that they were usually understood to be fertility aids. Their ability to increase bodily desire and pleasure was inherently tied to the effects they had upon the reproductive body and these effects made the body more fertile. Firstly, by increasing sexual desire, aphrodisiacs encouraged people to engage in intercourse, which was of course necessary for conception to occur. However, secondly, pleasure was also necessary as male and female seed was believed by many to be released during orgasm and mixed to form a foetus; without pleasure sexual intercourse would be empty and, in essence, pointless because it would not satisfy either party and would not result in conception. Throughout the early modern period, foods that stimulated desire and pleasure but came to be considered of little benefit to fertility and conception – notably windy and salty aphrodisiacs – were gradually dismissed as ineffective and lost their association with libido.[40] Lemnius argued that wind, long thought to be crucial to successful intercourse, provided a hollow sexual experience because sex facilitated by wind was not fertile. As he explained, these men 'have their veins puffed up with wind, but there wants seed'.[41] Similarly, Théophile Bonet (1620–89), the Geneva physician, was emphatic in his 1684 medical text that stimulants that worked through '*Flatus*' were not to be considered true aphrodisiacs because they did not make the seed 'turgid'.[42]

Increasing desire and pleasure was particularly crucial for improving the fertility of the female body, which was considered, in general, to be colder and less desiring than the male body. In the humoral model men and women were positioned along an axis of heat and cold that determined the strength of their gender characteristics and the strength of their sexual drive. Men, being naturally warmer and drier, had a greater sex drive, or as some writers stated, a greater propensity for and ability in the 'Sports of *Venus*'.[43] Women were not monolithically sexually numb, however. Warmer women were believed to be more lustful and some medical authors even warned men about thin, pale brunette women:

> Those Women are more hot, and prone to venery, and more mad after pleasure, that have more imbred heat, which is commonly found in pale & lean Women, & such as are of a brown colour, for their genital parts are full of a sharp salt biting humour … Wherefore men must make a good choice and not presently take what comes next to hand rashly. For he that hath got a lean slender woman of declining years, hath such a one as is alwaies itching, and will never be satisfied … she will stick to her Husband like a Horeseleach, and she will never let him rest, though he be tired out quite, nor give him so much respite as to recover his strength.[44]

Men's warmth also meant that they took less time to reach orgasm and release their seed. Some medical writers (who followed the model that proposed both men and women produced seed) argued that the best chance of conception occurred when both men and women released their seed into the woman's womb at the same moment. In 1636 John Sadler (1615–74), a physician in Norwich, informed his readers that conception sometimes failed because of 'the manner of the act: as when in the emission of the seed, the man is quicke and the woman too slow, whereby there is not a concurse [*sic*] of both seeds at the same instant, as the rules of conception require.'[45] Not all medical writers subscribed to the idea that women had to orgasm to release their seed. Yet some still noted that conception could only occur, as one text put it, 'when the Seed of both Sexes is mingled in the Womb'.[46] Nicholas Culpeper (1616–54), in his *Practice of Physick*, based on translations from Lazarus Riverius (Lazare Rivière) (1589–1655), provided a similar description but highlighted more prominently the important role pleasure played in this process:

> [a] Woman being averse from this kind of pleasure, gives not down sufficient quantity of Spirits, wherewith her Genitals ought to swell at the instant of Generation, that her womb skipping as it were for joy, may meet her Husbands Sperm, graciously and freely receive the same, and draw it into its innermost Cavity or Closet, and withall bedew and sprinkle it with her own Sperm, poured forth in that pang of Pleasure, that so by the commixture of both, Conception may arise.[47]

Using aphrodisiacs to increase women's desire and sexual pleasure, therefore, increased the likelihood that the two seeds would meet at the appropriate moment and that intercourse would lead to pregnancy.

Pleasure was thus an important element in fertile sexuality. Medical writers and others acknowledged that men and women could experience and indulge in this pleasure without intending to conceive a child. John Marten (d. 1737), writing in the early eighteenth century, explained that aphrodisiacs could be used in this way: 'Old Letchers thinking to improve their former Prowess, and Young Gallants willing to merit their Misses good Will, do oftentimes misapply those Medicines.'[48] In response, medical writers were at pains to emphasize that sexual pleasure was not frivolous but had a purpose and, importantly, was instituted by God. Perhaps the most vehement statement of this nature came from John Marten himself, who wrote:

> God Almighty has … endued each [sex] with natural Instincts, prompting them to the use thereof with desire, in order to perpetuate the Species, by producing new Creatures to supply the room of those who are gone; without which desire, what rational Creature would have taken delight in so filthy, so contemptible and base a thing as *Venery* is? And indeed, had not Nature tack'd a more than ordinary pleasing Sensation and Desire to each Sex, in the Act, by giving those parts such a quick tender Sense and transporting Titillation, and which with all the artillery of Reason we are not able to controul [*sic*], (so furious is our passion for the Embrace,) we should have no manner of incitement or inclination to the performing it; and consequently Procreation must soon cease and be at an end.[49]

Marten was adamant that pleasure was crucial to procreation. He was not alone in promoting this understanding of human sexuality. He followed in the footsteps of several earlier medical writers, including Helkiah Crooke (1576–1648), who had explained in 1615 that generation would not otherwise be possible

> were it not that the God of Nature hath placed heerein so incredible a sting or rage of pleasure, as whereby wee are transported for a time as it were out of our selves, what man is there almost who hath anie sense of his own divine nature, that would defile himselfe in

> such impurities? what woman would admit the embracements of a man, remembring her nine moneths burthen, her painefull and dangerous deliverance.[50]

Unlike Marten, Crooke noted that sexual pleasure did not just surmount the problem that intercourse was demeaning. He also emphasized its role in encouraging women to forget the pain and discomfort of pregnancy and childbirth.

Pleasure was central to early modern understandings of sexuality, but this was implicitly and explicitly framed by religious discussions of fertility and reproduction. God had instituted the feelings of sexual desire and pleasure to ensure that generation occurred: 'he put into them both force to love, and a greedy desire of procreating their like … he added allurements and a desire of mutual Embracing, that when they did use procreation, they should be sweetly affected, and pacified wonderfull wayes.'[51] Pleasure not only encouraged men and women to engage in intercourse, but caused the body to be fertile. Having children was thus, hopefully, in part, a pleasurable experience endorsed by God. Moreover, it was an experience that could be enhanced by consuming a range of aphrodisiacs, which were not only sexual curiosities but were fundamentally medicines intended to improve the body's fertility and the likelihood of conception.

Stilts

Jacqueline Mulhallen

(inspired by an historical account)

We were in a strange country –
Strange, unfamiliar, uncanny,
A treacherous land, too.
What we thought was land was watery quagmire
A man could go to his death in an instant.

Not that we're afraid of death, we are soldiers –
But such a death, sucked down to hell without warning!
And the water – the water was not always water.
Sometimes the land itself looks like water
It shines wetly.

There are fogs and mists covering it.
Suddenly birds start up;
A man could step near a swan's nest and they rise
Hissing, squawking and flapping their huge white wings.
Not that we're afraid of a swan, but we were often alarmed.

The people are strange too.
They don't labour in the fields, they have a boat,
They get what they can from the water.
Fish. Eels. They make houses from reeds.
They have cattle, and they know when to move them on to the higher ground.

Nothing is high. It is all flat. Reeds, mists, water.
Cold and wet. It breeds the ague.
They say if it were drained it would be good land.

So we were there. And then this came towards us.
A human being walking on the water.
Nay, I tell truly, walking on the water.
A woman by her skirts. Along by the reeds
Near where we found the swan's nest
And eels slithering in the mud.

Not that we're superstitious. We don't hold with miracles
Or such like papist stuff. But walking on the water?
Out of nowhere she came. What were we to think?
My father once saw a play where witches came out of a mist.
They led a man on to murder.
We didn't wait to see if she floated.

We did her down. There were four of us. She fought.
She fell immediately. She had sticks tied to her legs.
What else could she have been but a witch?

About the Poem

In September 1643, at the time of the English Civil War (1642–51), a number of publications reported that a witch had been found and killed by Parliamentary soldiers prior to the Battle of Newbury. One of the accounts appeared in an anonymous pamphlet which claimed to reveal *A Most Certain, Strange, and true Discovery of a Witch* (1643). A soldier discovers the woman 'treading of the water with her feet, with as much ease and firmnesse as if one should walk or trample, on the earth'.[1] His comrades and commanders, presented as credible witnesses, interpret her 'dance upon the water' as the act of a 'divellish woman'.[2] Believing her to be a witch, the soldiers attack, 'leaving her legacy of a detested carcasse to the wormes'.[3]

The accounts of the Witch of Newbury precede the notorious witch-hunts conducted by Matthew Hopkins (d. 1647), self-proclaimed 'Witch-Finder General', between the years 1644 and 1647.

Stilts is inspired by the story of the Witch of Newbury, but the tale is creatively re-imagined, with the setting transposed to the atmospheric landscape of the East Anglian fens, where the author lives. Historically, people used stilts and punts to navigate their way across the fens, a magical landscape long associated with superstition and witchcraft.

Chapter Four

Tweaking the Biography of Anne Finch

by Yvonne Noble

I first encountered Anne Finch, née Kingsmill, when, as a specialist on John Gay (1685–1732), I was asked to review Jayne Elizabeth Lewis's *The English Fable: Aesop and Literary Culture 1651–1740* (1996). Finch's witty female engagement with this subversive, seemingly naïve genre made me eager to know her other poetry and to learn about her life as well, for I live close to the part of Kent that Finch inhabited and wrote about during most of her life. On 15 May 1684 she married Heneage Finch (1657–1726), second son of the 3rd Earl of Winchilsea (1628–89), whose family seat, Eastwell Manor, was set in a park on the North Downs. I resolved to learn as much as I could about her life and writings. Recently I have been giving particular attention to what is being written about her, and this work has clarified some of the special dangers, as well as opportunities, for those of us who study early modern women. This endeavour has taught me how much more difficult it is to research an early modern woman's life than a man's, and the extra care scholars must take. In this chapter I will point out some of these difficulties, along with offering small additions or corrections to the existing record of Anne Finch's life.

Finch was circumspect about her poetry, far more reserved than a man with similar talents and commitment to the practice would have been, justly fearing that her work would provoke hostility because she was a woman. As she says in 'The Introduction' to her folio manuscript collection, not printed in her lifetime:

> Alas! A woman that attempts the pen,
> Such an intruder on the rights of men,
> Such a presumptuous Creature, is esteem'd,
> The fault, can by no vertue be redeem'd. (lines 9-12)[1]

Consequently, the verse that did get into print was scattered and generally anonymous. The main exception was the volume Finch was persuaded to publish in 1713 after she had reached a rather more secure status as a countess: her husband had become the 5th Earl of Winchilsea in the previous year. It appeared with the anonymity she preferred as *Miscellany Poems on Several Occasions. Written by a Lady*. This edition occurs with many different title pages, sometimes mistaken by the bibliographically innocent for multiple reprintings and thus evidence of popular success. On the contrary, poor sales caused the surplus sheets that had been printed to be sold on from bookseller to bookseller until, presumably to stimulate buyers, later issues replaced '*a Lady*' with '*the Right Hon*^{ble} *Anne, Countess of Winchilsea*'. This exposure, I feel sure, would have been made without her permission being sought and would have constituted a painful embarrassment to her. She had entered the market with great hesitation and had found, as she had feared, that there one loses one's control over one's words sometimes and over the presentation of one's own identity. The experience bore out the description of the fate of poets in the new commercial age that she had put into the mouth of the miser Mammon in 'A Tale of the Miser and the Poet, Written about the Year 1709':

> Instead of Honour'd and Rewarded,
> Are you not Slighted, or Discarded?
> What have you met with, but Disgraces?
>
> ……
>
> Now grant *no Worth in any thing*
> *But so much Money as 'twill bring.*
> Then, never more from your Endeavours
> Expect Preferment, or less Favours. (lines 51-3, 78-81)[2]

Instead of print, Anne preserved her poems at home in manuscript volumes. The earliest was an octavo, entitled 'Poems on Several Subjects, Written by Ardelia'. It is now in the Northamptonshire Record Office, as MS Finch-Hatton 283. Subsequently it was supplanted by a folio, entitled 'Miscellany Poems with Two Plays by Ardelia', now in the Folger Shakespeare Library as MS N.b.3, into which most of the poems in the octavo were copied and to which many further poems as well as the two plays were added. Finch seems to have regarded her *Miscellany Poems* as a comparable personal record, for many poems printed there do not appear in the manuscripts. Finally, near the end of her life in 1720 another manuscript volume was begun to record pieces written since the *Miscellany Poems* and others written earlier that were too informally personal or too outspoken politically to expose to most eyes. Most, perhaps all, of this manuscript was created after her death; it is now in the Margaret Clapp Library at Wellesley College and can be viewed online via Wellesley College Digital Scholarship and Archive as English Poetry Collection 43.

All these manuscript volumes have been thoroughly and carefully discussed by Gillian Wright in *Producing Women's Poetry, 1600–1730: Text and Paratext, Manuscript and Print* (2013). In 1903, when Myra Reynolds prepared her edition of Finch, the Wellesley manuscript had disappeared from public knowledge; it has since been published in a separate edition by Barbara McGovern, her biographer, and Charles H. Hinnant, author of the only book-length study of her writing.[3] Many worthy scholars – D.G. Neill, Ellen Moody, Carol Barash, Germaine Greer – have attempted a complete modern scholarly edition. At last Jennifer Keith, co-editing with Claudia Thomas Kairoff and with further assistance from Jean Marsden, may have succeeded: their edition, in two volumes, is promised this year from Cambridge University Press. Most students of the period agree with Paula Backscheider and Susan Staves that Finch is the foremost English woman poet of the eighteenth century.[4] She was acknowledged in friendship as a fellow poet by Alexander Pope (1688–1744), Jonathan Swift (1667–1745), and the dramatist Nicholas Rowe (1674–1718). Yet, because her poetry was written by a woman, it has taken 298 years from her death to gain comparable scholarly recognition.

Obscurity still hangs over the details of Anne Finch's life as well as her literary accomplishments. We know that in 1683 Heneage Finch was at court in his capacity as an officer in the Coldstream Guards and a groom of the bedchamber to James, Duke of York, younger brother and heir presumptive to Charles II. Anne was a maid of honour to the Duchess of York, Mary of Modena.[5] At her marriage Anne necessarily resigned her post, but Heneage remained in service after James succeeded to the throne as James II in 1685. We are not even certain where they lived as a couple. Barbara McGovern writes, without citation, that they 'lived in Westminster Palace', but specialists in court history I have asked tell me this idea is almost certainly mistaken.[6] W.J. Cameron, still acknowledged as the most informed Finch scholar, says merely that 'The young couple lived in Westminster.'[7] Finch so endorses a poem from this period, 'A Letter to Daphnis from Westminster, Ap: the 2d, 1685.'[8] Knowing that Heneage had court duties, McGovern must have attached to this the idea of the palace. Westminster Palace had been begun before the Norman Conquest by Edward the Confessor (c.1003–66), who moved his court away from the city of London; by Tudor times it housed certain law courts and Parliament as well as the royal court and residences. In the time of Henry VIII, however, the royal quarters had burned down. When Henry seized properties owned by Cardinal Thomas Wolsey (c.1473–1530), he moved the court to York Place, which the prelate had expanded to one of the grandest houses in London; it was renamed Whitehall Palace. In Finch's time residences of royal attendants would have been there or at St James's Palace. Anne's time as a maid of honour would have been at St James's, where we know the Duke of York first established Mary in London.

Positioned at the centre of influence, Anne and Heneage's prospects seemed happy in the 1680s. Heneage remained close to the king; he had also been promoted to lieutenant colonel in the Guards.[9] However, the political ineptitude of the Catholic James devastated their lives, as so many others'. Influential Protestants feared that his attempts to introduce broader religious toleration were the prelude to a Roman Catholic tyranny and welcomed an invasion by James's Protestant son-in-law William of Orange, who became joint ruler with James's elder daughter, Mary.[10] This put Anne and Heneage in a painful position: they remained staunch Church of England Protestants for their entire lives but considered that their loyalties lay with James and his heirs. They also faced difficult short-term problems: when the king fled to France, they lost their accommodation and stipends and had to seek somewhere to live and other means to live by. The family seat at Eastwell was an obvious base, but the couple may have preferred to stay somewhere else nearby, for the house could have been crowded with personalities potentially at odds: the old earl, disappointed in life and financially stressed, who had in the end abandoned King James and gone over to support William; the earl's fourth wife, Elizabeth née Ayres (1661–1745), near in age to Heneage and Anne; however many of the earl's numerous children down to toddlers were housed there; Heneage's older brother's widow (styled Viscountess Maidstone, née Elizabeth Wyndham [c.1656–96]) and her son Charles (1672–1712), the heir, still under age. Certainly, as the earl's biographer recounts, when he died the next year in 1689 the new widow and the mother of the heir squabbled over ownership of the household furniture.[11]

Anne and Heneage must have stayed nearby, however, for in 1690 at Hythe, a Channel port near Eastwell, with a few companions he attempted to sail to France to join James. He was arrested and imprisoned in the Tower under threat of being tried for treason from April to November 1690. Heneage was eventually released but lost his army commission. Till the end of his life Heneage refused to swear loyalty to William and Mary or any of the succeeding monarchs and therefore disqualified himself from patronage in public office. People in this position were known as non-jurors. During the anxious time when Heneage was imprisoned, Anne lived at Godmersham, a village about 6 miles from Eastwell on the Canterbury road, better known to literary scholars as the residence later of Edward Austen Knight (1768–1852), brother of Jane Austen. There Anne attempted to find solace by writing a play, *Aristomenes*, on a classical subject encoding topical issues; she explains in the 'Epilogue':

> when this was writt,
> 'Twas not for praise, or with pretense to witt:
> But lonely Godmersham th' attempt excuses,
> Not sure to be endur'd, without the Muses [.] (lines 10-13)[12]

McGovern and Wright suggest that it was at this time she began the formal collecting of her writing in the octavo manuscript volume.[13]

Outside Anne's poetry, little is documented about their life in the next two decades. It is often summarized in the terms used, for example, by Michael Gavin: Anne and Heneage were 'exiled from London as non-jurors' and 'went to live with his nephew, Charles Finch, then Earl of Winchilsea', placing them at Eastwell.[14] First of all, Anne was not a non-juror in the proper sense. She held no office, and it is doubtful she would have been required to swear allegiance to William; the regulations applied only to holders of civil, ecclesiastical, or military offices, though the words 'his or her said refusall' indicated that women might be included.[15] This matter, of course, might have arisen if she again became an attendant at court (but see endnotes 37-40). Next, their retreat to the country may have been due not so much to a forced 'exile' as to a wish to stay away from William's court, a choice shared by many of their friends and relations who had been willing to comply with the oath. On the other hand, they may have wished to avoid falling foul of the 'Act for the Amoving Papists and reputed Papists from the Cityes of London and Westminster and Ten Miles distance from the same.'[16] Anybody refusing to make a declaration renouncing the temporal or spiritual authority of any 'Forreigne Prince Person Prelate State or Potentate …. within this Realme' could be treated as a 'Popish Recusant' if they stayed within 10 miles of London.[17]

As for living with Heneage's nephew at Eastwell Park, Charles had to come of age and assume control of his property before he could invite them. Then it cannot be assumed that residing in the manor would put Anne in control of a 'new public space'.[18] Yet she certainly writes of Charles's invitation with becoming gratitude: 'an utter change in my Condition, and Circumstances, remov'd me into the solitude, & security of the Country, and the generous kindnesse of one that possest the most delightfull seat in itt; envited him, from whom I was inseperable, to partake of the pleasures of itt.'[19] The pair may not have stayed there long, but might have been instead accommodated at some other estate property nearby while still being able to enjoy the manor park and Charles's hospitality. While, as Anne wholeheartedly acknowledges, Charles treated them generously and without constraint as companions, expressing interest in and encouraging Anne's writing, nevertheless both she and Heneage would always have been aware that within the aristocratic context they were dependants, poor relations in a sense.[20] For in September 1692, near the time he issued the invitation, Charles brought home a wife, Sarah, née Nourse (d. 1730), and eventually the pair had a child, a son also named Charles who lived for only two years (1703–1705). Viscountess Maidstone, the earl's mother, also could have been resident. There is no sense of this domestic quotidian context in Anne's poetry or in the modern writing about her. One might regard it as significant that among the many poems Anne wrote to, or celebrating, friends and relations, no mention is made of Sarah Finch, who would have been a constant companion to anyone living at Eastwell.

Certainly by 1702 the invitation had modulated into residence at Wye, a village about 3 miles away, recorded in the title of 'An Apology for my fearfull temper in a letter in Burlesque upon the firing of my chimney At Wye College March 25th 1702', caricaturing her own overreaction. In retrospect she can see that her decision to wake everybody up and insist that they flee the house instantly was ill-considered: 'This hasty council and conclusion / Seem'd harsh to those who had no shoes on' (lines 71-2).[21] It is again from 'Wye Colege feb 14 170¾' that she inscribes the cover letter for a copy of her 'Pindarick Poem Upon the Hurricane in November 1703', sent to Heneage's brother-in-law, Viscount Weymouth of Longleat (1640–1714).[22] The couple may be documentable in Wye as late as 1710. Deborah Kennedy mentions that Heneage was an executor for Lady Margaret Coventry, née Tufton (1636–1710).[23] Also illustrating the principle that it is worthwhile to chase footnotes, one finds that the actual wording used by Edward Hasted, Kennedy's source, reads 'The Hon. Heneage Finch, of Wye', thus placing him in that village in 1710, or whenever the main part of the will was written (it has a codicil).[24] I have so far been unsuccessful in locating the will; more research is required.

In her poem 'A Contemplation' (of the justice expected to be found in heaven) Finch praises Lady Coventry's many benefactions to the church both at home and abroad:

> There Coventry of Tufton's Line
> For piety renown'd
> Shall in transcending Virtues Shine
> And Equally be Crown'd
>
> Around her shall the Chains be spread
> Of Captives she has freed
> And ev'ry mouth that she has fed
> Shall testify the deed
>
> Whilst Scools supplied to mend our youth
> Shall on the List be Shown
> A Daughter and a Mother both
> In Her the Church shall own
>
> The Gospell croste the seas rehearst
> By her diffusive aid
> And fifty-thousand pounds dispers'd
> Shall there be largely paid (lines 65-80)[25]

Lady Coventry's bequest reveals a common interest between herself and our couple that Anne's poem does not mention:

> She gives the moiety of the produce of her goods and chattels to Thomas Kene, late bishop of Bath and Wells, and the Rev. Nathaniel Spinckes, in trust, that they dispose of it among the deprived bishops and ministers of Scotland, according to the form of the church of England, and such deprived ministers of the church of England, whose several circumstances by reason of their not having taken the oaths, should be found most pressing and necessitous, and among such widows and children of them as should be left exposed to want.[26]

This reveals a particular link with Heneage, for he served as witness to the secret consecrations of non-juring bishops, including one of the trustees

Lady Coventry named for her bequest, Nathaniel Spinckes (1654–1727).[27] The other trustee was Thomas Ken (1637–1711), who had lost the see of Bath and Wells for refusing the oath to William and who had been taken in by Lord Weymouth to live at Longleat. He is the only person named in Anne Finch's hurricane ode: his replacement had been killed by a falling chimney in the episcopal palace during the storm, and Finch allows herself to wonder what would have happened if Ken had not been dismissed:

> Yet strictly pious KEN! had'st Thou been there,
> This Fate, we think, had not become thy share;
> Nor had that awful Fabrick bow'd,
> Sliding from its loosen'd Bands;
> Nor yielding Timbers been allow'd
> To crush thy ever-lifted Hands,
> Or interrupt thy Pray'r. (lines 100-6)[28]

Lady Coventry's will reveals Heneage as a more active agent linking her and his sister's household than we had known.

Anne Finch also did her part. 'To the Rev[d]. Mr. Bedford' is addressed to Hilkiah Bedford (1663–1724), whose consecration as a non-juring bishop Heneage attended in 1721.[29] She depicts her unsuccessful effort to obtain favour for him from an influential nobleman. She begins with a farcical sketch of a woman caught between urgent business and impending wardrobe malfunctions:

> Your note recieved down stairs I fly
> My gown unpin'd my hood awry
> With M[rs]. Mary at my heels
> Who as she this disorder feels
> Here gives a twitch there aims a pin
> But cannot reach to fix it in [.] (lines 9-14)

She then creates a satirically ironic speech for his lordship, who tries to sweep her aside into a private, feminine realm: 'Shall I conduct you to my wife / I have no interest on my life' (lines 33-4). At the conclusion, however, she resolves to keep up the struggle, her resolve strengthened by indignation:

> ……in the parlour I remain
> O'ercome with sorrow and disdain

Yet with a Roman virtue scorn
The Land depraved where I was born
Where men now wealthy grown and great
En bagatell our sufferings treat. (lines 49-54)[30]

It was not simply gender that made Anne keep works like this in an unpublished manuscript.

Lady Coventry has a close connection in another respect to Anne, who, we notice, writes of her as 'of Tufton's line'. Her brother Thomas Tufton (1644–1729) was the 6th Earl of Thanet, with a seat at Hothfield, about 3 miles – easy walking distance – from Eastwell. Like Heneage, the earl had been a groom of the bedchamber to James. His wife, Catharine, née Cavendish (1655–1712), was our poet's closest female friend, as attested by the dedication of 'The Petition for an Absolute Retreat' and many other poems written to and about her and her daughters.[31] It may have been in the Hothfield grounds that Finch saw the vision of their radiant daughter in her 'Nocturnal Reverie':

When scatter'd *Glow-worms*, but in Twilight fine,
Shew trivial Beauties watch their Hour to shine;
Whilst *Salisb'ry* stands the Test of every Light,
In perfect Charms, and perfect Virtue bright [.] (lines 17-20)[32]

There had also been three elder brothers who had inherited the title in succession prior to Thomas Tufton and who had died.

The mother of this large family, who had probably died before Anne could have known her, supplies a tempting lead to a possible source of one of Anne's poems. Hugh Jenkins argues strongly for 'A Description of Cooke-ham', the pioneering country-house poem by Aemilia Lanyer, née Bassano (1569–1645), as a model for Finch's 'Petition for an Absolute Retreat', though he admits that he was 'able to find no evidence beyond the poems themselves that Finch knew Lanyer's work'.[33] Through the kindness of WSG member Helen Hackett, I have learned from Paul Salzman, who is working on the reputations during the Restoration and eighteenth century of pre-Civil War women poets, that no evidence is known of any awareness of Lanyer in those later years, which gives no encouragement to suppose Finch could have known the poem.[34] Finch's friendship with Lady Thanet, however, suggests a direction that could potentially provide a link. Lanyer, the first woman to publish a book of original poetry in English, describes the lost female utopian retreat she shared at Cookham with Margaret Clifford, née Russell, Countess of Cumberland (1560–1616), and her daughter Anne (1590–1676). Anne later married Richard Sackville, 3rd Earl of Dorset (1589–1624), and their daughter Margaret (1614–76) in turn married the 2nd Earl of Thanet, thus becoming mother of the family known to Finch. Salzman warns that Anne Clifford, who is now studied by many scholars, never mentions Lanyer. Nevertheless, if a copy of the book in which Lanyer's poem appeared, *Salve Deus Rex Judaeorum* (1611), came down in the family to Margaret Sackville Tufton, it would probably have become part of the libraries at Hothfield or Thanet House in Aldersgate Street in the City of London.[35]

In the *New Atalantis* Delarivier Manley (c.1670–1724) makes clear the close access Finch had to Catherine Tufton's private spaces:

> Be pleas'd to look into the Coach. . . , there sits the proudest Woman in *Atalantis*. . . [who] carries her pretty Daughters to the Opera-Market and *Prado* for Husbands; her own has out-liv'd five Brothers of his to come to the Estate, and there's yet one remaining that hopes he shall be the seventh that survives the sixth. The Lady her self, tho' neither handsom or distinguishable, (for any thing but Pride) believes so well of her self, she scarce does any one below her the favour to rise when they come in. There seems nothing in her so commendable, as her value for that fourth Person which was with them in the Coach. The Lady once belong'd to the Court, but marrying into the Country, she made it her Business to devote her self to the Muses, and has writ a great many pretty things.[36]

As an example, Manley prints Finch's 'Progress of Life' following this passage. With the degree of personal intimacy Manley depicts, we can easily imagine Finch browsing the Thanet library, where she certainly would have been drawn to a volume of poetry by another woman poet.

As scholars we must always scrutinize our assumptions and look for sound sources of information. Short biographical summaries, especially when the writer is not a specialist conversant with the nuances of his subject's life, can easily repeat or even distort misleading assumptions. Oft-repeated 'truths' should often be scrutinized. The idea of Westminster Palace as a residence for the couple seemed to me to deserve such scrutiny, and similarly it seemed to me odd to think that after some years in Kent Anne Finch returned to service at the court of Queen Anne: Carol Barash, for example, says she was 'an attendant to Queen Anne', citing Roger Lonsdale, who says she 'became

Lady of the Bedchamber to Queen Anne'.[37] I wondered that the wife of a resolved non-juror, someone herself known for Jacobite sympathies, would be allowed to hold such an office as an oath might have been required. Finch would not have qualified to serve until she became an aristocrat, in 1712, when Queen Anne was near the end of her life, requiring exceptional care from her attendants because of her gross weight, inability to walk, and many ailments. Yet in her poetry here and there Finch makes clear that she does not care for the duties or pastimes typically expected of women. At this time she would be busy preparing copy for the *Miscellany Poems*, which was to come out the next year. For all these reasons formal attendance on Queen Anne seemed unlikely to me. I do not know from whom this idea arose: the sources Lonsdale cites include one I have not been able to check, the unpublished thesis of D.G. Neill which the author has barred from public availability (Lonsdale had been able to use it as a personal acquaintance of Neill's at Oxford).[38]

Fortunately, the answers to some questions like this can now be discovered online. From the Lord Chamberlain's accounts and from E. and J. Chamberlayne's *Angliae Notitia* (1669–1707) and *Magnae Britanniae Notitia* (1708–55), which annually presented the names of the occupants of a wide range of public offices, and from other reliable lists, Robert O. Bucholz, an historian at Loyola University of Chicago, has compiled a database naming every court officer from the Lord Chamberlain down to lowly kitchen workers.[39] It is accompanied by a gracefully-written, long, informative introduction, which I urge everyone to read. For many years this online database has been confined to the officers of reigning monarchs, but this year Bucholz promises to add officers for some ancillary courts, including that of Mary of Modena, a draft of which list he has generously sent me. Anne Kingsmill certainly appears as a maid of honour to Mary of Modena from Michaelmas 1682 until her marriage.[40] It is her absence from Bucholz's documents relating to Queen Anne, however, that confirms our poet was *not* one of her attendants.

My examples show how even scholars of the highest stature, who have contributed far, far more than most to our knowledge of women and whose critical judgement is subtle and informed, nevertheless can distort the biographical record when they are focusing on other aspects of their projects. We must remember that it is therefore always necessary to scrutinize what we are repeating, especially from a secondary source that fails to document its statements or merely cites another secondary source. With new online access to others' work and to images of early books and manuscripts we have resources earlier scholars could not have hoped for. As we work, it is difficult – but essential – to clarify what we know, to recognize others' often insightful inferences and speculations for their value and yet ensure that they do not harden into 'facts'. We need to remember then to recognize supporting or disproving evidence. With such standards we can honour the early modern women we study.

Chapter Five

'For ever shaded by oblivion's veil': Obituarizing Women in the Eighteenth-Century *Gentleman's Magazine*

by Gillian Williamson

This chapter is adapted from research undertaken for my PhD thesis, subsequently published as *British Masculinity in the 'Gentleman's Magazine', 1731–1815*.[1] It is an extended version of a five-minute paper presented at the 2014 Women's Studies Group, 1558 -1837, annual workshop. My research focused on how this leading eighteenth-century periodical and its large and broadly-based readership which supplied a major proportion of the magazine's contents, including obituaries of family and friends, framed the superior masculinity implied by the '*Gentleman's*' of its title. I concluded that the magazine played an important part in shifting the meaning of gentlemanliness from a traditional definition based on birth and lineage to a more aspirational definition that allowed middling-sort men to self-make gentlemanly masculinity status through education, industriousness and sensibility. This was a forerunner of nineteenth-century middle-class meritocracy.

This chapter looks instead at the way in which *Gentleman's Magazine* obituaries also framed a version of femininity.[2] I will take one example of a woman's obituary, that of Lady Smith in the February 1786 issue of the magazine, together with the surrounding context of other obituaries published that month and a poem commemorating Lady Smith in the magazine for January 1788, as a platform for considering how the magazine's obituaries of men and women differed and how this difference defined and naturalized social roles that were based on gender. For women that role was primarily centred on the domestic: on their lives as daughters, wives, mothers and makers of the home. For men, while a position as the loving and benevolent head of a household was important, there was also a strong focus on achievement in the public world of work and association beyond the home. Yet this gendered boundary between private femininity and public masculinity was not, in the lives of real men and real women, a rigid one.

Occasionally the obituaries provide evidence of women who did lead 'public' lives.[3] A brief look at the obituaries of people who died in March 1809 (see p.56 below) confirms that there was an increasing tendency to include women in general, and also, with the added evidence of supplementary biographies, shows that special attention was awarded to women writers.

The *Gentleman's Magazine*, incidentally the first periodical to use the term with its now current meaning, was founded in January 1731 by publisher Edward Cave (1691–1754) who lived and worked at St John's Gate, Clerkenwell, London. He originally promoted it as a handy and relatively inexpensive (6d for forty-eight pages, compared to 2d for a four-page weekly or twice-weekly newspaper) digest of the month's news – London, provincial and international – together with *'some other matters of Use or Amusement that will be communicated to us'* (such as poetry, books published, and other announcements).[4] It was shamelessly plagiaristic (not unusual in the period) and an instant success, selling some 10,000 copies and more monthly across Britain and beyond, keeping Cave's presses profitably employed and spawning many imitators keen for a slice of this market. In the eighteenth century none of the latter achieved either the sales figures or the longevity of the *Gentleman's Magazine* (which survived the death of Cave and changes in editorship and ownership until 1907, albeit by then in a much-diminished form).[5]

The magazine's cultural significance lay in two factors. Firstly, it was pretty much all-pervasive: most literate men, women and children of the period would have been aware of it and, as the essayist and philosopher William Hazlitt (1778–1830) nostalgically suggested, would probably have flicked through it at some time or another:

> Who, with the *Gentleman's Magazine* held carelessly in his hand, has not passed minutes, hours, days, in *lackadaisical* triumph over *ennui*? Who has not taken it up in parlour window-seats? Who has not ran [*sic*] it slightly through in reading-rooms?[6]

The readership extended from noble families through the gentry to the expanding middling sort, its bedrock, and into the artisan classes. Some read it from childhood to old age and saw it as a much-loved part of the routine of their lives: it was 'an old Chrony', even 'an agreeable Miss *Mag*'.[7] Secondly, it rapidly became a repository of contributions (many anonymous and pseudonymous) from its very loyal readership. Correspondence often continued over several issues, taking the form of a debate between readers. By the 1740s Cave had to produce nine supplements, entitled *Miscellaneous Correspondence, Containing Essays, Dissertations, etc. on Various Subjects, Sent to the Author of the Gentleman's Magazine*, to accommodate the deluge of correspondence sent for publication. In 1783 the magazine was doubled in size (and price) for the same reason, without apparently denting sales. There were women, albeit in a minority, among the correspondents. These included a number of prominent women writers who were regular contributors. In 1821 John Nichols (1745–1826), the editor from c.1778, listed nine such women (and 521 men) in an introduction to a new *General Index* to the magazine: they were Mrs Eliza Berkeley, née Frinsham (1734–1800), Mrs Hester Chapone, née Mulso (1727–1801), Mrs Hannah Cowley, née Parkhouse (1743–1809), Mrs Susanna Duncombe of Canterbury, née Highmore (1725–1812), Mrs Mary Knowles, Fair Quaker, née Morris (1733–1807), Miss Anna Seward (1742–1809), Mrs Charlotte Smith, née Turner (1749–1806), Miss Catherine Talbot (1721–70) and Mrs Thomas of Newbold.[8] These two factors – a large and robust readership base and the reflexive nature of its contents – mean that we can justifiably regard the *Gentleman's Magazine* as both influential and as representing far more than a simply editorial position.

The *Gentleman's Magazine* printed obituaries from the outset. In its first twenty years or so these took the form of notices which, with announcements of births and marriages, appeared towards the back, just after the news section. They were few and generally a single sentence. Like most of the early magazine's contents, they were usually lifted from elsewhere (the London papers, for example). For obituaries in the British press were not new: the earliest date from the seventeenth century.[9] Reflecting its sources, the overwhelming majority of the early *Gentleman's Magazine* death notices were of adult males and, within this group, of those who were traditional gentlemen by birth. Occasionally these elite men merited a slightly longer piece detailing their lineage. For example, it was said of Rt Hon. George Brudenel who died on 6 July 1732 that 'He married the Daughter of the E[arl] of *Aylesbury*, by whom he had 2 sons and 2 Daughters: Is succeeded by his eldest Son, *George*, yet under Age, married to the Duke of *Montagu*'s youngest Daughter.'[10] Females accounted for no more than 16 per cent of the notices in the 1730s, 1740s and 1750s, and also typically came from elite families.[11] Clearly this did not reflect the reality of death which afflicted males and females equally, and young children in particular, transcending social class. Indeed, the *Gentleman's Magazine* also printed the Bills of Mortality (the weekly mortality statistics for London compiled routinely by the parish clerks from 1611), which made this plain. The exception to this pattern in the early magazine came where there was an element of wonder or comedy in the deceased: 105-year-old Robert Bristow of Stamford was deaf but retained his other senses to the end; when the (unnamed) wife of 'one *Kirkeen*' of Dublin died, he 'immediately put her into a Coffin, had it nailed up and buryed her the next Day' as she had twice previously come back to life.[12]

As reader contributions grew, however, obituaries became an important correspondence format (alongside prose letters and articles, and poetry of often dubious merit). By the third quarter of the eighteenth century the obituaries section accounted for around 10 per cent of the magazine's approximately 100 pages. There were not only more obituaries but many were also longer, containing life stories and descriptions of the deceased, and most were now submitted by readers of the magazine. Stephen Howard has suggested that, regardless of the sex of obituarists' subjects, they were mainly composed by men.[13] However, there are many original letters to editor John Nichols from women enclosing or commenting on family obituaries.[14] Eleanor Tasker, for instance, sent Nichols a letter in February 1800 with unvarnished details of the death of her husband, the Revd William Tasker, 'in grat agony's [*sic*] after a total suppression of urine'. She chased the matter up in March as the notice had not appeared and the obituary was finally published that month (with her spelling corrected).[15] However, the death notices had not only expanded into fuller obituaries: there was also a notable change in the social profile of their subjects. They now represented more closely the magazine's core professional and commercial middling-sort reader-contributors and their values. The change is detectable from the opening of the Seven Years' War (1756–63) and was followed in other publications (which now often reprinted *Gentleman's Magazine* obituaries, as the *Annual Register* did, for example). It was noted and ridiculed by contemporary satirists. The *Gentleman's Magazine* itself reprinted in July 1755 an article from the *Connoisseur* lamenting that 'When an obscure grocer or tallow-chandler dies at his lodgings at *Islington*, the news-papers are stuffed with the same parade of his virtues and good qualities, as when a duke goes out of the world.'[16] In a satirical ode of 1790, 'Peter Pindar', the pseudonym of the Revd John Wolcot (1738–1819), imagined the dead begging to be spared a *Gentleman's Magazine* obituary: 'Oh! save us from JOHN NICHOLS!' is the cry: / 'Let not that death-hunter know where we lie.'[17]

However, despite the mockery, the change persisted. The *Gentleman's Magazine* was for many the publication place of choice for obituaries that would have a national impact. It was, in this respect, a journal of record, as the memorial to Lady Downe in the North Quire aisle of York Minster reveals. Unusually this refers the passer-by wishing to read a fuller account of her 'character and other particulars' to the *Gentleman's Magazine* for May 1812 (very much a back issue as the memorial was raised in 1836). By the third quarter of the eighteenth century, the lives of the middling sort were now memorialized in juxtaposition with those of their social superiors, such as Lady Downe. It was no longer merely ancestry that was praised, but rags-to-riches stories of personal advancement through hard work and moral virtues such as benevolence, tenderness as a husband and father, and kindness as an employer. The dead (or at least their nearest and dearest who sent in the notices) were often proudly self-made men. It is worth quoting almost in full the 1785 tribute to Mr Richard Atkinson, director of the East India Company, who was billed as an exemplar of the growing numbers of men whose standing was literally all their own work. Atkinson represented

> one of the many instances of good sense and persevering industry, well-directed, in a commercial country, like England, rising from the bottom of society to the summit of affluence. Mr. A. when he came from the North, was a mere adventurer, unsustained by any inheritance, by few family friends of any power, and by no acquisitions which education imparts, but common penmanship and arithmetic. Thus circumstanced, he came to London, and, passing through different 'compting-houses, and experiments in trade, accumulated that prodigious wealth of which he died possessed.[18]

We know too that these obituaries were eagerly read. 'A Traveller' thought this the 'greatest amusement and pleasure' and knew a man who always turned to them first, reading the magazine from the back, where they appeared, forwards.[19] One reader proposed that the information be arranged topographically (they were generally printed in chronological order of death), as in the *Monthly Magazine*, and another wanted each announcement to begin with the name picked out in capitals so that it was easier to spot those one knew.[20] Sometimes the magazine was the means by which news of a death was received, as poetic correspondent 'J.H.' versified in 1750: 'A public paper, in confusion read, / Brings the sad tidings that my friend is – dead' (lines 23-4).[21] The repetition of this new style of male obituary, often several to a page, must have created an impact for the readers.

How, though, were women's obituaries affected by this change? By the 1780s women were the subjects of an increased proportion of the magazine's obituaries – 26 per cent in that decade and 31 per cent in the 1790s – but they still remained in the minority, as at least one contemporary correspondent recognized. I now turn to the quotation used in the title of my chapter: 'For ever shaded by oblivion's veil'. This is taken from line 7 of an anonymous epitaph printed in January 1788:

Whilst man, proud man, demands the sculptur'd tomb,
The midnight taper, and the sable plume,
With all the solemn mockeries of death;
Shall female merit claim no cypress wreath?
Shall the soft virtues which the sex adorn,
(Pure and unsullied as the vernal morn)
For ever shaded by oblivion's veil,
Close hapless *woman's* melancholy tale?
Go, partial spirit, who deniest the claim,
Which thy fond help-mate dares assert to fame,
Go, and within thy social circle seek,
Affections ardent, virtues ever meek –
Hast thou no parent, sister, wife, or friend,
In whom the gentler passions sweetly blend?
If so unblest, with thee no female shares,
Thy swelling hopes, thy sad presaging cares,
Hither return, and with converted mind,
In this sad urn, their faithful emblem find –
See where pure Faith, in robe of spotless hue,
Points to the Heaven now opening to her view:
And Hope, warm Hope, that never-failing friend,
Who* travels thro', nor quits us when we end,
Spreds [*sic*] her white pinions to th'aetherial road,
To waft the spirit to its blest abode:
Whilst thou, O Charity, belov'd of Heaven,
Thou sweetest solace to frail mortals given,
Thou, who (in retrospective mirror shewn)
Canst make each past good deed again thine own,
Thou shalt her fame secure, refine, sublime,
Ev'n till yon arches close the wreck of time.

* 'Hope travels through, nor quits us when we die.'
Essay on Man, Ep. III.[22]

The poem commemorates the late Lady Smith, widow and second wife of Sir George Smith. Our poet compares her 'ever shaded' fate – to be forgotten like deceased women generally – with 'Man, proud man' who 'demands the sculptur'd tomb' (line 1). This line consciously evokes Isabella's plea for the life of her brother Claudio in Shakespeare's *Measure for Measure*:

> O, but man! proud man, 143
> Drest in a little brief authority,
> Most ignorant of what he's most assur'd, 145
> His glassy essence, like an angry ape,
> Plays such fantastick tricks before high heav'n, 147
> As make the angels weep. (Act 2, scene 7)[23]

The choice of a quotation that concerns a close sibling relationship indicates that the poet may well have been Lady Smith's brother, the Revd William Vyse (1741–1816), rector of Lambeth.[24] Shakespeare's Isabella contrasts man in the sense of mankind with the angels, whereas the epitaphist contrasts men with women. Both Isabella and our poet, however, use the conceit to talk about power: Isabella's 'man' (as a seventeenth-century authority figure, inevitably male) and the epitaph's 'man' both display an earthly vanity. Maybe we are intended to regard the 'soft virtues' (line 5) possessed by the hitherto uncommemorated Lady Smith and others of her sex as placing them closer to the angels.[25]

Lady Smith had died on 21 February 1786, two years before this epitaph was published. She had been obituarized in the *Gentleman's Magazine* in March 1786, but in a mere four lines:

> At her house in the close of the cath.
> church of Lichfield, Lady Smith, widow of
> the late Sir Geo. S. bart. of Stoke, Notting-
> hamsh. and sister to the Rev. Dr. Vyse.[26]

She was summarized as one man's wife/widow and another man's sister. She was allotted no given name (in fact Catherine), and there is no indication of her age (probably around 40 as her two brothers were born in 1741 and 1746). On the same page as Lady Smith's obituary were ten other death notices, with an eleventh continued from the previous page. Eight of these were for men and only four for women. For the month of March as a whole there were seventy-nine notices, forty-nine for males (of whom one was a child) and thirty for females. At 38 per cent of the total, March represented quite a good showing for women. In 1786 for my two sampled months (see note 11) 30 per cent of obituaries were for women. For the surrounding decade, the 1780s, the figure was, as we have seen, only 26 per cent. The epitaph writer had a point.

Returning to March 1786, the eleven obituaries immediately surrounding Lady Smith's were of varying length, but the longest were all for men. There was a whole column for naval officer Edward Thomson (or Thompson) Esq., commander of HMS *Grampus*, who had died off the coast of Africa 'in the discharge of his duty to his king and country'. He was, his obituarist told the reader, not only a courageous and zealous officer, but generous, cultivated ('extensively known in the polite and in the literary world'), and 'alive to the most virtuous sensibilities': the very model of the magazine's 'new gentleman' I have identified.[27] The Revd Thomas Marshal Jordan, Anglican rector of Barming, Kent, earned twelve lines. He had dropped dead of an apoplexy immediately after taking divine service and enjoying his dinner. He was 'a most valuable and affectionate member' of his circle, a 'rare, but useful example of genuine piety' and 'uniformly chearful and unaffected'.[28] Almost a page was devoted to John Jebb MD, physician, reformer and former fellow of Peterhouse, Cambridge.[29] Jebb was portrayed as both professionally distinguished and amiable. Lengthy details of his funeral hinted at a wide social circle where he would be sorely missed. All three deceased men were therefore described in terms that implied they had attained self-made merit through their occupational achievements, had contributed to the national wellbeing, and had distinctive, individual personalities. Of the shorter male notices, Samuel Mence was a gentleman of the Chapel Royal at St James's, T. Bristow Esq. an alderman and former mayor of York, and Mr Stephen Boone a surgeon. None of the eight men was defined by birth or family. Each had a very public persona. This was the context for Lady Smith's four-line, rather bare notice.

The poetic epitaph to Lady Smith indicated that female worth lay in 'the soft virtues which the sex adorn' (line 5). Some eighteenth-century commentators were reluctant to go this far. In his poem *Of the Characters of Women: An Epistle to a Lady*, Alexander Pope, whose *Essay on Man* Lady Smith's epitaphist quoted (line 22), wrote that '*Most Women have no Characters at all*' (line 2).[30] Regular magazine correspondent the Revd Samuel Pegge (1704–96) slightly misquoted Pope on women's characters in the heading of a letter printed in the magazine in 1770. While he went on in the main body to suggest that most men also had 'no character', he regarded it as characteristic of a man to at least aim at 'excellency in some way' that would 'distinguish himself above the herd'.[31] Death notices for women bear testament to Pope's and Pegge's beliefs.

An example from January 1789 gives a flavour of the rather interchangeable qualities, the 'soft virtues', that were typically recorded in the magazine's obituaries to women: Mrs Elderton was 'an affectionate wife, a tender parent, and an uniform promoter of happiness in others'.[32]

However, none of the women obituarized in March 1786 was allowed any personal attributes and almost all were, like Lady Smith (and indeed Lady Downe), defined by nothing more than their relationship to male relatives, to their husbands, brothers, sons, fathers and grandfathers. They were quite lucky to get off so lightly: sometimes in the magazine a woman's death was an excuse to trumpet the successes and virtues of these male relatives. Mrs Milicent Hammond, for instance, was recorded in 1787 as not only the wife of the Revd John Hammond 'late fellow of Queen's coll. and now lecturer of Trinity church' but also 'only dau. of the late Mr. James Essex, the inge[n]-ious architect and F.A.S. of whom see some particulars in our vol. LV'.[33] These were also the terms in which our poet had thought of Lady Smith and other women worthy of memorial. He exhorted his fellow men 'Hast thou no parent, sister, wife, or friend?' (line 13). These women portrayed in the *Gentleman's Magazine* obituaries were, then, the adjuncts, the useful help-meets of successful men in a man's world. I propose that in the second half of the eighteenth century the *Gentleman's Magazine* contained more obituaries of women, but of this limited type, because for the readership it underpinned their version of gentlemanly masculinity in which public success was allied to a paternal benevolence in which the gentleman was the guardian of the supportive but weaker sex.[34]

However, many eighteenth-century women below gentry status did work and had lives outside the home, as Amy Erickson, Bridget Hill and Margaret Hunt have pointed out.[35] The magazine's obituaries portrayed professionalism and individual merit as masculine, but this was a useful discourse rather than a reality. Sometimes in these obituaries, as in other sources, women's work was probably concealed behind the male head of household's occupation (where a couple ran a business together, for example), but from time to time it was more visible. In the March 1786 obituaries Mrs Chapman, the second woman on Lady Smith's page, was a businesswoman and not even in a traditionally female trade. She was mistress of the White Horse livery stable in Coleman Street in the City of London.[36] Two pages on, tucked within the obituary of Mr John Shield, the retired master of a school in Islington (the *alma mater* of magazine editor John Nichols) was a more detailed picture of female participation in the public world of work. Shield's academy had originally been a school for young ladies run by a Mrs Science whose husband had an entirely separate occupation as a watchmaker. On Mrs Science's death, the business passed to her stepdaughter and assistant, Miss Barker. John Shield's 'eminent' and lucrative career was in fact based on a foundation of women's work: he married Miss Barker, moved from a position as an assistant at a school in Ware to Islington and thereby acquired the school which he converted to 'his' academy for boys.[37]

Writing seems to have been the acknowledged female career *par excellence*. On 11 and 25 March 1809 respectively, Hannah Cowley and Anna Seward, two of the nine ladies in Nichols' list of *Gentleman's Magazine* correspondents, died.[38] Their obituaries in the magazine were short, but indicated impressive attainments: 'a very high degree of genuine poetic and dramatic genius' was attributed to Cowley, while Seward was referred to as 'justly-celebrated'.[39] Their achievements were further acknowledged in the April edition. A 'Biographical Character of the Late Mrs. Cowley' praises her domestic lifestyle and feminine reserve - 'soft virtues' - saying that 'she wore her laurels gracefully veiled', but pays much admiring attention to her publications.[40] The 'Biographical Sketch of the Late Miss Seward' is equally enthusiastic and, far from prioritizing family obligations, lays stress on her struggles to develop her poetic talents in the face of 'the chillness of maternal discouragement'.[41] It is interesting to note that the March 1809 deaths also confirm the tendency for the proportion of obituarized women to rise overall: with 86 females to 92 males, unusually it approached parity at 48 per cent.[42]

To conclude, then, *Gentleman's Magazine* obituaries were an important means by which readers created, circulated and absorbed a national, middling-sort masculinity of industry, success and sensibility. It was a masculine identity that prided itself on individuality and achievement. It did not rely upon differentiation from women and femininity. Women were much less likely to be obituarized. When they were, it was almost always as subordinate to a male relative. They were rarely described as rounded individuals. This was a construction in which women as obituary writers and readers were complicit. Occasionally, however, the veil drawn across women's public lives was pulled aside to provide a glimpse of a less neatly-gendered society in which a woman's work contributed to both her own identity (Mrs Chapman) and to that of men (John Shields). Lady Smith's 1786 obituary and 1788 epitaph therefore open a window onto the value of these two literary genres in revealing the often concealed ways in which women were both individuals and contributors to the success of British culture and commerce of the period.[43]

Chapter Six

Female Radicals in Bristol: The Three Marys and Mary Wollstonecraft's 'The Cave of Fancy'

by Marie Mulvey-Roberts

Across the centuries, Bristol has been associated with radicalism, yet the extent of the city's links to three leading female radicals has been neglected.[1] These key women are Mary Wollstonecraft, Mary Hays and Mary Robinson, née Darby, who argued for the rights of women during the 1790s and were connected to Bristol in varying degrees.[2] Here, Robinson was born and spent her early years, Hays came to live and Wollstonecraft visited. As this chapter will show, the time they spent in the city was conducive to the production of several works, including a Gothic romance and poems by Robinson, didactic novellas written by Hays and Wollstonecraft's early fiction.

Until their rehabilitation by feminist critics from the 1970s onwards, the importance of the radical writings of these women was not fully recognized, partly because the moral condemnation of their personal lives had eclipsed their literary achievements. Robinson and Wollstonecraft were seen in some quarters as fallen women, while Hays was ridiculed for her unconventional approach to courtship. All three were satirized in the poem *The Unsex'd Females* (1798), written by the reactionary Cornish clergyman Richard Polwhele (1760–1838). Wollstonecraft, depicted by Polwhele as a woman 'whom no decorum checks' (line 83), was the author of *A Vindication of the Rights of Woman* (1792).[3] Mary Hays was born in the same year as Wollstonecraft and published her *Appeal to the Men of Great Britain in* [sic] *Behalf of Women* in 1798; the following year, Mary Robinson published *A Letter to the Women of England, on the Injustice of Mental Subordination* (1799). For radically shaking up attitudes towards women at the end of the eighteenth century, Robinson and Hays were dubbed Wollstonecraftian.

Nevertheless, in spite of being influenced and inspired by the *Vindication*, Robinson was most insistent that she had not produced a 'servile imitation .... For it requires a *legion of Wollstonecrafts* to undermine the poisons of prejudice and malevolence.'[4]

Another admirer of Wollstonecraft was Robert Owen (1771–1858), founder of the co-operative movement and utopian socialism. A woman, born and raised in Bristol, who moved in his circles was Emma Martin, née Bullock (1811/12–51), the one-time editor of the *Bristol Literary Magazine*.[5] In the early 1840s, she was giving public lectures around the country on revolutionary and reforming issues, drawing in crowds of 2,000 to 5,000 people.[6] Despite her popular appeal, she was admonished for questioning certain religious tenets, and for taking a lover.[7] Indeed, similar condemnations of Wollstonecraft's private life, following her death, helped blight her legacy and likewise Mary Robinson was maligned for love affairs, the most well-known being the one with George, Prince of Wales (1762–1830).

Mary Robinson

Born in Bristol at Minster House next to the medieval cathedral, Robinson claims that early exposure to its Gothic architecture induced an over-developed sensibility that seems to have exacerbated her melancholic disposition. For as she wrote in her memoirs: '*Bristol!* Why does my pen seem suddenly arrested while I write the word? I know not why, but an undefinable melancholy always follows the idea of my native birth-place. I instantly beheld the Gothic structure, the lonely cloisters, the lofty aisles, of the antique minster.'[8]

Loneliness and despair permeate Robinson's Gothic poem 'The Haunted Beach' (1800), which appears in her *Lyrical Tales* (1800). The poem was a response to 'The Rime of the Ancient Mariner' (1798) by Samuel Taylor Coleridge (1772–1834), included in William Wordsworth (1770–1850) and Coleridge's *Lyrical Ballads* (1798). Since Robinson's *Lyrical Tales* was published in reply to *Lyrical Ballads*, it is rather appropriate that the printer and typesetter for both books was the same Bristol publisher, Joseph Cottle (1770–1853). A departure from Wordsworth and Coleridge's collection of poems may be found in the way Robinson uses the Gothic ballad to convey a female perspective, as in 'Golfre, A Gothic Swiss Tale' (1800) about a peasant girl pursued by a wicked baron. This more woman-centred approach is also apparent in an earlier poem, 'The Doublet of Grey' (1797), which tells the story of the ill-fated lovers, the wealthy Madeline and her swain Theodore. Because of the latter's peasant stock, Madeline's father is intent on preventing the marriage and ultimately murders his prospective son-in-law. In retaliation, the distraught Madeline, dressed in a grey doublet and armed with sword and spear, fatally wounds her father. By appropriating a masculine role and donning male attire, she vanquishes the power of the patriarch, but at a harrowing cost. The poem culminates in an evocation of 'horrors on horrors' (line 64), with the ghost of the blood-covered shrieking maid 'in *her doublet of grey*!' (line 115).[9]

Robinson embraced the Gothic romance for her first novel, *Vancenza; or, The Dangers of Credulity* (1792), for which she drew on her affair with the Prince of Wales, which ended when he left her for Elizabeth Armistead (1750–1842) in a mire of acrimony and accusations of blackmail. Years after he cast her off, towards the end of her life in 1800, she turned to him, desperate for financial help so that she could visit Bristol's supposedly healing waters at Hot Wells, pleading 'Without your aid I cannot make trial of the Bristol waters, the *only* remedy that presents to me any hope of preserving my existence.'[10] Not unexpectedly, the request fell on deaf ears. As the infamy of the affair had ended her career as an actress, Robinson turned to earning a living by her pen, becoming an acclaimed poet and best-selling novelist. However, her authorship of *A Letter to the Women of England* is far more obscure, presumably because it was published under the pseudonym 'Anne Frances Randall'. Through her polemical *Letter*, Robinson points out how women's capabilities were being underestimated and disadvantaged by the double standard privileging men.

Mary Hays

Conversely, Mary Hays addresses her radical female treatise towards men rather than women.[11] In her *Appeal to the Men of Great Britain*, she sets out to re-educate men about women and correct misconceptions. In the main body of the work, headed 'What women ought to be', she argues that they ought not to be regarded as inferiors to men but as 'companions and equals'.[12] In *The English Review*, Richard Polwhele described Hays as 'one of the boldest beneath the standard of Wollstonecraft', declaring that 'Proudly to vaunt their intellectual powers, and to exhibit, at the same instant, the most "damning proofs" of mental imbecility, has (providentially, we had almost said) been the fate of these literary ladies.'[13]

Over a decade later in 1814, Hays moved to Bristol for the famous 'healing' waters that had also brought Mary Wollstonecraft to the city and, as noted earlier, were the impetus for Mary Robinson's attempt to return to her birthplace. Hays lodged in the Hotwells area at the home of the facile Penelope Pennington, née Weston (1757–1827), wife of the Master of Ceremonies, who arranged balls and other entertainment for upper-class visitors to the spa. As the daughter of radical dissenters, Hays felt more at home in the company of the learned Revd John Prior Estlin (1747–1817), the minister at the Unitarian Lewin's Mead Chapel that she attended and to which she subscribed, declaring herself to be 'greatly pleased' with him and his family.[14] Dr Estlin also ran a successful school at the top of St Michael's Hill and moved in the literary circles of Samuel Taylor Coleridge, Cottle, Robert Southey (1774–1843) and Anna Laetitia Barbauld, née Aitkin (1743–1825), who published a memoir about him. The dissenting tradition encouraged and supported the education of women and was already well-established in Bristol by John Wesley (1703–91) and the early Methodists. This aspect of the city may well have resonated with Wollstonecraft, who also had connections with dissenters.

While in Bristol, Hays was drawn to The Prudent Man's Friend Society, founded in the city the previous year of 1813, whose goals included 'the establishment of a benefit club, particularly for females'.[15] She was impressed by this woman-friendly benevolent society's encouragement of 'provident habits' and self-reliance, for not only had it established a 'poor man's bank' where interest could be accumulated but it had also, from its subscriptions, made interest-free loans to the needy.[16] The society inspired Hays to write the short didactic novel, *The Brothers; or, Consequences: A Story of What Happens Every Day; Addressed to that Most Useful Part of the Community, the Labouring Poor* (1815). The 1818 edition even included a tract of related interest, 'A Short Account of Savings Banks'.[17] The novella, published by the Baptist William Button, is written in the form of dialogues to promote the values of frugality and self-discipline. It presents a radical vision of the future in which 'the necessaries if not the comforts of life are enjoyed by *all*'.[18] Hays's prime purpose in writing the book was to encourage the countrywide adoption of the principles governing this Bristol institution of 'active benevolence and enlightened charity', and to lay the foundations for a 'highly moral and religious national character'.[19] Yet this was not enough to preserve the fragile marriage between friendly society and charitable institution and prevent the eventual closure of the benefit club on the grounds that 'the minds of the lower classes are not yet sufficiently prepared by education to receive a plan which principally promises distant advantages'.[20] Evidently the poor had not yet been persuaded to make adequate sacrifices in the present to safeguard the future. Hays's novella enshrines the ideals of The Prudent Man's Friend Society, and underlines the perils of ignoring them in her subtitle *Consequences*, which aimed at deterring members of the labouring classes from making imprudent marriages for which insufficient financial provision had been made. A reviewer for the *Gentleman's Magazine* heartily recommended that every labourer's family in the kingdom should receive a copy of the book, insisting 'It would be infinitely more serviceable than the miserable trash which is ostentatiously obtruded on them by the intemperate zeal of illiterate enthusiastic visionaries, under the *misnomer* of Religious Tracts.'[21]

Hays's didactic outlook shared common ground with the teaching and writings of the evangelical Bristol writer Hannah More (1745–1833), who helped her sisters run a school in Bristol's Park Street, which had been attended by Mary Robinson.[22] More was the author of moralistic publications for the labouring poor, as in her series of *Cheap Repository Tracts*.[23] At first sight, the radical Mary Hays and the conservative Hannah More had little in common, but they were brought together through their religious sensibility and concern for the poor. According to Cathy Hartley, Hays's friendship with More encouraged her to write *The Brothers* and then *Family Annals; or, The Sisters* (1817), which appeared two years later.[24] The latter tells the tale of two sisters, the extravagant Charlotte and the prudent Ellen, directed this time at the middle ranks of society. In the same year, More published *Stories for the Middle Ranks of Society, and Tales for the Common People* (1817), which targeted the same social classes as did Hays's *Family Annals* and *The Brothers*. More's working-class protégée Ann Yearsley, née Cromartie (1753–1806), known as 'the Bristol Milkwoman',[25] prompted the poet Anna Seward to observe that 'Bristol seems the soil where poetic plants, of wonderful strength and luxuriance, spring up amidst the weeds and brambles of vulgar life.'[26]

Mary Wollstonecraft

A cultivator of this abundant local talent was the Bristol poet Robert Southey, a friend to both Hannah More and Mary Hays. For Southey, Hays's close friendship with Wollstonecraft, on whom he eulogized 'As for panegyric, I never praised living being yet, except Mary Wollstonecraft',[27] must have given an added sheen to their friendship. He had written a dedicatory verse to his idol, 'To Mary Wollstonecraft', dated Bristol 1795, which opens with the lines:

> The lily cheek, the 'purple light of love,'
> The liquid lustre of the melting eye,..
> Mary! of these the Poet sung, for these
> Did Woman triumph; …. turn not thou away
> Contemptuous from the theme. (lines 1-5)[28]

George Gordon, Lord Byron (1788–1824) rashly declared that Wollstonecraft was 'a former Love of Southey's', noting that this had not caused him 'to respect the fame of her daughter' Mary Shelley (1797–1851).[29] While Southey helped tarnish Mary Shelley's character by spreading rumours that she was part of a Byronic 'League of Incest',[30] he unreservedly championed Wollstonecraft's posthumous reputation after its inadvertent besmirching by her husband, William Godwin (1756–1836). This had come about because of Godwin's indiscreet account of her lovers and suicide attempts in his *Memoirs of the Author of A Vindication of the Rights of Woman* (1798). Leaping to Wollstonecraft's defence, Southey proclaimed the *Memoirs* to be a scandalous publication, which had exposed Godwin's 'want of all feeling in stripping his dead wife naked'.[31]

Southey first met Wollstonecraft ten years after her visit to Bristol during the summer of 1787, when she had been employed as governess to Margaret, Caroline and Mary, the daughters of Robert and Caroline, Lord and Lady Kingsborough of Mitchelstown, Ireland. The family had come to Hot Wells, Bristol, 'one of the best frequented and most crowded watering-places in the kingdom', for the start of a Continental tour.[32] Wollstonecraft disliked the subordinate role that she was expected to play as governess to a noble family and resented being offered Lady Kingsborough's discarded poplin gown and petticoat, regarding this charitable act as more appropriate for a lady's maid than a governess.[33] She complained: 'My nerves daily grow worse and worse – yet I strive to occupy my mind even when duty does not force me to do it.'[34] At Hot Wells, she tried distracting herself by netting purses for her younger sisters Eliza and Everina; writing would soon prove to be a more effective remedy.

During her time in Bristol, between June and August 1787, Wollstonecraft worked on her first novel, *Mary: A Fiction* (1788), which she sent to her London publisher, Joseph Johnson (1738–1809), the following September.[35] This was her only fictional work to concentrate on the upper classes, which she was able to observe at close quarters in Ireland and at Bristol's Hot Wells. It was reported in *Felix Farley's Bristol Journal* that more than 1,000 persons of quality visited the resort that year, which saw the opening of a new elegant colonnade connecting the old Hotwell House with the Rock House that served as accommodation.[36] It was also during her stay in Bristol that Wollstonecraft made a start on another novel, 'The Cave of Fancy', which was never completed.[37] Most affecting in this fragment is the description of a child lamenting over the drowned corpse of her mother.[38] The theme of parental abandonment parallels how Wollstonecraft would leave her beloved pupil Margaret, following her dismissal by Lady Kingsborough at Hot Wells that August,[39] and is also eerily prophetic of her own premature death, which left the infant Mary Shelley motherless. The original version of Shelley's second novel, *Matilda*, written between 1819 and 1820, is entitled 'The Fields of Fancy', which, as the draft indicates, had started life as a reworking of Wollstonecraft's projected second novel, 'The Cave of Fancy'.[40] There are further similarities with her dead mother's incomplete fiction and Mary Shelley's novel *The Last Man* (1826), written in response to the deaths of her husband Percy Bysshe Shelley (1792–1822) and friend Lord Byron. Shelley's dystopia opens in the cave of the Ancient Greek prophetess, the Cumaean Sibyl, in which the narrator comes across a collection of prophetic writings. This corresponds to the inspiration described in Wollstonecraft's tale, 'The Cave of Fancy', where an old sage for whom 'nature had unlocked her most hidden secrets' gains mysterious entry to a nearby cavern full of spirits that he is able to control: 'One side of the hut was supported by the rock, and at midnight, when the sage struck the inclosed part, it yawned wide, and admitted him into a cavern in the very bowels of the earth, where never human foot before had trod.'[41]

There used to be an old hermitage or chapel dedicated to St Vincent at the narrowest point of the Avon Gorge in Clifton by Hot Wells. High up the gorge is a cave which, according to tradition, was once inhabited by a hermit, and this may have given rise to both Wollstonecraft's sage and the Cave of Fancy. This Avon cave has a variety of names including St Vincent's Cave, Ghyston's Cave or the Giant's Hole or Cave, and is associated with a legend of two brothers, the giants Goram and Vincent, each of whom is in love with the beautiful Avona, whose name is a Latinate version for that of the River Avon. Situated 250ft (76m) from the floor of the gorge, the cave could be reached only with the utmost difficulty via the cliff face until 1837 when William West (1801–61) constructed a tunnel from the observatory above that was opened to the public. Today, a platform jutting out from the cave can be seen high above the Portway, the road hugging the course of the River Avon.

The Avon Gorge runs through a limestone ridge which, by the end of the eighteenth century, posed a danger from falling rocks, loosened by blasts from quarrying for building work in Bristol. In 'The Cave of Fancy', Wollstonecraft writes that

> a ponderous mass, loosened from the cliff, to which it scarcely seemed to adhere, always threatening to fall, fell into the flood, rebounding as it fell, and the sound was re-echoed from rock to rock. Look where you would, all was without form, as if nature, suddenly stopping her hand, had left chaos a retreat.[42]

The Avon Gorge, with its steep cliffs set in greenery on either side of the river, was celebrated for its picturesque scenery and the sublimity of its aspect, attracting poets and painters, including J.M.W. Turner (1775–1851).[43] Edmund Burke (1729–97), the MP for Bristol (1774–80), represents the sublime as an encounter with untamed nature and its overwhelming forces, as in a deep chasm.[44] While the Avon Gorge may have provided Wollstonecraft with the sublime setting for her 'Cave of Fancy', another landmark in her story, next to the sage's 'rude hut, formed of stumps of trees and matted twigs', can be linked topographically to Bristol:

> A clear spring broke out of the middle of the adjacent rock, which, dropping slowly into a cavity it had hollowed, soon overflowed, and then ran, struggling to free itself from the cumbrous fragments, till, become a deep, silent stream, it escaped through reeds, and roots of trees, whose blasted tops overhung and darkened the current.[45]

The spring described above may well be a fictionalized version of the natural spring, known as St Vincent's Spring, lying not far from the bottom of St Vincent's Rock, the steep cliffs on the easterly bank of the River Avon running through the gorge where St Vincent's Cave is located.[46] This bubbling spring serviced the old Bristol Hotwell House spa, a rival to the Pump Room in Bath, which attracted upper-class visitors such as the Kingsborough family.[47] The classical encomium 'A Hymn to the Nymph of the Bristol Spring' (1751) by the future poet laureate William Whitehead (1715–85) with its reference to a hermit 'sealed the arrival of the Hotwell as a premier watering place fit for gentility'.[48] Nevertheless, Wollstonecraft's description of how a stream 'rushed out of the centre of the earth ... for ever bubbling along the cave', where the spirits living there purified themselves from 'the dross contracted in their first stage of existence', which 'flowed in black waves',[49] can be interpreted as a tongue-in-cheek description of members from the privileged classes, such as Lord and Lady Kingsborough, with whom Wollstonecraft had little affinity, taking the Bristol waters, which were believed to have health-giving and curative properties. At the same time, the purity of the spring was being corrupted by the polluted tide and river-water which 'threatened to seriously disrupt the daily therapeutic regime upon which the medical arm of the resort ultimately depended'.[50] Furthermore, visitors were invariably confronted by the distressing spectacle of the terminally ill or dying for whom the spa had literally become the last resort.

A juxtaposition of life and death appears in 'The Cave of Fancy' when the sage, after rejoicing in the life of herbs growing around him (and the Avon Gorge was, and still is, renowned for its rare and abundant flora),[51] is confronted by the horror of carnage from a shipwreck. He witnesses bodies washed up on the beach, some hanging from rocks. The year in which Mary Wollstonecraft spent the summer in Bristol, the brig *Piltown* sank due to a dangerous shoal in the Bristol Channel, running aground on Scarweather Sands. The drowning of fourteen crew and passengers was reported in *The Times* of 10 April 1787, two months before Wollstonecraft's arrival at Hot Wells, situated next to the River Avon which flows into the Bristol Channel. Recent local memory would still have been scorched by this tragic loss of life. Wollstonecraft's sage, after seeing the shipwrecked bodies of male and female passengers, observes that 'Another part of the beach was covered with sailors, whose bodies exhibited marks of strength and brutal courage.'[52] The only survivor of the historical disaster was the Revd William Glascott (1756–1829), thought to have been a part-owner of the vessel. In Wollstonecraft's 'The Cave of Fancy', the sole survivor of the shipwreck is a young girl, whom the sage finds kissing the lips of her mother's corpse. He decides to adopt and educate her by transforming the Cave of Fancy into a classroom in which moralizing stories are told about the wider world beyond. A similar pedagogical method is adopted in Wollstonecraft's *Original Stories from Real Life* (1788) in which the pupils Margaret and Caroline, modelled on Wollstonecraft's Kingsborough tutees, are given a moral education through the edifying tales told by Mrs Mason. In later life, Margaret Kingsborough even adopted for herself the name 'Mrs Mason' in homage to her former governess.[53] In *Thoughts on the Education of Daughters* (1787), Wollstonecraft advocated that children be instructed through stories aimed at improving and amusing them,[54] though she was only able to put these precepts into practice for her elder child Fanny, for she died ten days after the birth of her other daughter Mary.

Nearly thirty years later, Mary Shelley came to Bristol and stayed in Clifton. At that time, she was pregnant with William, the grandson Wollstonecraft would never know. When William died a few years later in 1819, he would have been around the same age as his namesake, strangled by the creature Shelley had created several years earlier in her best-known novel. Mary Shelley visited Bristol in 1815, the year before starting work on *Frankenstein* (1818), and the city may have played a formative role in its gestation.[55] If so, she should take her place alongside Wollstonecraft, Hays and Robinson as another notable Mary during the Romantic period, whose connections with Bristol deserve greater recognition.[56]

Chapter Seven

A Quest for Female Sexual Agency in the Eighteenth-Century Novel

by Sarah Oliver

This chapter discusses some of the ways in which novelists in the long eighteenth century made efforts to describe women whose behaviour asserts both agency and sexuality.[1] In order to illustrate my argument I have used selected novels, most of which were written by women, but I also consider male-authored texts when their works contribute to the discussion. However, 'agency' assumes the right, and the freedom, to choose; and I shall argue that this notion presented problems, particularly for the eighteenth-century woman writer.

In the late seventeenth and early eighteenth century, women amatory novelists paved the way by attempting to present a picture of female power and sexual independence, but their task was made difficult by societal prejudice against desiring women. Literary conventions therefore dictated that women had to be seen to suffer the consequences of their perverted behaviour: 'impropriety' not only damaged a female character's reputation but also her physical being, as it often resulted in rape. Furthermore, in early woman-authored fiction it is possible to trace a series of physical factors that limit women's sexual agency, or punish them for acting on it.

As early as 1688, Aphra Behn (1640–89) reversed traditional gender roles in *The Fair Jilt*, positioning Miranda as the aggressive seducer of a handsome young priest who is the object of her lust: 'The trembling young Man … demanded what she wou'd have him do.'[2] However, by placing *her* at *his* feet during Miranda's attempt to seduce him, Behn addresses the reality of the unequal power structure, for her readers are well aware that Miranda cannot achieve her goal since, physically, she is incapable of overpowering him and actually committing rape. He is rescued by his fellow priests and Miranda is disgraced and punished.

In 'Fantomina: Or, Love in a Maze' (1725), Eliza Haywood (c.1693–1756) creates a pleasure-seeking protagonist who exploits the masquerade's advantages for women, since it enables Fantomina to entertain her lover in hired lodgings during the day and appear in her actual persona at the balls and assemblies. According to convention, however, Fantomina's bid for sexual agency is short-lived and, as with Behn's Miranda, physically thwarted. In Fantomina's case, her sexual career is ended by pregnancy. She goes into labour at the ball, and her fall from grace is made horribly public:

> She could not conceal the sudden Rack which all at once invaded her; or had her Tongue been mute, her wildly rolling Eyes, the Distortion of her Features, and the Convulsions which shook her whole Frame, in spite of her, wou'd have reveal'd she labour'd under some terrible Shock of Nature.[3]

Fantomina's humiliation is brutally corporal and an exclusively female fate: no male hero's amorous adventures could ever be physically disrupted by the pains of childbirth.

In *The Reformed Coquet; or, Memoirs of Amoranda* (1724), Mary Davys (1674–1732) uses cross-dressing and disguise to fuel her plot and underline her warning to women. The beautiful Amoranda is about to be raped by her new female friend Berintha, who is really a man named Biranthus. He is operating with the aid of his servant Formator, who is really the gentleman hero. Formator rescues Amoranda, but in order to do this he leaves the rape scene and reappears as a handsome young stranger. Incredibly, the hero/protector has left the terrified young heroine during the attempted rape in order to change his clothes! However, although this man of sense is sometimes ridiculous and inappropriate and his attempts at protection often place the heroine in danger, Formator explains that his strange behaviour was in Amoranda's best interests:

> I put on an Air of Cruelty, which, Heaven knows! my Heart had no Hand in, and rode from you; I knew it would give you double Terror, to see a Prospect of Relief, then find yourself Abandoned: And I likewise knew, the greater your Fear was then, the greater your Care wou'd be for the future to avoid such Enterprizes: But I had yet a View in favour of myself, and had Reason to believe, the greater your Deliverance was, the greater Value would you set upon your Deliverer.[4]

Amoranda's would-be rapist and her seducer are both using their physical strength at her expense. Furthermore, Davys' Formator saves the heroine from rape, but he was also teaching her how to behave: she is dependent on him for both physical protection and moral education.

Throughout the long eighteenth century the rape theme presented difficulties for both male and female writers since, in literary convention, a raped woman – regardless of her virtue – had to marry her rapist, starve, fall into prostitution or die. For example, in his epistolary novel *Clarissa* (1748), Samuel Richardson (1689–1761) describes a heroine who chooses death after she is abducted and raped by the aristocratic libertine Robert Lovelace. Clarissa feels so defiled by her experience that she has to die: she is convinced that death is her destiny, that is, the consequence of her defilement and that she is not committing suicide, which by contemporary standards was a deadly sin. The direct cause of her death is starvation, and Richardson makes it clear that, consciously at least, Clarissa cannot prevent it. She tells her friends: 'I have no appetite. Nothing you call nourishing will stay on my stomach. I do what I can.' She also acknowledges that to indulge in 'wilful neglects' would be 'unpardonable'.[5]

Attitudes towards female sexual desire and agency in eighteenth-century society – especially towards raped women – were underpinned by the strictures in polemical writing, conduct literature and novels. The warnings they contained perpetuated the view that men, particularly wealthy and influential men, could do what they liked, but a woman had to mind her manners and her virtue. This viewpoint had a profound effect on women's behaviour. The warnings also linked negative ideas of female sexual desire to raped women, virtuous or not. A rape could be revelatory or transformative, or both. Since she had placed herself in a position where her physical chastity could be taken from her, the victim must already have been a whore before the rape. On the other hand, the very fact of the rape could make her previous circumstances, character and motives irrelevant. Anna Clark describes how the rape itself defined and settled the victim's social status: 'After her uncle raped fifteen-year-old Ann Bradshaw on a North Riding moor, the men to whom she ran for aid merely asked, "if he had made a whore of her".'[6]

Besides the warnings to women contained in contemporary conduct literature and novels, the negative attitude to female sexual agency was supported by the prevailing law under which a woman was deemed to be the possession of a male relative: her father, husband or brother. Rape *was* a crime perpetrated against the woman but it was also considered to be theft: of a man's goods. Importantly, the prevailing punishment for '*rape, raptus mulierum*, or the carnal knowledge of a woman forcibly and against her will' was death, and since the defendant's life was at stake and perjury regarded as a serious problem, accusations of rape caused a high level of concern.[7] As a result, female victims were reluctant to give evidence in court, and the novels of the period suggest that a woman violated by a gentleman rapist had little chance of redress.

Therefore a woman's all-important reputation was intimately linked to her behaviour, because her reputation was not only crucial to her and her future, but also impacted personally on her husband, father or brother as well as on her male relatives' standing in society. Yet the responsibility for her virtue rested with the woman. Early in the eighteenth century Penelope Aubin (c.1679–1738) illustrates this point in her novel, *The Strange Adventures of Count Vinevil and his Family* (1721). While Count Vinevil and his daughter, the unfortunate Ardelisa, are staying in Constantinople, she is threatened with rape by the captain of the Sultan's guard. Vinevil's reaction is to beg for death so that he can be released from the disgrace of his daughter's violation and Ardelisa's husband, De Longueville, expects his wife to preserve her virtue by preferring death to rape: 'Permit not a vile Infidel to dishonour you, resist to death, and let me not be so compleatly curs'd, to hear you live, and are debauch'd.'[8] Ardelisa dutifully replies, 'Why, my dear Lord, do you anticipate Misfortunes? …. Fear not my Virtue, I'm resolv'd never to yield whilst Life shall last.'[9] Not only does Aubin link the heroine's reputation with her male relatives' fears in this plot, but she also highlights contemporary attitudes to rape.

Towards the mid-eighteenth century, Samuel Richardson's *Pamela: or, Virtue Rewarded* (1740) also raises questions regarding contemporary attitudes to rape as well as a woman's selfhood. The virtuous young servant girl Pamela manages to avoid her master Mr B's attempts to rape her and, in the end, her virtue is rewarded by marriage to him. However, Richardson's gentry accept the notion that since she is her master's property and therefore nobody of consequence, any lower-class girl who objects to yielding her virtue to him is simply a hypocrite. Crucially, Pamela herself raises the question of who owns a woman's body: her master, her male relatives or herself. 'And pray, said I, walking on, how came I to be his Property? What Right has he in me, but such as a Thief may plead to stolen Goods?'[10]

Despite the challenges posed by cultural convention and societal norms, there were late seventeenth and eighteenth-century amatory novelists who made attempts to depict female sexual desire and sexual independence. However, their efforts to dismiss conventional restrictions and explore women's agency often offered accounts of male sexual aggression, couched in the language of seduction, in which the heroine played an active part. As a consequence, these narratives are problematic as they blur the distinction between seduction and rape, while complicating and limiting the concept of female desire. In amatory novels such as Aubin's, the heroine is seen as the persecuted innocent, representing virtue in distress; on the other hand, in novels such as Eliza Haywood's best-selling *Love in Excess* (1725), the heroine is seen as the desiring, seduced and betrayed virgin, easily coaxed into intercourse because she wanted the sexual experience.

Haywood's rape narratives often explored female sexuality in stories involving aristocratic or powerful males and innocent young girls that stimulated erotic fantasy via the trope of the persecuted victim. In *Love in Excess*, the wealthy young woman Amena is attacked, betrayed and assaulted by the amorous Count D'Elmont, who is known for his romantic escapades. Haywood depicts D'Elmont as a combination of scintillating hero and aggressive libertine-seducer; inevitably, Amena feels strong sexual passion: 'he found her panting Heart beat Measures of Consent, her heaving Breast swell to be press'd by his, and every Pulse confess a Wish to yield.' Only a chance interruption preserves her chastity.[11] In the same story, another young girl, Melliora, who has been entrusted to D'Elmont's care, is powerfully attracted to him and excited by his advances, but at the same time she is disturbed by her feelings. When he gazes at her sleeping body, Melliora cries out in a dream, 'D'ELMONT, cease, cease to Charm, to such a height – Life cannot bear these Raptures!'[12] Encouraged, he tries to have intercourse with her. As soon as she awakes, she resists him, but he uses force; luckily for her, 'a loud knocking at the Chamber Door, put a stop to his beginning Extacy.'[13] Since the heroine has made her sexual desire obvious, the episode *could* be seen as seduction, but as she is asleep at the beginning of the episode and overpowered at the end, she has no agency, which clearly signals rape.

Although Haywood's earlier novels attempted to suggest the idea of female sexual agency, *The History of Miss Betsy Thoughtless* (1751), written more than twenty years after 'Fantomina' makes the point that girls like Betsy must learn the consequences of impropriety. Sir Frederick Fineer lures her to his bedroom under the pretext that he is dying. There, she is forced into a sham marriage and sexually assaulted. When her rescuer, Mr Trueworth, explains matters to Betsy's brothers, they 'began to consider what was to be done for the chastisement of the villain, as the prosecuting him by law would expose their sister's folly'; they are aware that legal proceedings would damage her reputation, which must be preserved at all costs.[14]

Progress regarding the idea of female sexual independence was slow but, by the end of the eighteenth century, ideas regarding a woman's agency and selfhood were changing in stories produced by novelists such as Mary Wollstonecraft, Mary Hays and Jane Austen. Mary Wollstonecraft's *Maria: or, The Wrongs of Woman* (1798) criticizes the marriage laws that restricted a married woman's choice of sexual partner; Mary Hays's unconventional raped heroine Mary Raymond refuses to marry her baronet rapist, determines to find work and resolves to move on with her life in *The Victim of Prejudice* (1798); and in her novels, Jane Austen changes the image of the beleaguered heroine.

In their polemic and novels, radical writers Mary Hays and Mary Wollstonecraft railed against the kind of femininity and masculinity advanced in *Emile* (1762) by Jean-Jacques Rousseau (1712–78). As far as Wollstonecraft was concerned Rousseau's Sophie, the young girl bred to be Emile's wife, was the antithesis of the woman she envisioned in the new order. She thought the notion of natural female modesty and physical and mental weakness would only ever be an excuse for male sexual aggression.[15] However, Wollstonecraft's novel, *Maria: or, the Wrongs of Woman* (1798), focuses on contemporary marriage laws that stifled the married woman's economic and sexual agency. According to Sir William Blackstone (1723–80), the law of *coverture* decreed that 'the very being or legal existence of the woman is suspended during the marriage.'[16] 'Upon this principle, of an union of person', the married woman's existence was figuratively 'covered' or subsumed by her husband.[17]

The Wrongs of Woman describes a married woman's unsuccessful bid to divorce a cruel husband and marry another man, illustrating the kind of injustice meted out to married women by legislation, because men held the power. Wollstonecraft's novel links a married woman's lack of freedom and choice with her sexuality and associates marriage with prostitution by allowing her heroine to explain that duty should not force a woman into sex: '"we cannot, without depraving our minds, endeavour to please a lover or a husband, but in proportion as he pleases us".'[18] In the letter used as a preface to the novel, Wollstonecraft argues that 'a woman of sensibility', married to a husband she did not love, would be 'obliged to renounce all the humanizing affections'.[19] Maria leaves her selfish, violent and merciless husband Mr Venables, who married her for her fortune and tried to prostitute her to one of his friends to whom he owed money.[20] However, she is arrested and finds herself in prison where she falls in love with a fellow prisoner, Henry Darnford. Since marriage and property law regard her chosen relationship as illicit, her lover has to pay damages to Mr Venables for seducing his wife, but when she attempts to defend Darnford in court her argument serves to highlight the injustices she suffers. The judge's response to her plea alludes to 'the fallacy of letting women plead their feelings'.[21] He objects to women being allowed to plead emotion as an excuse or palliation of infidelity, on the grounds that it will open the floodgates for immorality, for 'What virtuous woman thought of her feelings?'[22]

Wollstonecraft's friend Mary Hays pushes the subject of female sexual agency even further in her fiction and questions society's attitudes to violated women. Inspired by her friendship with William Frend (1757–1841), the charismatic Unitarian dissenter, Hays perceived that men and women were drawn to each other through shared beliefs and feelings.[23] Furthermore, research by Erasmus Darwin (1731–1802), claiming that consciousness is located in the brain and the brain is connected to the body by sensory and motor nerves, led her to consider mental activity as an organic process in the physical body, representing a link between intellect and feeling.[24] Hays became fascinated by the idea of a woman's sexual independence and the link between intellect and feeling since, in this view, sexual desire is natural and not depraved.

In *The Memoirs of Emma Courtney* (1796), Hays linked her own sexual experiences and feelings with her emerging understanding of societal prejudices and sexual politics, which she had been discussing in correspondence with William Godwin as she wrote the novel. William Godwin was Mary Wollstonecraft's husband and author of *Things as they Are; or, the Adventures of Caleb Williams* (1794), which criticizes patriarchy, aristocracy, the legal system and the government. In her novel, Hays focused on the idea of a virtuous desiring female, but contemporary readers ridiculed the work, seeing it as the product of the author's sexual obsession with William Frend.[25] Since the cornerstones of her sexual politics were equality and a desire to redefine the nature of 'masculinity' and 'femininity', the embittered Hays embarked on a second novel, *The Victim of Prejudice* (1799), which interrogated contemporary assumptions about a woman's right to choose or not to choose her sexual partner. Importantly, it also offers the possibility of a woman's survival after rape.

Hays's depictions of virtuous but desiring women in her novels attempted to turn the current situation on its head by lifting her heroine out of the limits imposed by contemporary assumptions of women's weakness, madness, quivering sensibility and ideal femininity that were designed to control women's behaviour. Hays's first heroine Emma Courtney shattered literary and social conventions when she pleaded with her reluctant lover, Augustus Harley: '*My friend – I would give myself to you* – the gift is not worthless.'[26] As I have suggested, fictional heroines had long been prevented from declaring their sexual longing, and Hays's audacious move paved the way for a more self-sufficient heroine to emerge in the nineteenth century, since Emma's actions and words would have signalled impropriety and the risk of violation in a conventional narrative. Yet, when Emma breaks tradition by articulating her sexual desire and writing about it, she is not raped. Unlike the cynical rake heroes portrayed in the typical rape text, Harley fails to act on her impropriety. Harley obviously is not interested in Emma's offer but his reluctance serves to emphasize the extraordinary nature of the heroine's declaration of her sexual desire. In this reversal of conventional portrayals, Hays's virtuous heroine takes control of the seduction scene, voices her agency to a silent hero, is rejected and moves on.

Hays explores this theme not only in her portrayal of Emma's relationship with Harley, but also in Emma's interpretation of the maid Rachel's plight. Following the discovery of Augustus Harley's imprudent marriage, Emma Courtney reluctantly marries Mr Montague, whom she does not love. When Harley is wounded and dies in her arms she makes a home for the dead Harley's son and her own daughter Emma. Obsessed by his jealousy of Emma's unconcealed love for Harley, Montague contracts a liaison with Rachel, Emma's maid-servant. When she finds Rachel in a compromising position with her husband, Emma takes an unusually detached, rational and objective view of the situation: 'One morning, going suddenly into Mr. Montague's dressing-room, I surprised Rachael [*sic*] sitting on a sopha with her master: – he held her hand in his, while his arm was thrown round her waist; and they appeared to be engaged in earnest conversation. They both started, on my entrance.'[27] This scene revisits and addresses the problem of distinctions between seduction and rape, as rather than having her heroine confront and dismiss her maid with the familiar accusations of romantic illusions and sexual depravity, Hays simply allows Emma to leave the scene. Even more unusually, Emma later turns on her husband and makes it explicit that she regards the responsibility for the scene she has witnessed as his and not the unfortunate girl's. She warns him that his behaviour will do the servant untold harm: '"Should you corrupt the innocence of this girl, she is emphatically *ruined*. It is the strong mind only, that, firmly resting on its own powers, can sustain and recover itself amidst the world's scorn and injustice."'[28] The words in this passage foreshadow the appearance of Mary Raymond, the heroine of Hays's second novel, *The Victim of Prejudice*

(1799). Mary Raymond is destined to possess the 'strong mind …. firmly resting on its own powers' that Emma describes. In *The Memoirs of Emma Courtney*, however, Hays's focus is on Rachel; she is a servant and therefore has no power, however strong her mind might prove to be.

I suggest that Emma's reaction to her husband's sexual behaviour with the maid destabilizes the eighteenth-century view that a master's sexual abuse of a servant girl is acceptable. It also poses questions regarding the very notion of seduction in cases such as Rachel's. Since Emma places the blame for the incident on her husband, and since she realizes that her servant had little chance of avoiding a master's sexual attentions, Emma sees the 'seduction' as sexual coercion because her husband has the power in this scenario. By presenting her heroine in this way, Hays undermines some of the assumptions and devices on which the conventional rape narrative is based. In a reversal of the conventional narrative, the master-seducer and not the raped woman dies: ultimately, Montague commits suicide.

Having raised the issue of female sexual agency in her first novel, Mary Hays returns to the question of attitudes to seduced women in *The Victim of Prejudice*. Here, the language Hays deploys undermines the familiar trope because it accuses contemporary prejudice of being the author of a violated woman's disgrace. It is the heroine's mother, the first 'victim', who makes this accusation in a letter revealing her story of desire, abandonment and prostitution. Imprisoned for the murder of her lover, Mary Raymond's mother feels that she is '"the victim of the injustice, of the prejudice, of society, which, by opposing to my return to virtue almost insuperable barriers, had plunged me into irremediable ruin."'[29] The law is the cause of her destruction: '"*Law* completes the triumph of injustice. The despotism of man rendered me weak, his vices betrayed me into shame, a barbarous policy stifled returning dignity, prejudice robbed me of the means of independence."'[30] When Mary hears what happened to her mother, she fears that she herself will follow in her mother's footsteps; the tragedy is that even before her landlord assaults her, Mary has been victimized by her mother's reputation.

In her first novel, Hays's depiction of a sexually independent heroine set the scene because the unusually strong female characterization had a profound effect on the nature of the hero figure. Conversely, the creation of an unusually silent and passive Harley enabled the vocal Emma to achieve a semblance of sexual identity and freedom. On the other hand, according to convention, the woman writer of a rape narrative has to protect her heroine's reputation, which in turn obliges her to represent the fictional sexual encounter as a matter of force. Hays revisits the question of the hero in her second novel, and tackles the question of what makes a *hero* a *hero* in a rape story, by examining the way the depiction affects the behaviour of the heroine, and vice versa.

In her characterization of Osborne in *The Victim of Prejudice*, Hays presents us with a much more convoluted relationship between the baronet and his victim than we usually see in eighteenth-century rape narratives. The worldly rake figure is combined with the image of a man of feeling to present a reasonable man who persistently claims to adore Mary. The various mental and emotional disturbances Osborne suffers suggest that he is both confused by, and drawn to, Mary's mental strength, self-reliance and fortitude. In spite of his rank and her past, he offers multiple declarations of love and reasonable offers of marriage and fortune.

Unconventionally, and yet critically, Hays's image of the baronet is one of a confused, frustrated but passionately involved man who is completely unlike the cynical rakes of the familiar rape text. Yet the unusual heroine refuses to consort with an attractive and plausible rake and she rejects the idea of solving the problem of her tainted reputation by marrying him. Unlike Richardson's Clarissa, Hays's raped heroine resolves to survive, and determines to find work in order to move on; but however hard she struggles, she is ensnared in a net of intolerance and prejudice. Osborne is aware that his wealth, influence and power will protect him from society and the law, and like Richardson's Mr B and Robert Lovelace, he knows that his sexual crimes will be overlooked in accordance with the double standard exploited by his class. Threatened with court action, he cynically responds to his victim's demand for justice by using her disgrace to silence and humiliate her: '"To whom and where would you go, foolish and unhappy girl? – Let not passion and woman's vengeance blind you to the perils of your situation!"'[31] However, the novel's unusual and intriguing theme is the *potential* of female autonomy. After her capture and rape, Mary confidently and defiantly tells her rapist, '"I demand my liberty this moment … No one has a right to control me. … Think not, by feeble restraints, to fetter the body when the mind is determined and free."'[32]

Hays's heroines undermined the conventional narratives because, as we have seen, throughout the long eighteenth century the traditional text had presented sexual violation in a way that heightened its figurative elements and manipulated ordinary responses to the events described by suspending or interrupting them. The effect was to displace the reader's focus onto other formal or thematic elements. These elements in turn expressed anxieties and patriarchal priorities, including perceptions of femininity and masculinity, governmental authority, aristocracy, the sexual double standard and a host of related issues that impacted on women's lives.

Within this scheme, and since fictional representations of women during the period frequently provided a vehicle for debate concerning property (the ownership of material things), fictional rape episodes became a method of reminding women readers of the negative consequences of female sexual desire. The ultimate aim was to reinforce the view that it was not only improper but also unnatural. More importantly, the familiar rape story demonstrated ways in which eighteenth-century novels textualized male anxiety. They encapsulated economic, cultural and religious priorities that were intended to validate the importance of chastity and proper female sexual behaviour in the exchange of property and the preservation of family honour. In short, the warnings underpinning the trope functioned as a tool to suppress female sexual desire. If images of women with agency were to be achieved in future texts, then the image of the heroine had to change, as did the figure of the wealthy and influential rake.

Jane Austen began her writing career at the same time that Hays was revising the story of her independent heroine Mary Raymond. However, although Austen's novels shared many of the social preoccupations of the mid-eighteenth century, rather than those of the early nineteenth century, Julia Prewitt Brown suggests that Austen had a 'feminine consciousness' that demonstrates how 'women find ways to develop and assert their womanhood despite the restrictions placed on them'.[33] More recently, in the Preface to *Romancing Jane Austen*, Ashley Tauchert argues that Austen continues to be popular because 'she narrates the daydream of the heroine's persistent desire to be *somehow* saved by an ideal gentleman: a common desire to be rescued from "all this", and to live "happily ever after".' However, 'The "*somehow*" seems to involve a feminine power to transform an animalistic masculine desire into civility, or gentlemanly action.'[34]

Throughout this chapter I have suggested that certain novels written during the long eighteenth century, particularly those produced by women writers, criticized prevailing attitudes to women's sexual agency and there were attempts to change the way feminine power should be viewed. I also suggested that if representations of the after-effects of rape were to move on, the image of the weak and simpering heroine had to change, as well as the picture of the wealthy and influential rapist. What is needed is a strong-willed heroine with a sense of self and sexual agency, and a fictional hero who is capable of feeling.

Although Austen tended to write about individual young women in the heart of close-knit communities, most of her heroines are strong-willed. In Austen's first published novel, *Sense and Sensibility* (1811), the romantic Marianne is a new kind of heroine: although she falls passionately in love with Willoughby, she puts the unfortunate love affair behind her and moves on. Margaret Doody points out that Austen does not go so far as to advocate on behalf of violated women, but she is certainly pointing in that direction. In her portrayal of Marianne's ability to reject an inconstant lover, 'she is definitely joining in an argument about female sexuality'.[35] In contrast, Marianne's sister Elinor represents a continuation of the traditional role of a heroine who speaks only of the man she will eventually marry. This has the effect of simultaneously presenting two heroines: the traditional type, who can love only one man, and a new heroine who can fall in love again. Austen's Marianne, like Hays's Mary Raymond, obviously believed that marriage without love was no marriage. Therefore, while Austen's novels tend to centre on the effects of the prevailing laws governing inheritance and its importance to the stability of the community depicted, the importance of love and a woman's sexual agency is also made apparent.

In *Sense and Sensibility*, the strong-willed Marianne is romantic and passionate and expects to fall in love with a handsome suitor. Mr Willoughby appears to fit the role and he charms Marianne's mother and sister, 'in a manner so frank and so graceful, that his person, which was uncommonly handsome, received additional charms from his voice and expression.'[36] However, the aristocratic libertine that haunted eighteenth-century novels and was abhorred by Wollstonecraft and Hays has not entirely disappeared. Willoughby proves to be a liar, and he has a secret that is revealed to Elinor, Marianne's more sensible sister, by Colonel Brandon. The colonel explains that many years before, he had himself been in love with a girl called Eliza, but his father married her to Brandon's brother for her money. Brandon's father and brother mistreated her and, while he was away with his regiment in the East Indies, she ran away with a lover, who abandoned her. On his return Brandon found her dying of consumption and took her child, a second Eliza, into care. The young Eliza grew up and was seduced by Willoughby, who repeated the pattern by abandoning her and her baby. When Brandon heard of their plight 'on the morning of our intended party to Whitwell', he removed them to safety in the country: 'I was called away to the relief of one, whom he [Willoughby] had made poor and miserable; but *had* he known it, what would it have availed?'[37]

While Willoughby is cast in the traditional role of heartless rake, Colonel Brandon is characterized as wealthy, powerful, yet feeling. Elinor tells her sister, 'He has seen a great deal of the world; has been abroad; has read, and has a thinking mind.'[38] In Austen's romance, both the abandoned heroine Marianne *and* the wealthy and powerful hero Brandon seize the opportunity to choose a second partner. They marry each other and move on with their lives: 'Marianne could never love by halves; and her whole heart became, in time, as much devoted to her husband, as it had once been to Willoughby.'[39] Although Austen does not allow any of her other heroines such a thorough change of heart, her questioning of sexual conventions continues. One of her most explicit critiques occurs at the end of *Mansfield Park* (1814), when the narrator discusses the fate of Henry Crawford, who has seduced a married woman: 'That punishment, the public punishment of disgrace, should in a just measure attend *his* share of the offence is, we know, not one of the barriers which society gives to virtue. In this world, the penalty is less equal than could be wished.'[40]

In the nineteenth-century romantic novel, we see the emergence of a more confident and self-possessed heroine who expects to discuss her future destiny with her family and voice her preference when a man offers marriage; she is also allowed to change her mind without imperilling the happy ending. Furthermore, within the romantic novel the aristocratic rake figure is replaced by a stronger, more cultured, more mysterious, more thinking and, crucially, more feeling hero who is engaged in intellectual and economic pursuits. This progression suggests that female authors were themselves growing more confident, self-possessed and rational.

Chapter Eight

Scold, Punish, Pity or Seduce? The Confused Rhetoric of *Advice to Unmarried Women* (1791)

by Tabitha Kenlon

To observe that conduct manuals in the eighteenth century (and indeed most centuries) vehemently opposed premarital sex, especially for women, is a statement bordering on the redundant. Likewise, to point out that not everyone followed this advice demonstrates an impressive grasp of the obvious. Most of the audience for advice literature of the period were proper young ladies who wanted (or whose parents wanted them) to achieve a little extra polish, to be perhaps mistaken for someone of slightly higher quality. Readers of Jane Austen might remember the scene in Chapter 14 of *Pride and Prejudice* (1813) in which Mr Collins volunteers to share some passages from *Sermons to Young Women* (1766) by James Fordyce (1720–96) with the Bennet sisters. Only the fastidious Mary meets the suggestion with enthusiasm, while Jane and Elizabeth exude polite resignation and Lydia rebels, not for the first or the last time in the novel. In this brief tableau, Austen encapsulates the eighteenth-century attitude towards conduct manuals. They were part of a well-brought-up young lady's life, delineating ideal behaviour in chapters devoted to topics such as modesty in dress and deed, humility, friendship, love, motherhood, old age and much more, but they were not always taken seriously. Though popular books that went through multiple printings, they were often lampooned by novelists and playwrights.

Austen also takes a jab against the warnings about female education given by Dr John Gregory (1724–73) in *A Father's Legacy to His Daughters* (1774): 'Be even cautious in displaying your good sense … But if you happen to have any learning, keep it a profound secret, especially from the men, who generally look with a jealous and malignant eye on a woman of great parts, and a cultivated understanding.'[1] The narrator in *Northanger Abbey* (1818), Chapter 14, observes somewhat tartly, 'A woman especially, if she have the misfortune of knowing any thing, should conceal it as well as she can.'[2] In *The*

Rivals (1775) by Richard Brinsley Sheridan (1751–1816), the heroine bids her maid hide her more salacious reading and display her chaste conduct books: 'put *the Innocent Adultery* into *The Whole Duty of Man* … and leave Fordyce's *Sermons* open on the table' (Act 1, scene 2).[3]

For the most part, conduct manuals were intended to reinforce the lessons young ladies would have been already receiving at home and in church. The books frequently offer explanations for the rules. Young ladies could see appropriate women all around them, so they knew how to behave; the conduct manuals would tell them why. The authors of conduct books were thus content to speak to the larger audience, warning the innocent and ignoring the guilty. The guilty, or the fallen woman, however, was not without allure. She was a figure that both disgusted and intrigued; even the upright Dr Gregory suggests, 'Shew a compassionate sympathy to unfortunate women, especially to those who are rendered so by the villainy of men. Indulge a secret pleasure, I may say pride, in being the friends and refuge of the unhappy, but without the vanity of shewing it.'[4] Some writers went beyond such brief references and wrote either about fallen women, in order to provide a cautionary tale, or directly to them. It might be expected that condemnation of the fallen state would be universal and, outwardly, most texts would seem to agree.

A close reading of a 1791 pamphlet published by an anonymous clergyman from Hackney, however, provides a more complicated example of the forbidden fruit embodied by the sinful woman.[5] The writer blends stern denunciation with an almost erotic description of the crime, betraying conflicting male desires for both the chaste female ideal and the titillation promised by a (presumably) sexually-available fallen woman, all the while perpetuating her subordination.

The forty-four-page pamphlet is titled *Advice to Unmarried Women: to Recover and Reclaim the Fallen; and to Prevent the Fall of Others, into the Snares and Consequences of Seduction*. The writer explains that he has had success helping fallen women in his parish and now has written the pamphlet to assist others; he hopes that a familiarity with the situation of fallen women will serve as a warning to those of a 'better character' and help them resist temptation.[6] From the beginning, therefore, his tone is fraught with contradictions, as he professes a desire to help those who have fallen, but almost immediately insults them by mentioning the 'better character' of others. Then, a page later, his approach shifts as he expresses compassion when he describes women in the 'fallen state' as 'a part of the community who are too often left to perish unpitied in their sins, for want of some timely interposition of means ... to reclaim and save them.'[7] Throughout the remaining pages, he continues this ambivalence as he moves between blame, sympathy, encouragement, condemnation and, at times, perhaps even a hint of titillation.

Given the eighteenth century's eager consumption of 'true stories' contained in the burgeoning form of the novel, an attitude that combines denunciation with fascination is not surprising. *Pamela: or, Virtue Rewarded* (1740) by Samuel Richardson purports to be letters written by the eponymous heroine during her detention by the son of her now-deceased employer. This man, whom she refers to as Squire B, is determined to seduce Pamela and even tries to rape her on more than one occasion. Though Pamela emphasizes her purity throughout the book, it is not really a prim cautionary tale of the rewards that await virtuous young women, but rather a long narrative of imprisonment, attempted rape, fainting, stolen kisses and, ultimately, capitulation. That Squire B's satisfaction does not occur until the wedding night is, for the imaginative reader, almost beside the point. The chase, the teasing, the foreplay, provide the focus of the book.

Similarly, *Advice to Unmarried Women* combines a moral message with relatively detailed descriptions of how seduction can take place. The writer decides he must remind his readers of their sin and he speculates on the reason for their situation. His first theory is excessive love for and trust in a man who promises marriage. He spends three pages explaining how the man gradually wore down 'the guards of principle and duty' until the young lady 'yielded to the temptation of the moment, and [was] undone'.[8] Although the language is as modest as would be expected from a clergyman addressing a female audience in the English language, there is a slow sensuality in his description: rather than simply summarizing the process, he spins a little story of love betrayed and uses the second-person form of address to place the reader as his audience, his heroine and his victim. His recital forces the woman to re-live the events, once again helpless to defend herself against male manipulation, as she reads: 'His regard for you, you believed to be the same as your's for him … You gave him credit for the most pure and honourable intentions ... The fences of modesty once broken down, the repetition of your shame became easy to your seducer.'[9] The account of female shame is simultaneously a chronicle of male triumph, and the writer becomes a kind of accomplice as he performs in words what his predecessor enacted in deed.

Although the author briefly characterizes the man as a thief, saying that the women were 'robbed' by their seducers, he also casts the women as easy prey, calling them 'Young and inexperienced' and noting that they 'had not the judgment to discover nor discretion to escape' the trap their lovers set for them.[10] However, this excuse is cold comfort as it reinforces the original act of victimization and then infantilizes the women by stealing their free will and ability to make decisions. Rather than absolving them of responsibility, this explanation depicts women as helpless and entirely controlled by men, yet still culpable and deserving punishment.

The writer's patronizing sympathy disappears when he admits another possible reason for a woman's fallen state: financial necessity. He claims that no healthy young woman is unable to find an honest job. To him, those who prostitute themselves use the need for money as an excuse when the real reason is their own lust. He can accept a foolish faith in men and love as explanation for a fall, but nothing else. He refuses to acknowledge the existence of truly desperate situations, confident that respectable women would rather die than become prostitutes. He invokes centuries of tradition that offer death as the only honourable option, either as an alternative to sex or as a punishment for it. He declares that 'a virtuous woman' would

> suffer any thing rather than prostitute her person, and barter her modesty for bread. And indeed, whenever it comes to this, the wretched remainder of life is scarcely worth preserving. It is better to perish for want, than prolong by infamy a life that has nothing but the sinful wages of prostitution for its support.[11]

Those who choose a life of shame, according to him, are motivated by 'lust' and 'vanity': discontented with their 'humble condition', they have yielded to 'the foolish desire of being finer clothed, of being raised above their companions'; indeed, he seems to believe them all to have become mistresses of gentlemen who provided the luxurious lifestyle and fine clothes they desired.[12]

Up to this point, the author has clearly assumed that his readers are members of the serving class, maids with secure positions in respectable households whose employment prospects have been damaged by their fall, and to them he can proffer some modicum of understanding. However, for the women who sin wilfully, with the goal of crossing class lines, he has nothing but scorn. Women should be content with their humble lifestyles and hard work and not aspire to more. In fact, the two offences seem inseparable and compose a strange opposition of a deliberate fall undertaken in the hope of rising.

After detailing the possible causes of the seduction, the writer moves on to a tangible effect: the illegitimate child. His description of the situation, from a speculation about a woman contemplating infanticide to a mention of the shameful baptismal record, lacks sympathy for any party involved. He condemns mother, father and child with Old Testament severity: 'That register which will hereafter inform him of his birth, will tell him of his mother's crime ... and the sin of his father will be visited upon him, in scornful reproaches, to the third and fourth generation.'[13] The writer has used the word 'shame' fairly frequently to describe the woman's deeds, and now he introduces harsher rhetoric, characterizing it as a 'crime', and the man's actions as a 'sin'.

In earthly terms, the words 'sin' and 'crime' seem evocative of the obvious double standard applied to men and women in matters of sexuality (and almost everything), wherein the woman can expect instant and ongoing public humiliation while the man carries on unscathed. The eternal damnation that awaits him, though severe, is intangible and in the distant future. To a clergyman and his flock, however, the distinction between a crime and a sin might have been negligible, if not non-existent. For example, in *Thelyphthora; or, A Treatise on Female Ruin* (1780), Martin Madan debates women's sexuality within and without the bonds of marriage, arguing against distinguishing between moral and legal crimes:

> Can any person ... imagine that it was unlawful in the sight of GOD ... three thousand years ago, to take a virgin and then abandon her, but that now it is lawful? or, because there is no law of this land against it, it is therefore less offensive in the eyes of GOD, than at the instant He forbad it? or that GOD's law is only binding on the consciences of men, where it has the sanction of human institutions to inforce it?[14]

In this construction, there is no difference between a sin and a crime: a sin against God's law is in effect a criminal offence on heaven and earth.

The castigation of the woman is both a departure from the sympathy exhibited in previous pages and a continuation of the subordinate position assigned to her, as she moves from infantile victim who lacks the power of reason to a criminal who has damaged the society that so generously employed and sustained her. After a recitation of how miserable her life will be, how hard it will be to take care of the child and how society will scorn her, the writer ends as though pronouncing the sentence at the conclusion of a trial: 'Such, unhappy female, is your situation; such the difficulties and troubles which you have brought upon yourself.'[15] Again, there is no trace of kindness, no allowance for innocent foolishness, only the judgement of a vengeful god penalizing one who has, in effect, asked for such harsh treatment. The excuses the writer offered on her behalf in previous pages – too much love and trust, too little discernment – have apparently been dismissed. There are echoes here of Eve's banishment from Eden after succumbing to temptation; for centuries, conduct manuals and other literature held contemporary women guilty of their predecessor's failings and debated whether women were inherently predisposed to evil, some of the fiercest critics even accusing Eve of purposely collaborating with Satan to undo Adam and all his descendants. For example, a satirical poem, *Love Given O're* (1682), variously attributed to Robert Gould (1660?–1708/1709) and Thomas Brown (1662–1704), maintains that Eve was created not by God but by 'some banish'd Fiend' (line 36), and does not think one woman can be found 'That does not envy *Eve* the glory of the Fall' (line 55).[16] By the eighteenth century, most conduct books depicted women as innocent and in need of manly protection, but, as seen here, writers remained wary and ready to punish.

The shifting rhetorical pattern, from sympathetic understanding to outraged condemnation, mirrors the situation described in the pages theorizing the progress of the seduction. Assuming the reader is a fallen woman, both her lover and the pamphlet's author draw her in with kind words. Both ask for her trust. Both offer assistance, a way out of her current situation. And then, both men turn on her. It could be said that she is physically abandoned by one and now emotionally forsaken by the other. The writer had already forced her to recall the details of her seduction, and he confines her still to the role of victim, repeatedly betraying her trust and demonstrating her inability to resist. For readers who have not fallen, the warning is clear: one misstep results in never-ending victimization.

However, the title of the pamphlet states that it will 'reclaim the fallen', and the author does at last offer the remedy. The advice given by a clergyman is predictable. He recommends that his readers pray all the time and amend their behaviour; he also cautions that the change must be sincere and no mere performance. Only a thorough and sustained alteration will redeem these women in the eyes of God and society. While he exhorts his readers to repent and reform, he does not think such a transformation is possible for the men who seduced them. He advises no contact between them, saying, 'He means only again to seduce and to abandon you. Suffer none of his plausible tales of remorse and promises of marriage to reach you.'[17] This could be a reflection of his limited faith in a woman's ability to say no, but the remaining pages illustrate a relatively low opinion of men in general; he shifts therefore from a tolerant attitude towards the male half of the seduction equation to one of disgusted resignation; men are just like that and he cannot change them.

The writer maintains a wariness of his fellow men as he first cautions readers that it might be difficult to find a new employer and then warns them about the males of the household they could eventually join.[18] These men, he points out, might think a woman once fallen will be easier to seduce, so he advises an even greater distance and reserve to make it clear that she is not available and has reformed. Earlier in the text, the well-meaning clergyman observed certain deficiencies in women's judgement of men's intentions, and he now admits a similar fault in men. He explains that men are not skilled at understanding female behaviour: 'Vanity leads them to interpret your civilities into affection for themselves … however free from suspicion or design they may be, familiarities tend to loosen the restraints of modesty, and insensibly lead you into danger.'[19] Although the man is a guilty party here, due to his own lack of discernment, it is clear that a significant share of the blame would be placed on the victim, as the woman is being held responsible if the man misbehaves.[20] Even when she behaves appropriately, 'civilities' and innocent 'familiarities' might be enough to cause suspicion, so that baseless allegations of provocation would probably be believed of a woman who had already fallen once. The writer thus establishes a perplexing future for the women he is attempting to reform. There seems to be no solution. Men cannot be trusted, and apparently a simple 'good morning, sir' might be interpreted as an invitation.

In such a doomed scenario, it is difficult to identify where the writer truly places the blame. Is it the man, with his optimistic translation of simple pleasantries? Or is it the woman? Is she so stained by her sin that no word she speaks can ever be free of it? Does it emanate from her every pore, like a tarnished but sensual nimbus? Although the writer criticizes male thinking, he nonetheless places responsibility on the woman for anticipating and correcting it. True, his pamphlet is addressed to women, so he has no reason to speak to men in these pages, but by requiring women to bear alone the burden of conducting appropriate relationships with other parties, he draws out her punishment and nullifies the promise of forgiveness made when he counselled repentance and reform. Regardless of the purity of her intentions, she is continually at risk. The writer has not given a promising illustration of redemption.

To strengthen his point, the author lists some reasons why men will be especially eager to be in the company of a known fallen woman. He explains that men might think it would be easier to persuade a woman who has given in before, a point of view that contains a certain logic, but he also presents some more complex reasons, concluding that men 'will have less reluctance to bring [a fallen woman] again into such a situation than they would have to debauch a virtuous character'.[21] Not only will the man have an easier time ensnaring his victim and alleviating his conscience, but he will also face less censure from the world at large, 'because the world expecting no good of you will think very lightly of the crime of bringing you again to shame.'[22] The writer has provided no evidence that the world ever thought more than lightly of the seducer's actions, and he demonstrates the interchangeability of the words 'crime' and 'sin' by this time describing the man's actions as the former rather than the latter. He also indicates that a woman's prayers and reformed behaviour really do very little to convince the world that she is once again virtuous. She may be reconciled to God, but here on earth she remains a criminal and a sinner who only bides her time before she strikes again. She is not Eve after all, but the snake.

Yet again the writer alters his approach. After pages of punishing descriptions of the cruel reception they can expect from the world, he asks his readers to look inward. He adopts the tone of a teacher of morals, hoping that the woman will reflect and learn from her mistakes and discover where her 'greatest danger lies'.[23] Did she trust too much in the restraint of the man she loved? Or did he gradually wear down her objections until after a while 'passion was left exposed to passion, to artifice and temptation, and you insensibly yielded to his lust'?[24] Once more, the writer re-enacts a seduction scene, providing vaguely suggestive details that might serve to entice rather than repel his readers.

It is ironic to see a clergyman's conduct book imitating the sentimental novels of the period, even if inadvertently. Conduct manuals generally discouraged young women from reading novels, believing such fictions to be dangerous influences that would corrupt female minds and give them unrealistic expectations in matters of romance. Yet the manuals were often conflicted. *The Female Mentor* (1793) suggested that ladies read only histories and other morally informative material, providing an example of an old maid who had refused several offers of marriage because the men did not measure up to her ideal, the protagonist of Samuel Richardson's *The History of Sir*

Charles Grandison (1753). A couple of pages later, though, the kindly mentor recommends *The Female Quixote* (1752) by Charlotte Lennox (c.1730–1804) as an appropriate novel, because it tells the story of Arabella, a young woman who lives her life according to the rules she finds in 'romances and novels', which almost leads to disaster.[25] The mentor evidently thinks that Arabella will serve as a cautionary tale, but she seems to forget that the book is highly entertaining and is more likely to whet a literary appetite than curb it.

The clergyman's next theory snaps readers back to reality. He suggests that alcohol could be to blame for a woman's fall from grace; he does not accuse his readers of regular drunkenness, just a momentary slip, saving his most severe condemnation for women who are repeatedly drunk. They seem to be even worse than fallen women, for he says, 'If I thought you such [a drunkard], I should spare myself the trouble to advise or reason with you: it would indeed be casting pearls before swine to do it.'[26] It is unlikely that he considers drinking a more serious offence than premarital sex; the repetition of the act of drunkenness seems to be his chief complaint. His address to his readers from the beginning appears to assume that their transgression was limited, either to one time or to one man. He warns against the dangers of prostitution in language that suggests he does not expect his audience to possess intimate knowledge of the profession, and here he is able to dismiss a single episode of excessive drinking, but not more than that. He continues to see-saw between indulgent forgiveness and implacable condemnation.

Vanity is the final reason the writer proposes for causing a woman's fall, and he has little tolerance for this shortcoming. He scolds women in general for vanity in dress and his readers specifically for aspiring to situations to which they were not born. He advises, 'Root out therefore from your heart the very wish of dressing or aspiring beyond the state in which the providence of God hath placed you.'[27] In the great chain of being, their positions as servants have been determined and they have no right to question it. He also reminds women of their true purpose: to be a wife and mother. He says women spend too much money on clothes, and he suggests that they save money for their future families. Addressing the women who have already fallen, he reminds them that they should spend their money not on themselves but on their child, particularly since they cannot depend on the father for support.

The final pages unite the unfeeling judge with the sympathetic counsellor. The writer seems to assume that even one transgression in the name of love will ultimately result in a life of prostitution, which he describes with revulsion, but his harsh words are intended to prevent this unhappy way of life and its eternal consequences. A clergyman may mourn for a soul lost, even as he condones its punishment. The concluding paragraph is almost a prayer, as he first wishes that God might grant his readers 'wisdom and grace' and then refers to Luke 19:42 in closing, hoping that readers might 'see in this your day the things which belong to your peace'.[28] He leaves the discussion on a spiritual note, but his treatment of his subject and his audience lacks the predictable consistency that might be expected from a man of the church tending to his flock. His varying tone and ambivalent chastisement betray the complexities of sexual morality, a problem faced by every society in every century. The writer's unacknowledged struggle is not an anomaly; many eighteenth-century conduct manuals, regardless of author or audience, demonstrate a kind of push-pull internal argument about appropriate female behaviour. We may well recognize the contradictions as the matter has yet, more than 200 years on, to be decided.

Gretchen's Answer

Tabitha Kenlon

(inspired by Goethe's *Faust*)

I

Is he a seducer? Am I a whore?
He asked – silently;
I said yes – invisibly.
Words damned us, yet there are none for what we felt.
For what I feel still.

The Street

No. No. No!
This is what we are taught, from the cradle to the well.
Wherever there are women gathered, the word most discussed
is no. It is pounded into a young girl's head.
It is forced into a young girl's mouth.
It issues forth automatically,
for the first time, at least.
But the old women, with their wise chatter and wagging heads,
do not explain one particular thing.
They tell us why.
They describe the shame in gleeful detail. They cast their stones
with precise enthusiasm. They point at examples with gnarled fingers
decorated with forgotten wedding bands. But they never, ever, not even once,
pause for a moment to tell a young girl
how.

How do you say no to a man whose smile makes you feel whole and holy?
How can you answer when he isn't really asking?

Why should you say no to a man whose eyes
have already undressed you?
When I met him on the street that first time,
I did what I'd been told. I said no.
I was unkind. I was obedient.
But the word that had been pounded into my head and forced into my mouth
had not quite got to my heart.
So even while my mouth spat forth the word it was supposed to,
every other part of me trembled in fear lest the man believe my mouth
and not hear the wild
yes yes yes, oh, yes
that sang like a bird from my fingers, my hair, my eyes –
indeed, from every part of me.

The Chamber

There were jewels. I will not lie.
There were jewels. And yes, I like jewels.
Every girl does. But the jewels are inconsequential.
(That is a word he taught me.)
I had, remember, already said yes.
So I gave them to my mother,
not really knowing what else to do.
There had been no mention of jewels
in the stories the women told by the well.
The jewels frightened me more than they persuaded me.
I did not want to be bought.
I wanted to be loved.
Perhaps, I thought, this is what the stories leave out.
All those sad, abandoned women – why had they said yes?
If it was for jewels – well then.
They might not have deserved their fate,
not really, but when a girl says yes because a man
gives her gifts, how can she trust his intentions?

Then there were more jewels.
I will not lie. These I kept.

The Garden

How foolish I must have looked to him.
A peasant girl in simple clothes
and ostentatious jewels.
(He taught me that word as well.)
He was pleased to see me.
I needed no education to recognize that.
When he took my hand, I let him.
When he kissed me,
I kissed him back,
dislodging the word no,
the word that had been pounded into my head
and forced into my mouth.
Now it fell away, forgotten and unrecognizable.

What had I been praying for all those mornings in church,
thinking of Christ on the cross?
Why would I want a man who would die for me
when I am so full of life?
I've watched the garden around me;
the blossoms undulate and unfold to the waiting bees,
and the bee loses itself in the fluttering embrace of the flower.
Is this what the priest means when he speaks of passion?

II

I am afraid.
His absence may cast him as a seducer.
But my yearning is not that of a whore.
I am – in love. There is,
I think,
a difference between a lover and a whore.
I am afraid the women at the well would
not agree.

The Garden

A reunion is no time for doubts
or questions. And yet.

And yet,
I question. Fearing for my own soul,
I ask after his.
Eternity is such a long time to be
alone.
I feel simple beside him. I feel able
to be encompassed.

But there is sorrow in his eyes, even as he
evades my questions, hoping, I think,
that in my simplicity I will not notice.
But I do, and I am afraid.

If I was not good,
I would not fear evil. And his friend
is evil. Not the kind the women tell young girls about at the well.
This is the kind that no one speaks of,
because to speak of it is to invite it.
This is something not told. Just known.
His eyes are hollow and cruel and tormented,
like one who has knowledge of paradise
but is barred from it forever,
and is trying to believe that it does not even
exist.
He is the devil in my garden,
but it is my love who has shown me
knowledge.

The Chamber

He is gone again and now I know.
He is a seducer.
Indeed. In deed.
I love him still.
I believe he loved me – once.
And now there will be a part of him
that will love me always,
and call me mother.

My brother is dead.
With his dying breath he condemned me.

When shall my regrets begin?
I still treasure every meeting, every kiss.
I wake each day wailing, wanting him.
I end each day weeping, wishing him
pain and tears and then praying for his soul.
O, how I have tried to hate him!
I have recounted his wrongs. I have listened
to gossip and insults about other young girls,
knowing that soon my belly will betray me too
and I will be damned.
But still my love remains. The flutters of his child
remind me of his love.
I invent excuses for his absence. I imagine
with imagination I never knew I possessed
the moment of our happy reunion,
his kisses, his embrace, my feet leaving the ground
as he spins me in the air.
His joy, his rapture, his own kind of religion.

He gave me once a potion to help my mother
sleep.
Now I give her more and more each night,
and I creep to the window, calling his name.
"Come, my love! 'Tis safe! She sleeps! She sleeps!
The world is our own. There is nothing to fear!
Come, my love, come."
And each night passes silently by until my own sobs
awake me in the careless morning light that casts
a straggled shadow of the tree outside
my window, slowly dying in the garden.
Dying. Slowly.

The Street

I swooned in church.
I could not pray. The words were strange
and held nothing.
Like jewels.
A price above rubies.
What price must I pay for love?

Is the cross my fate as well? Are the wages
of love death?

I wait for his rescue, I wait for salvation.
But Christ does not hear me.
He refuses to listen.
Just as all the women at the well
will not listen when I try to explain
that I am not a whore.
I am in love.

What are words? There is no difference
between yes and no, whore and lover.
It is just a question of knowledge
If no one knows what you've done,
they cannot tell you that you are evil.
And I know I am not evil. Even if Christ
ignores me, even if the town hates me,
even if my brother condemns me.
I said yes. Yes, I said yes.
Perhaps I am not an angel. No one is.
If we were, what need would we have
for God?

III

I have forgotten what I am.
My mother is dead, so I am not
a daughter.
My brother is dead, so I am not
a sister.
My child is dead, so I am not
a mother.
I am nothing.

The Prison

My heart says yes to the executioner.
But somehow my mouth remembers
how to say no.

It is too late for that now.
I want death. I do. It seems so soft and full.
I want to be an angel after all.
Perhaps if I could speak to God,
in person,
I could explain everything better.
Perhaps then he would understand
that love is not as simple
as it might seem there in heaven.
That love, here, on earth,
is really quite complicated.

But even so, when a man came for me,
all I could say was no. The unfamiliar word
came from my mouth again and again,
only the second time I had ever told him no.
because it was him.
Not the executioner.
Although, in some way, I suppose he was.
He had finally come to save me.
This had been beyond my imaginings.
I grasped at him, mad with relief and fear.
I begged him to kiss me, to bring me back
to life.

He did not say no.
He did not have to.
I felt it. O, I felt it.
I was not the first.
Nor am I the last.
But I kissed him anyway. I had to.
It was not a kiss. It was death.

I had borne everything the best I could. I had not
rued him, even after all the deaths and the
torment. I had loved him still.
I could have died loving him and in some way
been happy, dreaming of our garden.

But this – how could this be endured?
I had never thought, not once throughout
his absence, that he repented of me.
What cruelty. And what is death now?
What is there to fear when such a horror
stands before me?

It was so easy now to say no to him,
knowing that he loved me not.
(Foolish girl, to rely on the wisdom
of daisies.)
If he wanted to save me, it was not me
he wished to save. It was himself.
A guilty conscience, even to a man
who befriends the devil, is
an inconvenience.

It was this devil, not my love,
who saved me. His presence terrified my poor
heart, surpassing everything, even
love.
Now I was able to pray. Save me from this
creature, dear God.
Though I do not know which one I meant.
Through fear are we saved.

Faith and fear are closely related,
and in the end,
the word itself is less important
than the consequence.

IV

The women at the well,
I am sure, tell my story. The young girls listen,
ashamed and appalled. They swallow the no
that is forced into their mouths

and they believe that they will never say yes.
Not the way that I said it.
For if they should meet a man, they will say no.

Unless, of course, he loves them.

About the Poem

The story of Faust, the man who sells his soul to the devil in exchange for power and knowledge, has been told for centuries. One of the best-known versions is the two-part verse play *Faust* (1808, 1832) by Johann Wolfgang von Goethe (1749–1832). Goethe devotes a great deal of attention to Faust's temptation by Mephistopheles (Satan's messenger), his questionable behaviour and his influence on the people he meets. Gretchen is Faust's tragic love-interest, whom he seduces and abandons.

This poem was written during Dr Inez Hedges' post-graduate seminar course at Northeastern University, which focused on various permutations of the Faust legend in literature and film. I wrote this dramatic monologue in an effort to give voice to a character who seemed to be little more than a casualty of Faust's heartlessness in Goethe's story. To me, and I suspect to many women, Gretchen embodies the turmoil that can result when emotions are subject to judgement and double standards, when society tells women how to think, how to act, how to feel.

I must also acknowledge a debt to Carol Ann Duffy's *The World's Wife* (1999), a collection of poems providing the woman's perspective on stories dominated by male figures, which I discovered through a riveting stage adaptation at London's Trafalgar Studios in 2010.

Chapter Nine

Friendships: Commonalities across the Centuries

by Julie Peakman

I am loath to abandon all Thoughts of Friendship, both because it is one of the brightest Vertues, and because I have the noblest Designs in it.

Mary Astell[1]

Musing over thirty years of the Women's Studies Group (I have been a member for half that time), I wondered what to say about the things I have gained from the group. I realized that one of the reasons our group has been important to me is the support its members have given me, especially in my early career, encouraging me to give papers and providing the opportunity to speak about my work. The meetings also allowed me to meet with other women scholars, hear about their work, and connect with other women with similar interests to share visits to archives, libraries, exhibitions and galleries. However, the group has given much more than that: members have provided a support network, a group of friends in a sometimes hostile academic world, a sisterhood that (whatever we have been given to believe) is not always present 'outside' our own universities. While my own History and English departments at Birkbeck College, University of London, is full of supportive, sharing friends and colleagues, not everyone is so lucky. Over the years, the Women's Studies Group has provided a safe space where we can share information, air our papers and receive unbiased feedback, and share our grievances. Nor do we feel the need to seek protection in exclusivity: an important indicator of the group's self-confidence is our willingness to include those discerning male scholars who share our interests.

I wondered how important groups of this type have been for women, and surprisingly found a parallel between the WSG and my research working universe of eighteenth-century whores (although this may seem an unlikely comparison). One close personal friendship I explored was the relationship between Emma Hamilton, née Lyon (1765–1815), and Maria Carolina, the Queen of Naples (1752–1814). This research I turned into a chapter for our first Women's Studies Group collection, edited by our stalwarts Carolyn D. Williams, Angela Escott and Louise Duckling.[2] After working on Emma Hamilton's biography, I realized what an extraordinary woman she was, and how she utilized the opportunity to establish firm relationships with her friends, notably the queen. This particular alliance gave her a confidence that she might otherwise not have gained. This, in turn, enabled her to gain some leverage to assist Horatio Nelson (1758–1805) in his battle for Malta by encouraging the queen to provide ships for him. The relationship between the queen and Emma was an unspoken arrangement for the betterment of both parties, a mutually supportive rapport that enabled both women to gain control of political affairs: Maria guided her husband's affairs, while Emma used her influence to aid her diplomat husband William Hamilton (1730–1803), her future lover Nelson, and her country. Without each other, these women would have gained none of these benefits. Yet their friendship was more than a mutually-beneficial linkage enabling them to operate in the world of male-governed politics and war; it was also a caring, nurturing relationship that gave them protection and allowed them both to develop their personalities and their skills.

Female Friends

A broader network that mutually enhanced women's lives was revealed to me when I found Peg Plunkett, aka Mrs Margaret Leeson (she followed the common brothel-keeper's custom of taking the name of one of her elite lovers and prefixing it with a married woman's title), successively mistress, whore and brothel-keeper to the many men in her life.[3] While writing her biography, *Peg Plunkett: Memoirs of A Whore* (2015), I discovered the inner world of the eighteenth-century prostitutes' collective. Although men were important to Peg as providers of love, sex and financial security, and there were some painful episodes when female colleagues and relatives were unwilling or unable to help her, it was the women who remained a constant, both as sources of companionship and as last resorts in times of desperation. A brief account of Peg's life, highlighting her relationships with women, will be followed by some more general observations on eighteenth-century representations of prostitution as an organized sisterhood: her narrative can be set in context as part of a spectrum of stories about prostitutes' relationships with each other, and with men and women in general.

Peg was much maligned and ill-treated during her life, mainly by men (although the women in her life sometimes also let her down). Her elder brother squandered her family's estate and beat her constantly until she fled County Westmeath to seek protection in the house of a married sister in Dublin. Yet even sisterhood failed her when she fell pregnant by her seducer, a Mr Dardis, her brother-in-law's best friend, and needed shelter and support for herself and her baby daughter; as she puts it, 'My harsh sisters indeed, might have saved me from ruin, but that their *outrageous virtue* disdained.'[4] This ensured her a place as an outcast from society, the usual fate of women who bore children outside marriage. With no reputable means of making themselves independent, women were reliant on their families or male protectors. There was no possibility of employment, even in domestic service, for a woman in Peg's position: 'their characters being blasted, they have no means of support from any industry they may be willing to fly to for bread.'[5]

After going through a series of men, bearing more children, each successive lover abandoning her as they tired of her or wanted to marry another woman (for Peg was no longer bridal material), she found love. However, this was not to last. After five years together, her lover's income was cut off by his father because of his debauched and profligate lifestyle; he eventually abandoned Peg to chance his luck with a relative in New York, leaving her with their five children to look after.[6] Peg was left with only her jewellery and her clothes to sell to feed them all. With a steely grit few other women could show, Peg threw herself into the world of prostitution, working her way up to buy her own establishment of which she would be in charge, enabling her to control her own destiny. No longer prepared to rely on any one man, she played coquette to many and succumbed only to those who had enough money to pay extortionate sums for her company. Her clients included David La Touche (1729–1817), Governor of the Bank of Ireland, Captain John Hayes St Leger (1756–99) and various dignitaries from Dublin Castle, as well as barristers, wealthy merchants and the chief constable of the local watch. The pinnacle of her career was marked by the visits of Charles Manners, 4th Duke of Rutland (1754–87), during his administration as Viceroy of Ireland: 'the gay, the witty, the gallant, the convivial Rutland, whose court outrivaled that of Comus himself.'[7] John Fane, 10th Earl of Westmorland (1759–1841), one of his successors, did not fare so well: disapproving of his treatment of his late wife, she rejected his advances with '*hauteur and contempt*'.[8] Peg could pick and choose. She revelled in her success: 'I still encreased in celebrity, and was esteemed the first woman in Ireland in my line. I was visited by nobles and gentlemen of the first rank in the kingdom; for it became quite the fashion to be acquainted with me.'[9] More importantly, in the long run, she was 'looked up to as a kind of pattern to the ladies of the *sisterhood*': the word is generally used with ironic overtones, but in fact she found in their ranks a degree of support that her blood relatives failed to provide.[10]

The first trustworthy woman she connected with was Sally Hayes, who not only enjoyed the same lust for life and high living as Peg, but could also be relied upon to share the running of her business. Peg set up a high-class brothel in Drogheda Street, one of the finest in Dublin, and Sally lived with her; their partnership provided Dublin with glamorous public spectacles that must have provided an excellent advertisement:

> I hired an handsome chariot, and we dashed away, cared for nobody, wanted for nothing, had numerous presents, frequented every public amusement, were every night at the play superbly dressed, and lived like princesses. We constantly drove to the Curragh races, in a coach and four, my servants in liveries of scarlet and gold, and Isaacs, the dulcimer player in our rear.[11]

Later on, Sally moved in when Peg fitted up, at what even she admits was 'very great expence', a house in Wood Street.[12] Here Peg, 'spirited' up by a government ban on masquerades, held one of her own, inviting 200 distinguished guests.[13] This event attracted a huge mob, drawn by the irresistible combination of controversy, celebrities in fancy dress, and glamorous decorations, including 'five hundred coloured lamps, of blue, lilac and green'.[14] According to Peg, 'About seven they began to be somewhat riotous, and swore they would demolish all the windows, if I and Sally Hayes, did not come out and shew ourselves immediately.'[15] They hastily changed into their costumes and appeared on 'the upper step of the door'; the mob waited for a few minutes, then gave a huzza, and told them to go in, 'for they were satisfied, and no damage should happen.'[16] Undaunted by this experience, Sally was still at hand when the two women 'took possession' of Peg's next establishment, in Pitt Street.[17] It was 'elegantly fitted out' with 'lustres, gerandoles, branches, *elastic beds*, lascivious prints and paintings, and every matter that genius and fancy could suggest to the most heated and eccentric imagination.'[18]

At a time when any independent woman was seen as unruly and immodest, life was difficult for a group of single-minded hard-working autonomous women. As such, even when they were not organizing spectacular parties, they were open to masculine exploitation and aggression. With expensively-furnished houses in the most fashionable neighbourhoods in town and the

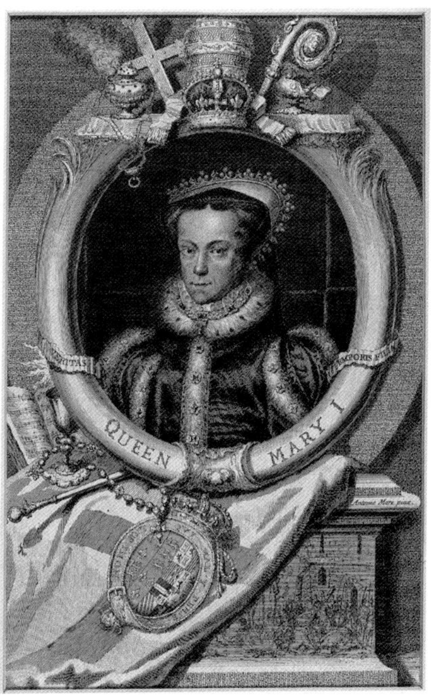

Mary Tudor, Queen of England from 1553-58, who was sometimes known as Bloody Mary. Engraving by George Vertue, 1710. (*Wellcome Collection*)

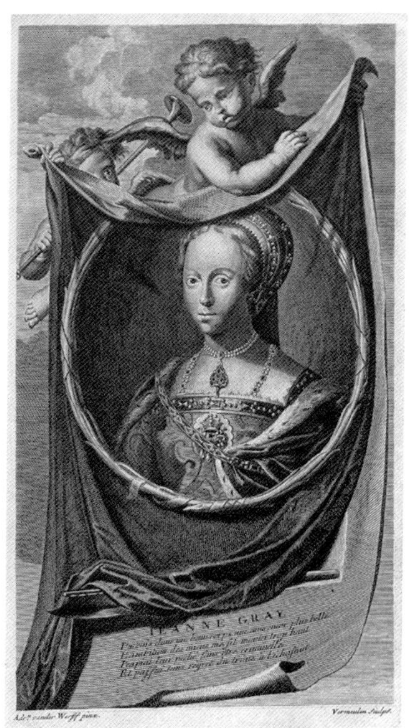

An eighteenth-century engraving of Lady Jane Grey, Queen of England for nine days in July 1553. She was executed on 12 February 1554 aged 16 or 17. (*Wellcome Collection*)

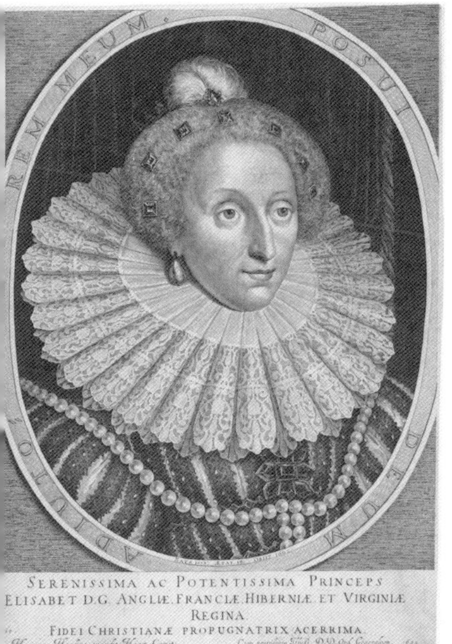

Elizabeth I of England by Hendrick Hondius the Elder, 1632. Elizabeth ruled England from 1558 until her death in March 1603, aged 69. (*Rijksmuseum, Netherlands*)

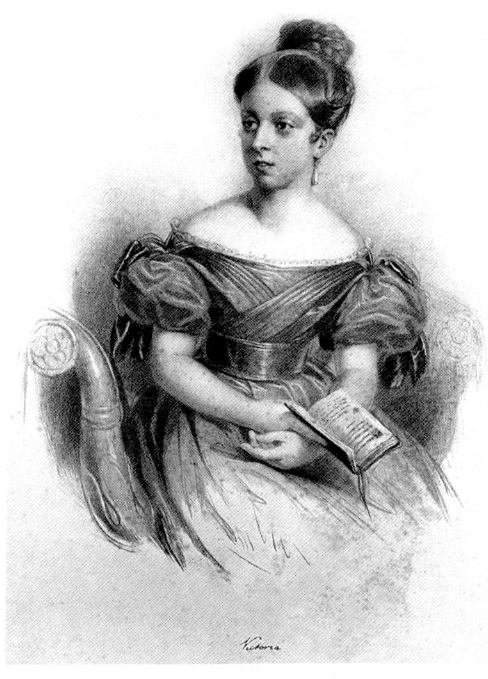

Queen Victoria as a young woman by F. W. Wilkin. Victoria inherited the throne at the age of 18 and reigned from 1837-1901. (*Wellcome Collection*)

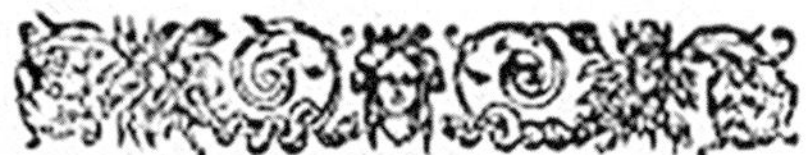

THE

COVNTESSE

OF LINCOLNES

NVRSERIE.

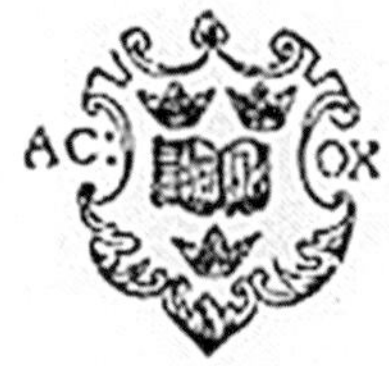

AT OXFORD,

Printed by IOHN LICHFIELD, and IAMES SHORT

Printers to the famous Vniversitie. 1622.

Title page of *The Countesse of Lincolnes Nurserie* (1622), written by the dowager Countess of Lincoln and introduced by physician Thomas Lodge. (*Image via 'A Celebration of Women Writers'*)

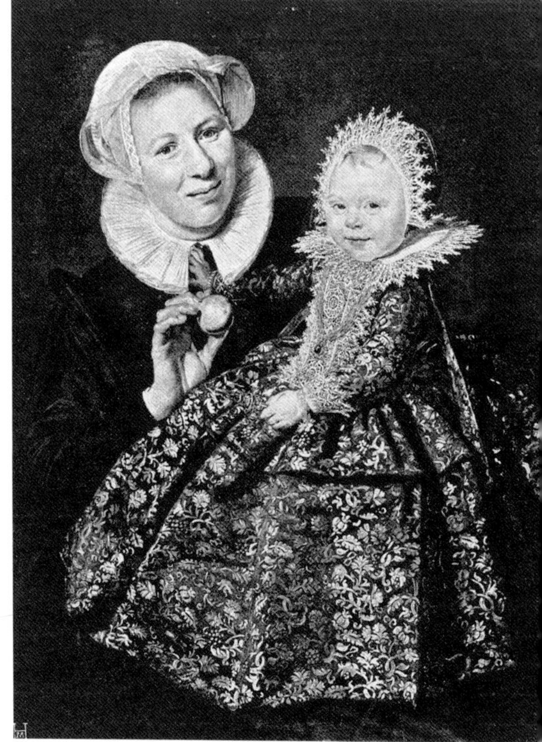

A plainly dressed wet nurse with an elaborately dressed infant, representing the traditional practice of high ranking people employing women to breastfeed their infants. After Frans Hals, 'Catharina Hooft with her Nurse', *c.*1620. (*Wellcome Collection*)

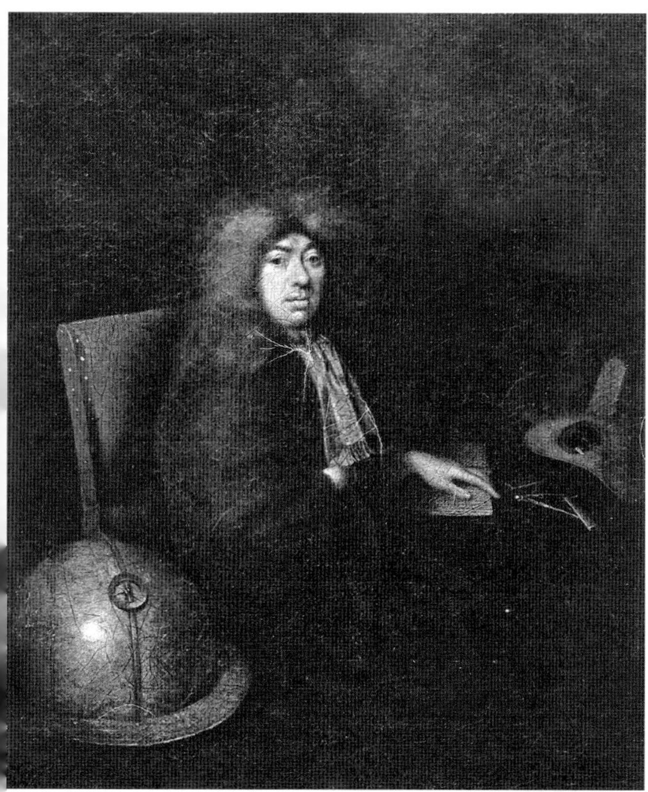

Naval administrator and diarist, Samuel Pepys (1633-1703). (*Wellcome Collection*)

Elisabeth Pepys (1640-69). Elisabeth married Samuel just prior to her fifteenth birthday. The marriage was a love match and the couple hoped for children throughout their fourteen year marriage. (*The New York Public Library Digital Collections*)

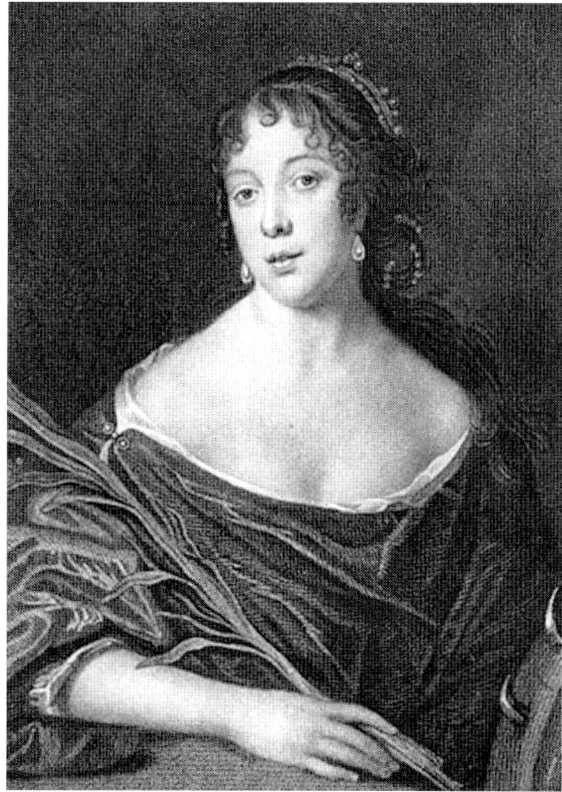

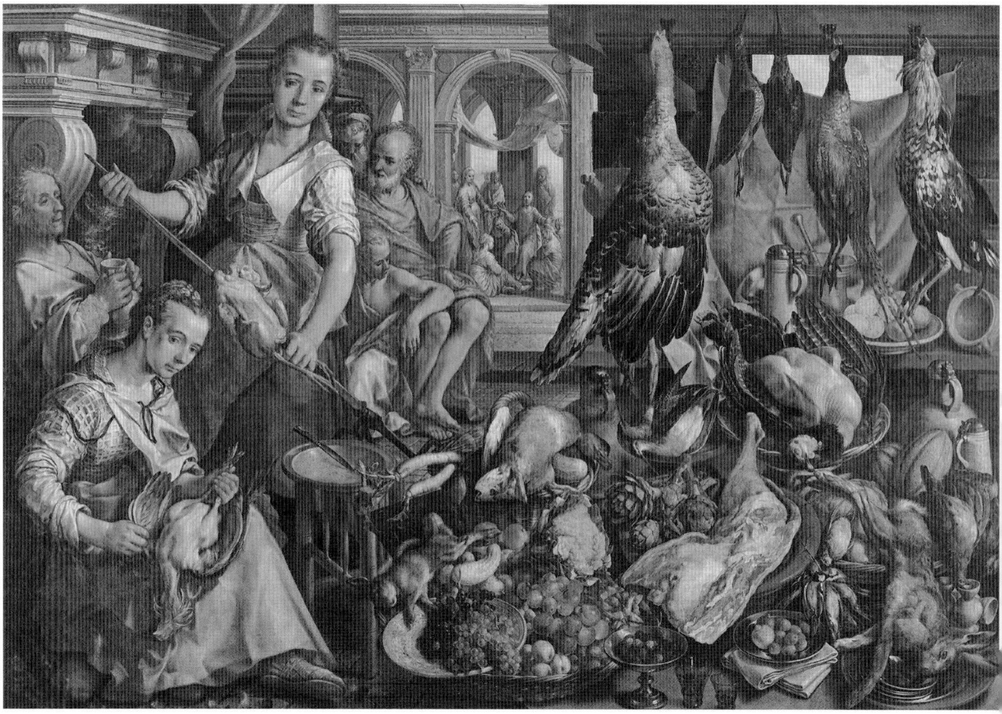

MISCELLANY

POEMS,

ON

Several Occasions.

Written by the Right Hon[ble] *ANNE*, Counteſs of WINCHILSEA.

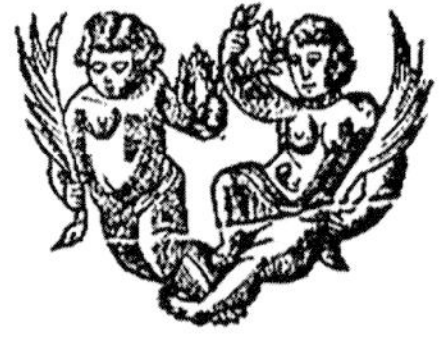

LONDON:

Printed for *J. B.* and Sold by *Benj. Tooke* at the *Middle-Temple-Gate*, *William Taylor* in *Pater-Noſter-Row*, and *James Round* in *Exchange-Alley*, *Cornhil.* 1713.

'The Well-stocked Kitchen', Joachim Bueckelaer, 1566, showing the types of everyday ingredients that might be used to manufacture aphrodisiacs in the home. (*Rijksmuseum, Netherlands*)

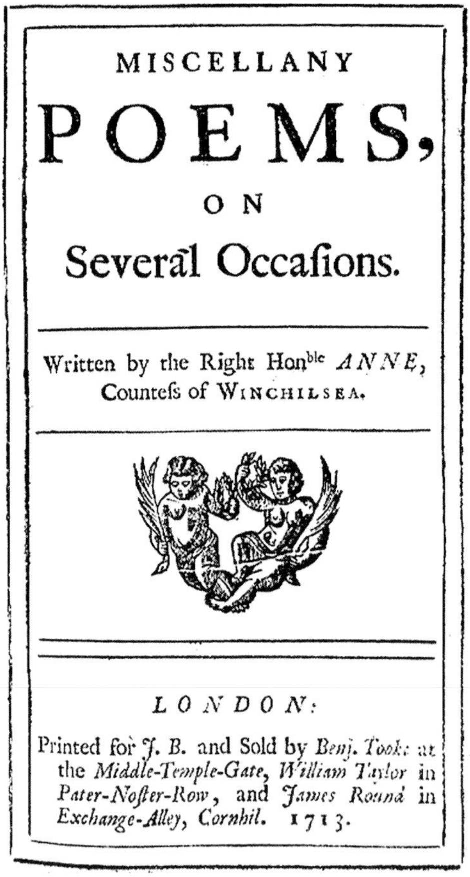

The title page of *Miscellany Poems, on Several Occasions*, by the Right Honourable Anne, Countess of Winchilsea (London, 1713). (*Image via 'A Celebration of Women Writers'*)

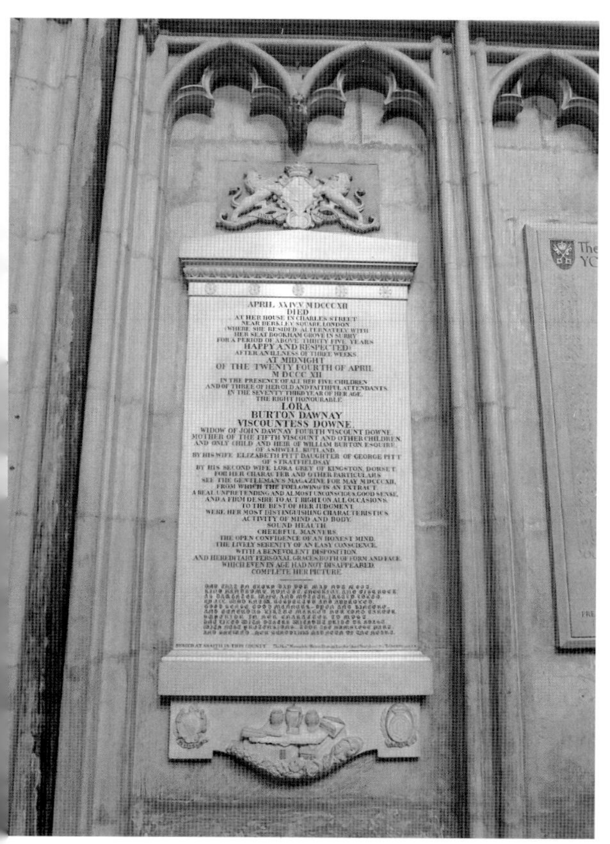

The memorial stone of Lora Burton Dawnay, Viscountess Downe, in York Minster. 'A DAUGHTER, WIFE AND MOTHER': Lady Downe's son installed her 'sculptur'd tomb' in the North Quire aisle of York Minster in 1836, a belated 24 years after her death. (*Photograph © Chloe Victoria Howard*)

Detail showing that the memorial refers the passer-by to Lady Downe's longer obituary in the *Gentleman's Magazine* for May 1812. (*Photograph © Chloe Victoria Howard*)

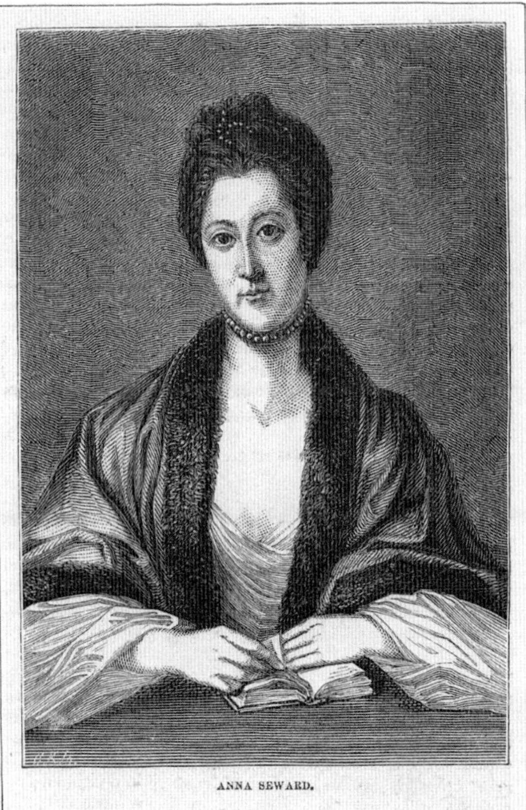

The writer Anna Seward (1742-1809) enjoyed considerable acclaim for her poetry and was known as the 'Swan of Lichfield'. She was a regular contributor to periodicals, especially the *Gentleman's Magazine*. (*The New York Public Library Digital Collections*)

Hannah Cowley (1743-1809) was a successful and innovative dramatist, celebrated for her witty comedies. She contributed regularly to the *Gentleman's Magazine*. (*Photograph © Angela Escott, print in her personal collection*)

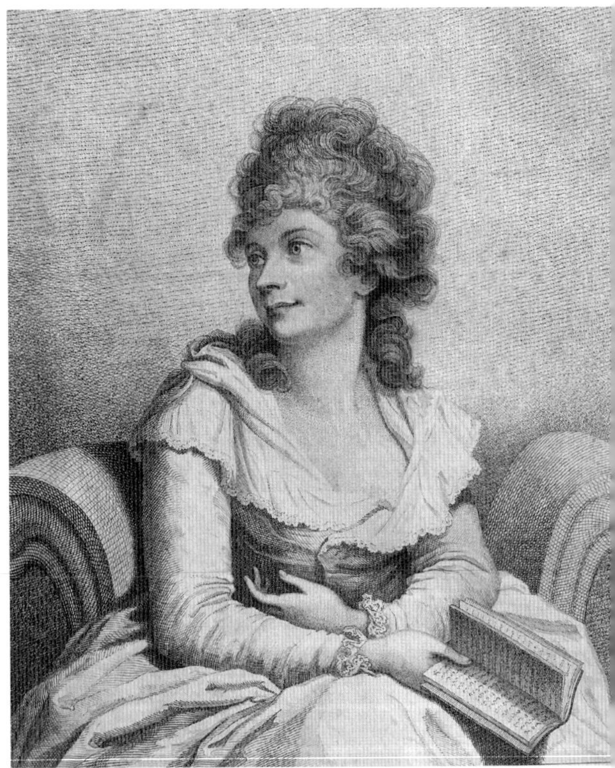

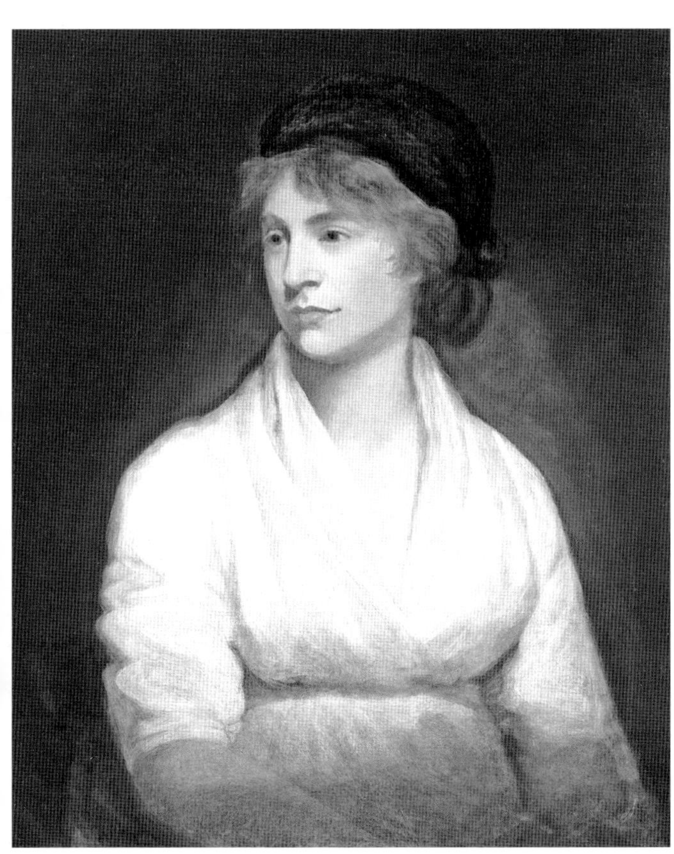

Portrait of Mary Wollstonecraft (1759-97), by John Opie, 1804. (*The New York Public Library Digital Collections*)

'St Vincent's Rock, Clifton, Bristol, with Hotwell's Spring House in the Distance', undated, by Francis Wheatley (1747–1801). Mary Wollstonecraft visited Bristol in 1787, when she started work on her unfinished novel, 'The Cave of Fancy'. The story contains topographical links to St Vincent's Rock and the Avon Gorge. (*Yale Center for British Art, Paul Mellon Collection*)

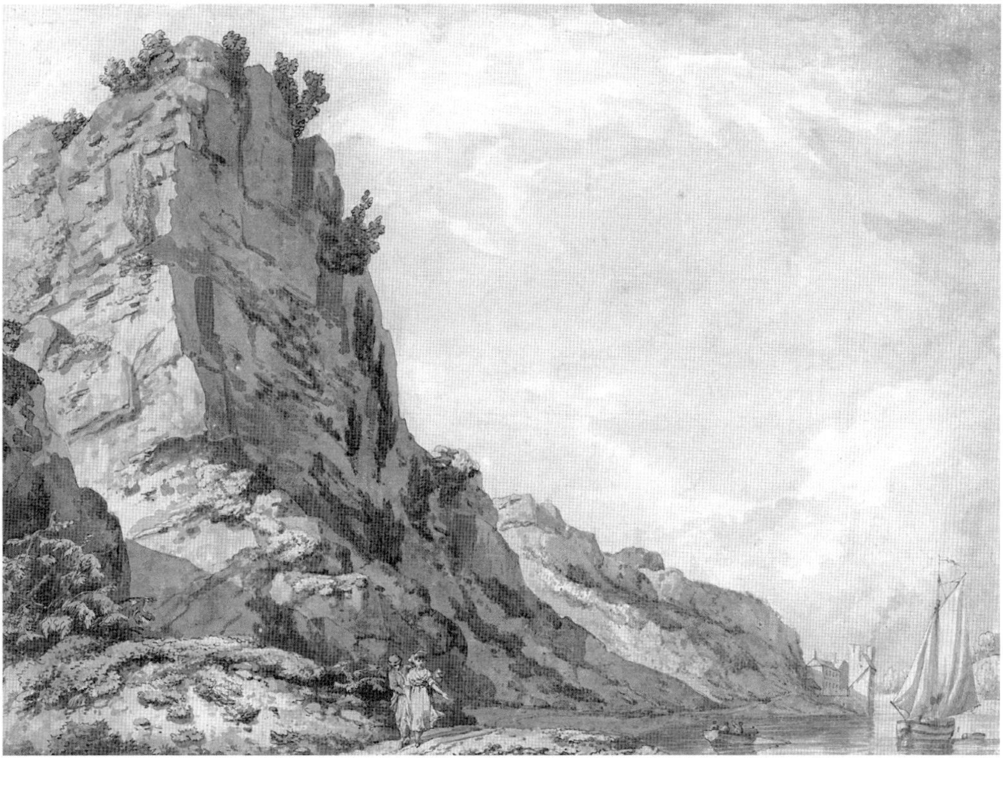

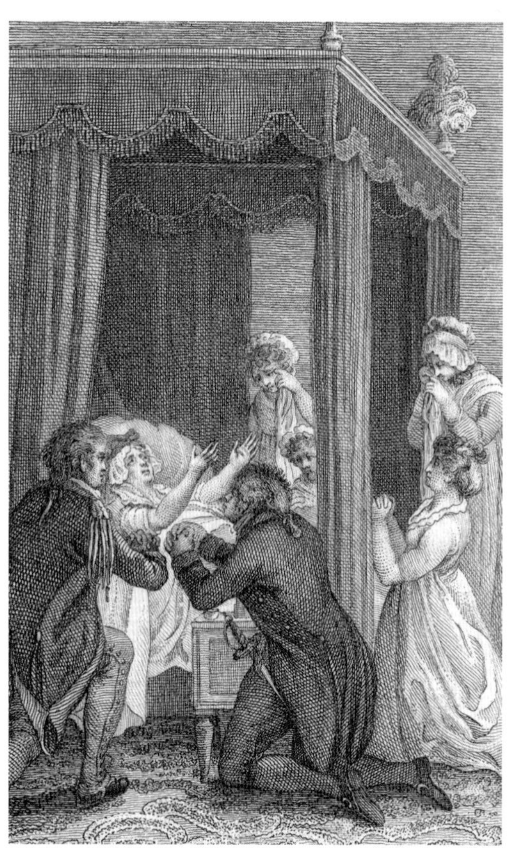

‘Praying and crying figures at Clarissa’s sickbed’, Reinier Vinkeles, 1805. In Chapter 7, Sarah Oliver discusses the treatment of the rape theme in Samuel Richardson’s *Clarissa. Or, the History of a Young Lady* (1748). (*Rijksmuseum, Netherlands*)

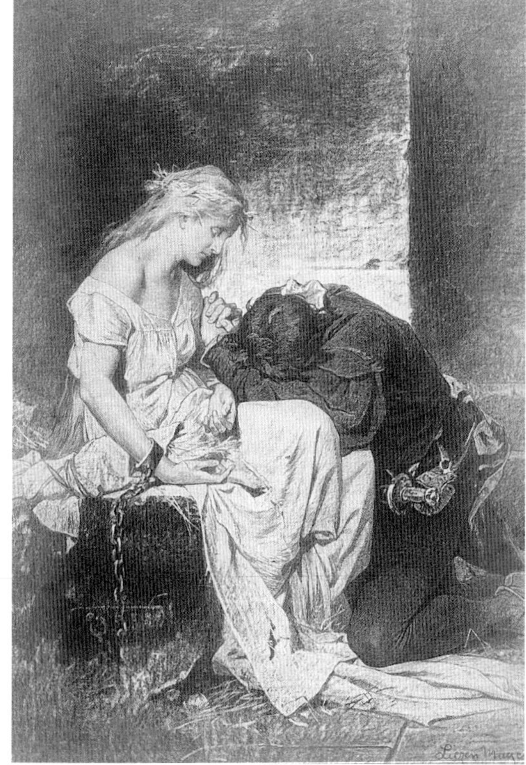

‘Faust and Gretchen in the dungeon’, Anonymous, after Alexander von Liezen-Mayer, 1878. (*Rijksmuseum, Netherlands*)

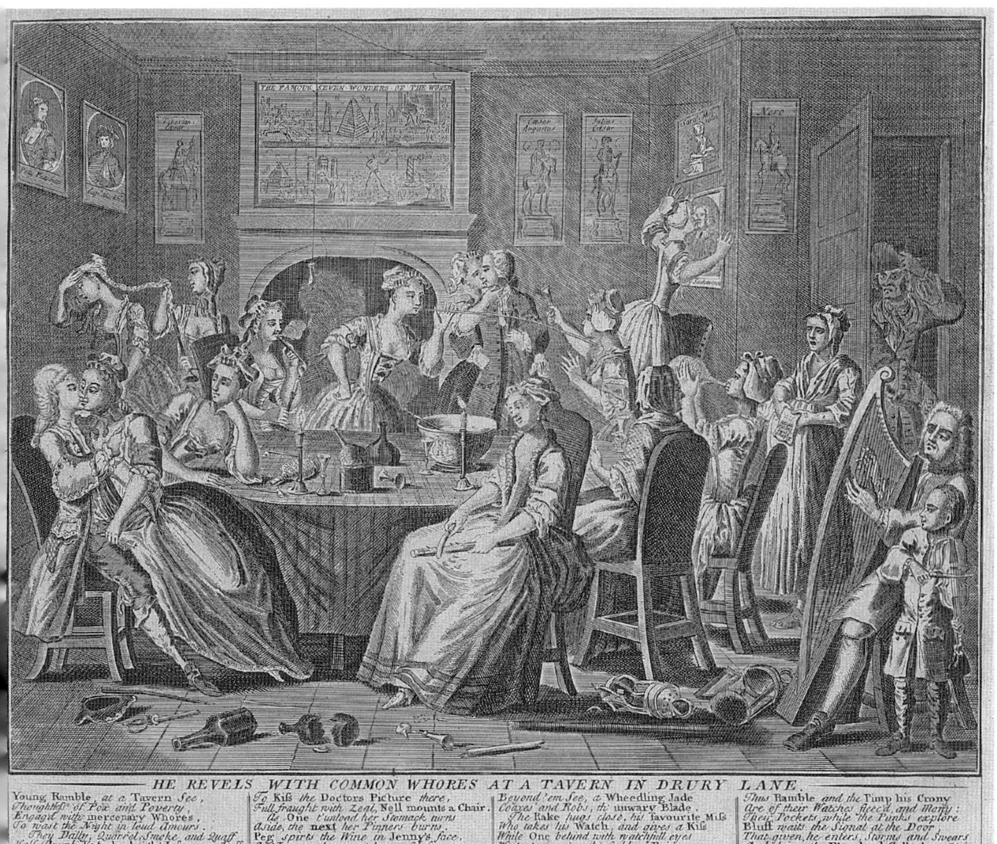

The rake carouses in a tavern full of
·rostitutes', Thomas Bowles, 1735.
Wellcome Collection)

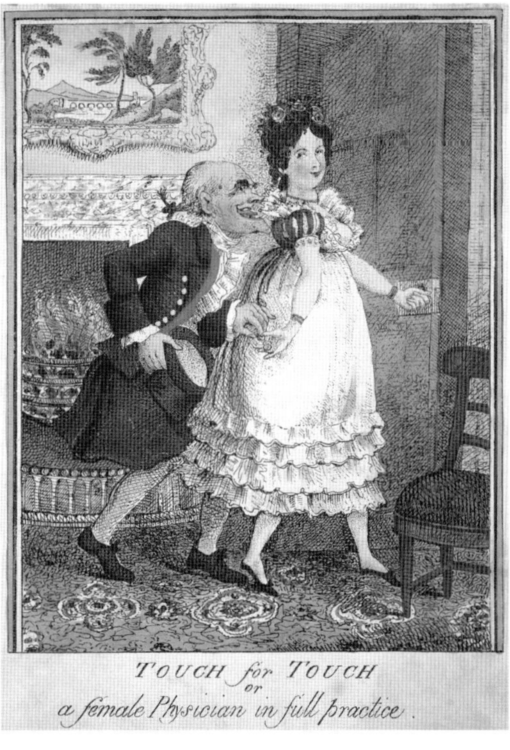

TOUCH for TOUCH
or
a female Physician in full practice.

A prostitute leading an old man into
ıe bedroom and taking money from
ım', after Thomas Rowlandson, 1811.
Wellcome Collection)

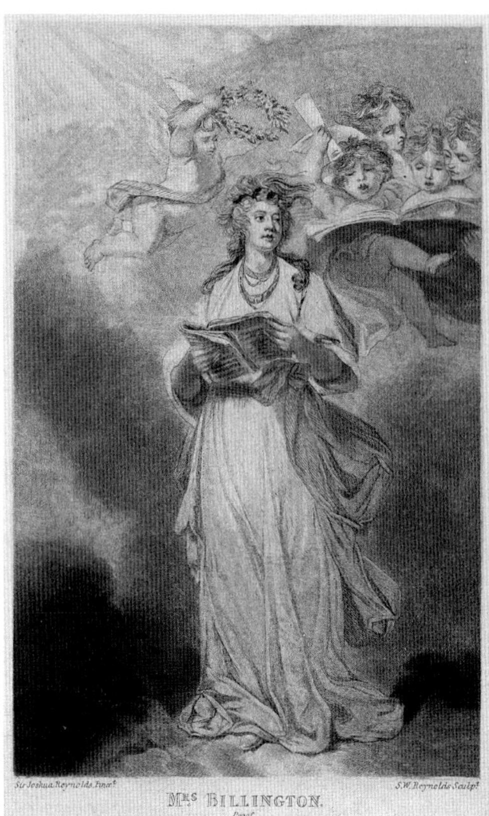

'Mrs Billington as Saint Cecilia', S. W. Reynolds after Sir J. Reynolds. Elizabeth Billington (*c.*1768-1818) was a British operatic soprano, described by Anna Seward as having a voice of 'great sweetness' (*Wellcome Collection*)

German operatic soprano Gertrude Mara (1749-1833), who was renowned for her great technical ability. (*Folger Digital Image Collection*)

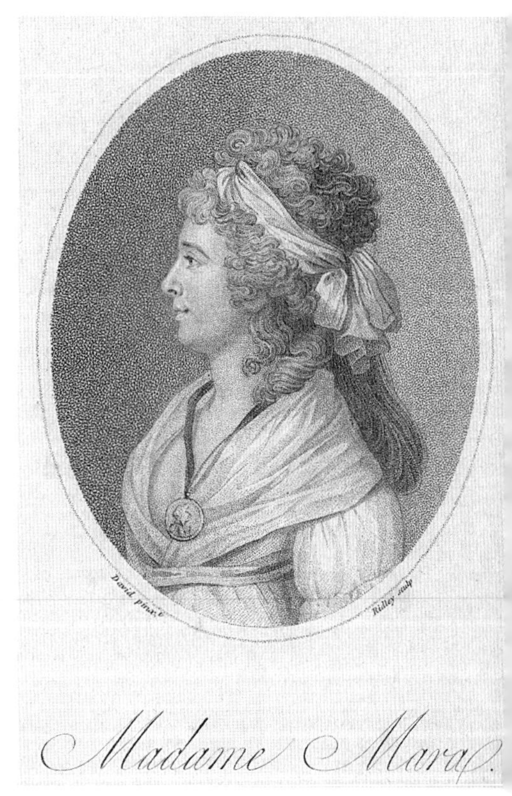

The actress Eliza O'Neill (1791-1872) as Juliet. In 1814 she took London by storm in that role. (*Folger Digital Image Collection*)

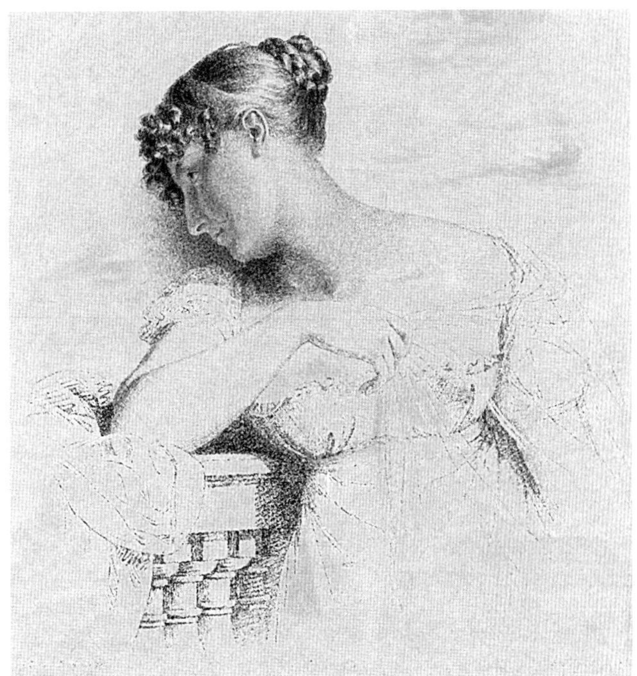

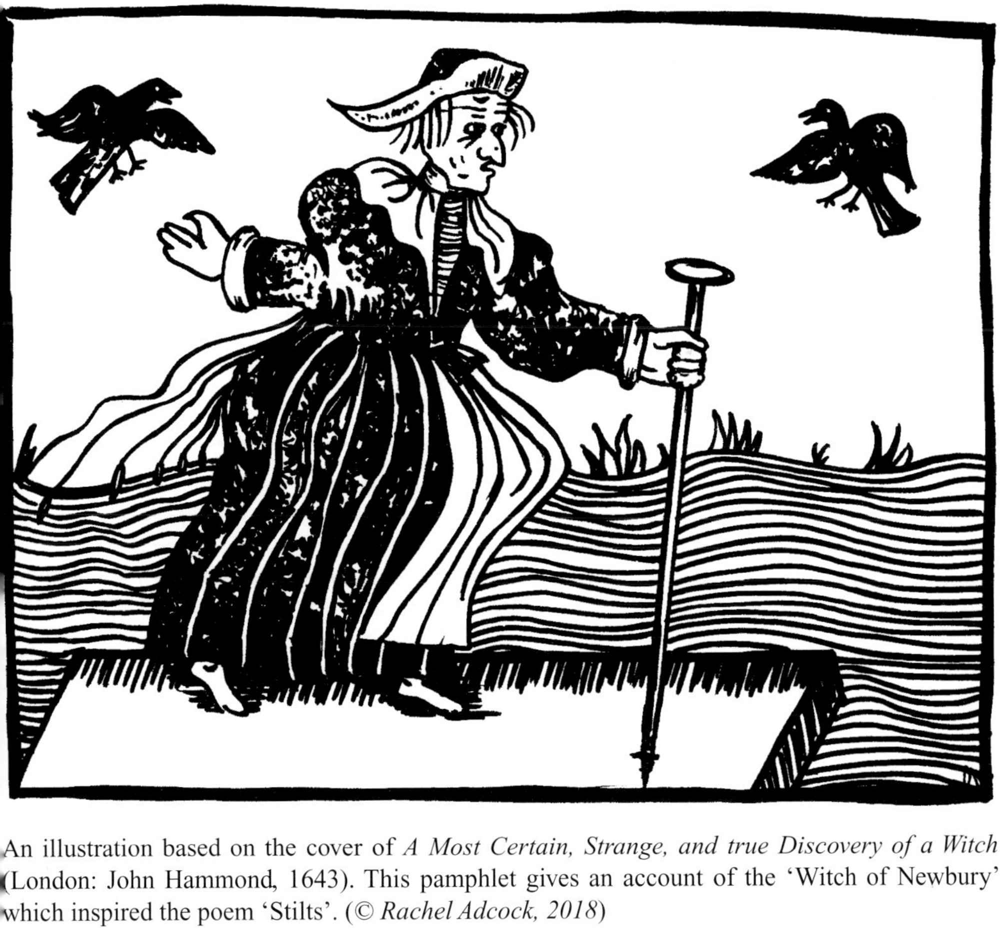

An illustration based on the cover of *A Most Certain, Strange, and true Discovery of a Witch* (London: John Hammond, 1643). This pamphlet gives an account of the 'Witch of Newbury' which inspired the poem 'Stilts'. (© *Rachel Adcock, 2018*)

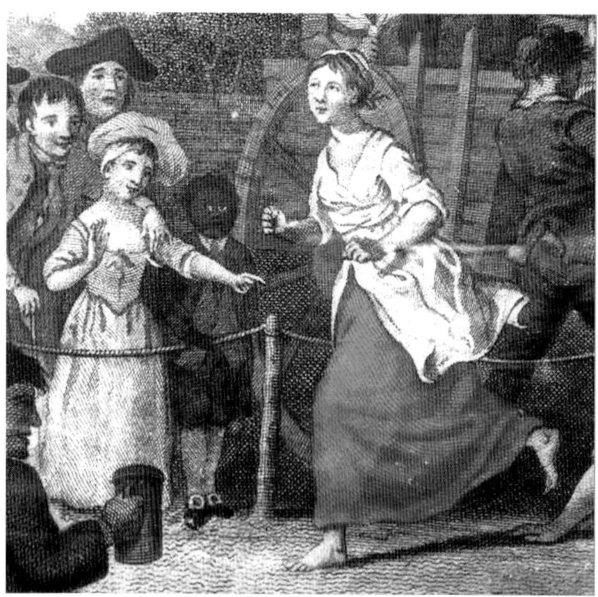

A detail from 'An Holland Smock to be run for, by any Woman born in this County: The best Woman in three Heats', John Collett, 1770. (*Photograph © Peter Radford, print in his personal collection*)

A poster (measuring approx 6 x 12 in) for the Prince of Wales' birthday celebrations in Brighton in 1789. Thought to be the only surviving copy. Some estimates suggest 20,000 people attended the celebration. (*Photograph © Peter Radford, print in his personal collection*)

Jack-Afs Racing, &c.

ON WEDNESDAY the 12th of AUGUST, 1789, the following RACES will be run on the *Level*, at *Brighthelmfton.*

Fuft Race. A Saddle and Bridle for Jack-Affes: The Afs that wins two Heats, to have the Saddle; and the fecond beft to have the Bridle.

Second Race. Saddle and Bridle: The *laft* Afs to have the Saddle, and the *firft* the Bridle *and each Perfon to ride his Neighbour's Afs.*

FOOT-RACE for LADIES:

A handfome Gown to be run for by Girls, under *Twenty-five* Years of Age.—Heats.

A handfome Gown for Women, above *Thirty-five* Years of Age.—Heats.

Many other PRIZES for Men to run in Sacks, &c.&c.

And a MATCH at STOOL BALL.

N. B. The Perfons that run their Affes,——the Women that run for the Gowns,——and the Men that run in Sacks, muft be on the Ground by NINE *o'Clock in the Morning, and give in their Names to Mr.* HENWOOD, *who is appointed to manage the whole Bufinefs.*

A SAILING MATCH, *in* Honour *of* His Royal Highnefs *the* PRINCE *of* WALES's BIRTH-DAY.

ON WEDNESDAY the 12th of this inftant *Auguft*, will be given, by the Right Honourable Colonel PELHAM, *a compleat SET of SAILS*, to be failed for by Boats employed in the Brighton Fifhery.

The Boats to be divided into THREE Claffes.

The *firft Clafs*, to confift of Boats from 24 to 27 Feet in Length; the Winner, in this Clafs, to receive a *Fore-fail* and *Main-fail*, large enough for the Ufe of fuch winning Boat.

The *fecond Clafs*, to confift of Boats from 21 to 24 Feet in Length; the Winner to receive a *Square-fail* and *Gaff Top-fail.*

The *third Clafs*, to confift of Boats of every Defcription, under 21 Feet; the Winner, in this Clafs, to receive a *Gib* and *Mizen-fail.*

To ftart at THREE o'Clock.

BRIGHTHELMSTONE: PRINTED BY W. AND A. LEE.

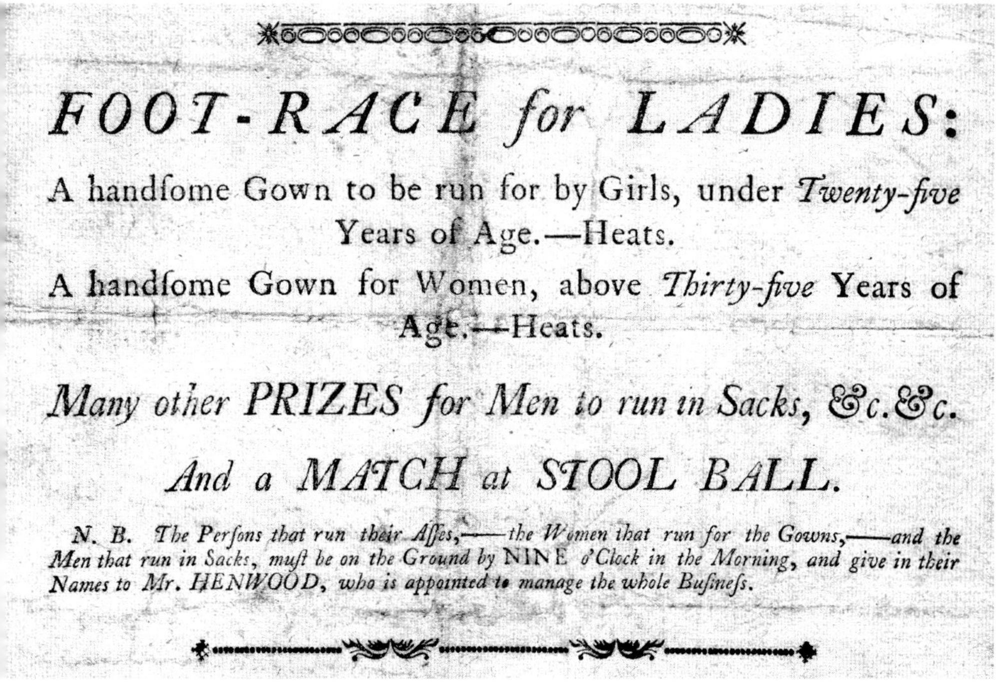

FOOT-RACE *for* LADIES:

A handſome Gown to be run for by Girls, under *Twenty-five* Years of Age.—Heats.

A handſome Gown for Women, above *Thirty-five* Years of Age.—Heats.

Many other PRIZES *for Men to run in Sacks, &c. &c.*

And a MATCH *at* STOOL BALL.

N. B. *The Perſons that run their Aſſes,——the Women that run for the Gowns,——and the Men that run in Sacks, muſt be on the Ground by* NINE *o'Clock in the Morning, and give in their Names to Mr.* HENWOOD, *who is appointed to manage the whole Buſineſs.*

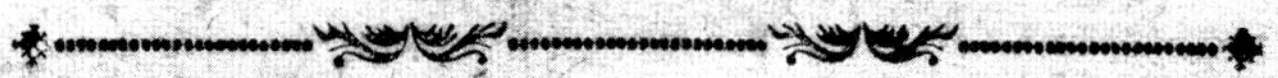

Detail from the poster showing the age classes and prizes for the ladies' foot-race. (*Photograph © Peter Radford*)

Detail from 'A Village Scene with Girls Spinning', Thomas Rowlandson (1756-1827), undated. (*Yale Center for British Art, Paul Mellon Collection*)

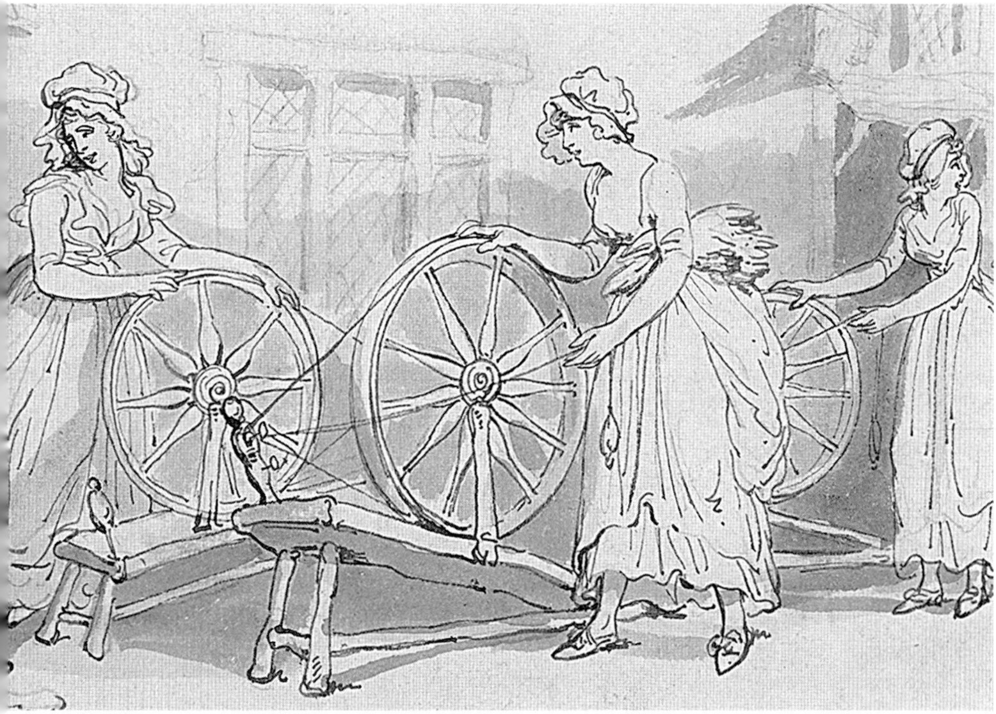

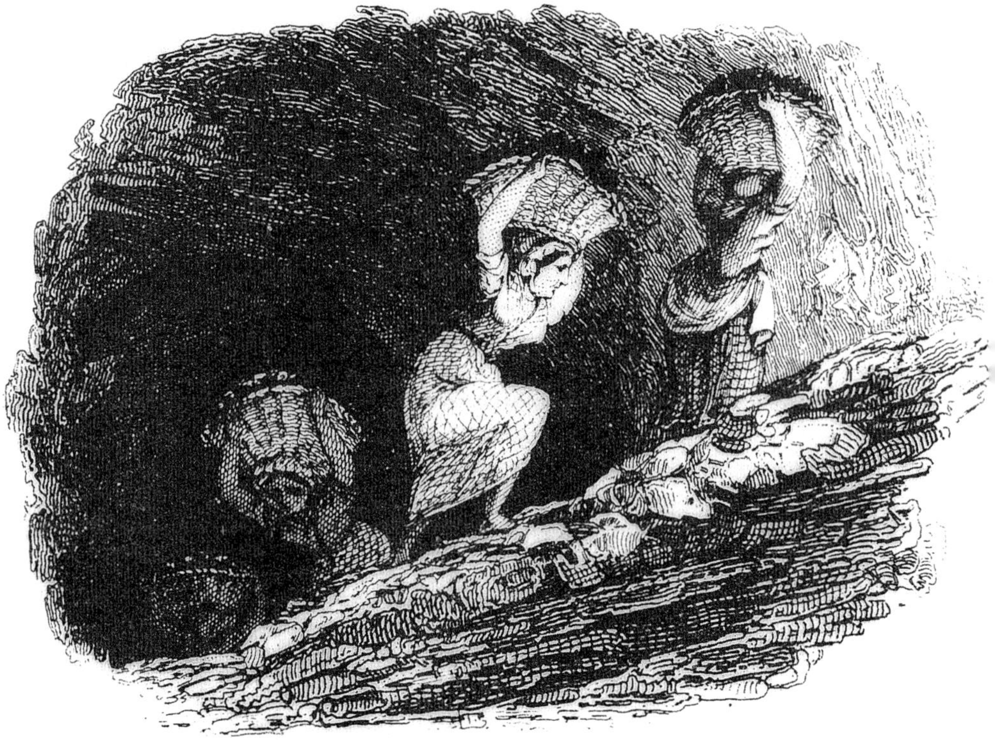

‘Women coal bearers’. (*Wellcome Collection*)

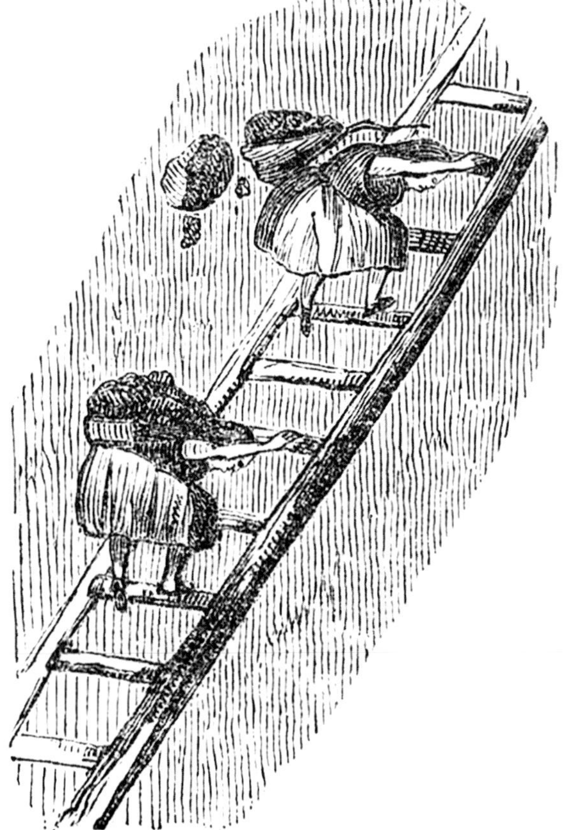

‘It is very dangerous to be under a load’. Report of the Children’s Employment Commission, 1842. (*British Library, Shelfmark 1509/353*)

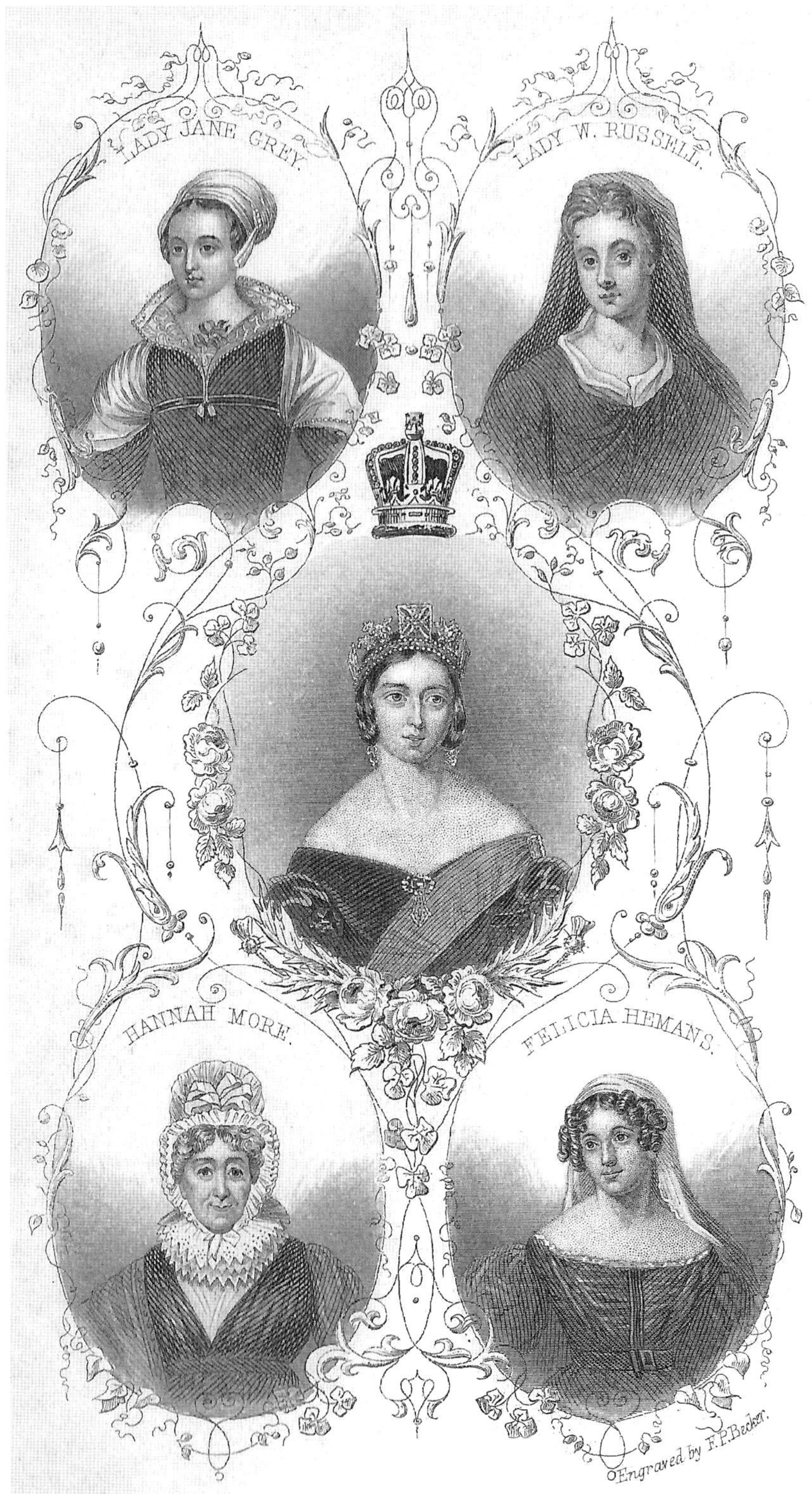

'rontisplate to *A Cyclopaedia of Female Biography* edited by H. G. Adams (1866), featuring
)ueen Victoria surrounded by women of 'moral virtue' (clock-wise from top left: Lady Jane
irey, Lady W. Russell, Felicia Hemans and Hannah More).

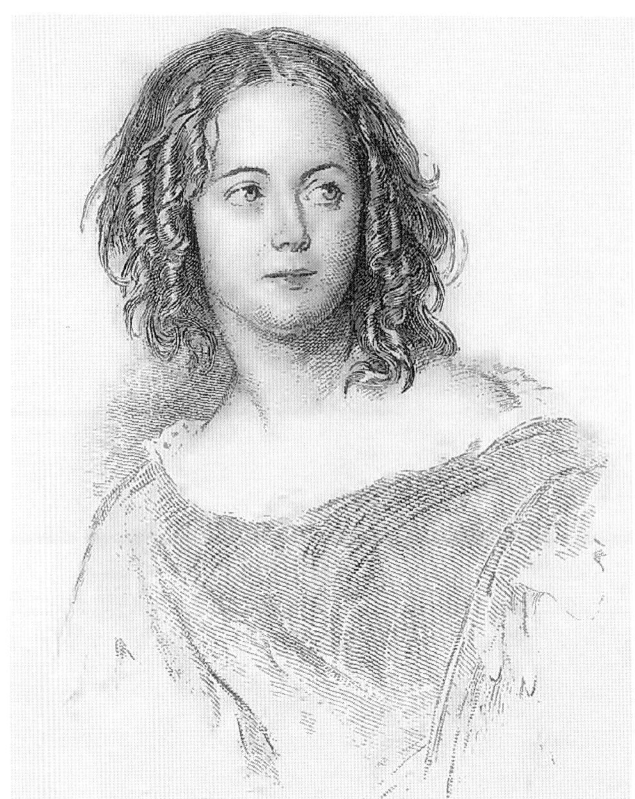

Mrs S. C. Hall (1800-81) was ar
Anglo-Irish writer who became a household name with her *Sketches of Irish Character*. She tested early public opinion of he writings in the annuals and gift books edited by herself and her husband, Samuel Carter Hall. (*Open Library, OL5652855W*)

'A Change for the Better', Sir Joseph Swain, after Sir John Tenniel. Satirical engraving in which the ghost of Queen Elizabeth I boasts of her potent political force to Queen Victoria. Published in *Punch*, 31 July 1869.

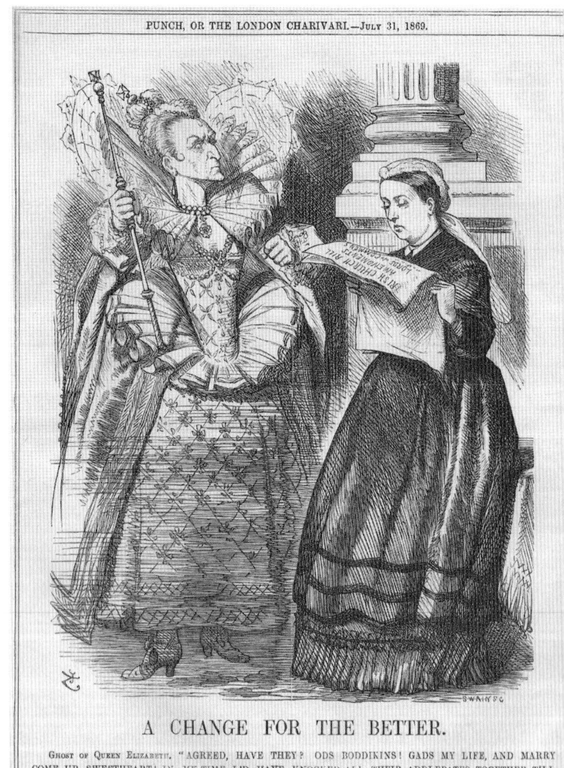

best furniture and silverware a person could buy, they were obviously doing well for themselves. As a result, although their establishment generated a huge income from elite men, it also attracted the attention of men who behaved badly. The women were frequently troubled by drunken men who believed they had a right to the women's company at any time of the day or night and awkward, sometimes violent, situations arose. Sally was always there to help. On one occasion, a drunken captain of the guards and three companions hammered at their door demanding entrance, interrupting a small dinner party the women were holding. Without hesitation, Sally (no doubt used to such incidents) 'seized an horse-whip, with a long lash, which lay on the chimney-piece, whipped the Captain round, and round the table, which was pretty large; and then turned him and his comrades out and locked the street door', contributing greatly to the night's mirth.[19] In a life of dissipation and lechery, it was more important than ever for a woman to have a loyal friend at her side.

Unfortunately, death dissolved their partnership. Peg declared:

> Miss Sally Hayes was my constant companion whilst she lived, and the woman I loved best, as she had a spirit congenial with my own. But alas! I lost her; for … she contracted some bilious complaints from vexation, at the loss of a favourite captain who went abroad, which carried her off [although it is more likely to have been some sort of disease or infection that caused the death which so devastated Peg].[20]

Peg, however, was no longer isolated: she knew women who could be sociable companions, sources of help in times of trouble and, when the exigencies of business required it, capable colleagues.

Peg found a valuable friend in another brothel-keeper, Moll Hall. It was to her she turned when she returned from a trip to London, landing back in Dublin 'ten pounds worse than a beggar'.[21] Moll gave her a place to stay and allowed Peg to entertain clients from her own house, thereby giving Peg time to rebuild her own clientele. The women frequently had get-togethers over a cup of tea to socialize, play cards and gossip on their nights off. When Moll died penniless at the age of 49, it was Peg's turn to come to her assistance. Her debtors had emptied her house of every stick of furniture, but Peg was determined to give her friend a respectable funeral and wake; she loaned a table and some chairs, and ordered in candles, pipes, tobacco, cold meats, wine and porter. She hired six funeral coaches, each carrying four whores dressed in full mourning, with Peg at the head of the procession. Peg had Moll's body interred in St Anne's churchyard and wrote her epitaph:

Here lies honest Moll Hall,
Who once had a great call,
And a fig for you all.[22]

Peg was not the best poet but her meaning was well-intentioned.

Peg also took good care of the '*nymphs*' who worked for her.[23] Her treatment combined a genuine regard for their welfare with sound sense: at the height of her success, money was rolling in, but without the women who were the backbone of the business, none of this would have been possible. She hired a theatre box for the use of herself and her 'young ladies', which was a good way to advertise their attractions, but also allowed them to enjoy some first-rate performances.[24] She also took them out on trips to the country, like an outing to Rathfarnham on the Little Dargle river where, after 'very minutely examining all the beauties of that enchanting spot', they spent the afternoon dining and drinking 'choice champaign' in the garden of Laughlin's tavern.[25] As it turned out, this was not an entirely unprofitable venture: 'by accident the company of Printers and Booksellers, amounting to upwards of fifty persons, happened to be there also', and joined their party.[26] 'A select party of these gentlemen' supped with Peg that evening, 'and generously laid down a guinea each for their entertainment'.[27] In Peg's line of work, it was not always possible to distinguish clearly between business and pleasure.

Peg's capacity for disinterested kindness appears more clearly in the stories that reveal how her young ladies entered her employment in the first place. Many women sought her financial assistance, often wishing to be allowed to live and work with her, when they had no other recourse. She was good enough to see their plight could be her own. However, she was no procurer: she never 'consented to the deflowering of virgin innocence' or 'the seduction of a married woman'.[28] She would engage only those who had already been seduced. They might have also got themselves into more dangerous scrapes, like Mrs Wrixon, who stole 200 guineas from a man injured in a duel in England, escaped on a packet boat to Dublin in August 1789, and spent her first night in Ireland under Peg's roof.[29] Elizabeth Bennett, who had 'a face like an angel', was also in urgent need of help.[30] She had been caught red-handed smuggling goods through the Dublin docks. Unable to pay the fine, she had traded her body with the principal tax officer in order to have her goods restored to her. With her husband in prison, Bennett had no means of supporting herself and had ended up living with another man, an indiscretion for which her husband never forgave her; once he was released, he took to beating and generally misusing her. Unable to endure the situation, she worked for Peg until she found a devoted lover who took her to live with him and, on Mr Bennett's death, 'made an honest woman of her, as the poor dear simpleton termed her marriage to us, which at once shewed my girls and I the *naivéte* [*sic*] of the heart.'[31] Peg claimed that she sometimes acted out of pure altruism, as in the case of Miss Molly McPherson, former mistress to the Marquess of Downshire (1718–93), whose death had left her destitute. Peg saw nothing in Molly 'that could promise any emolument', but ''twas my constant study to alleviate the miseries of all the *woe-worn animals* who applied to me for relief.'[32] So she invited Molly to come and live with her brood, first lending her 5 guineas to buy some new clothes. In this case, however, her kindness received a financial reward: Molly made 'upwards of three hundred pounds' and paid Peg 'very genteely and honourably'.[33]

An appeal to Peg's sense of humour might also pay dividends. Molly's friend was mistress to the Marquis of Abercorn (1756–1818), and although he drank too much, he was an amiable fellow. One day on a visit, she told Molly and Peg of the marquis's sexual proclivities: an obsession with feet. She told them '"of picking, washing, and cleaning my pretty little toes, which he took great delight in, and in which pleasurable, innocent, and inoffensive pastime he [h]as often spent hours".'[34] She added he had never even kissed her. Peg was so taken with the tale of this '"whimsical letch"' that she invited her to come and live '*en-famille*' with her and the other working women in her house.[35]

Wisely, Peg placed a high value on friends who displayed a capacity for gratitude. A glowing example was Mrs Robinson, an Englishwoman brought to Ireland by her keeper, who subsequently abandoned her, at which point she was robbed of £500 worth of plate and 'almost all her *wardrobe*' by her landlady, and so unscrupulously swindled by a jeweller that she was left with 6 guineas and desperate to 'get as soon as possible to her own country'.[36] Peg gave her 20 guineas, and two months later received 'a package of calico, worth fifty pounds', and a 'beautiful edition' of *Memoirs of a Woman of Pleasure* (1748–9) by John Cleland (1709–89), 'with some of the finest cuts I ever beheld'.[37] Peg possibly got the idea for her own memoirs from John Cleland's novel about the world of prostitution.

Another faithful former protégée was Fanny Beresford, who (like some of my WSG friends) would end up offering her skills as an editor; according to Peg, 'she was of a most reputable family, who gave her an excellent education; she was my principal amanuensis, and who [*sic*] prepared these my adventures for the press.'[38] Fanny performed a vitally important service: when Peg gave up brothel-keeping, she failed to rein in her extravagant lifestyle, and until she thought of publishing her life story, her retirement plan consisted solely of recovering debts from people who had no intention of paying her. The *Memoirs* were her 'only resource for profit and revenge'.[39] The second volume contained a warning about the contents of the third: she would 'enumerate those, of what rank soever, who have been so ungenerous as to continue in my debt, for money truly and lawfully due; that those who have defied justice, may not escape shame.'[40] There was a clear implication that people who paid her off could have their names withdrawn. In this way, Peg hoped to squeeze some money out of her former clients.

Even when she was in a debtors' prison, Peg's friends did not forsake her. Elizabeth Falvey (formerly Bennett) was set to repay the kindness Peg had shown her earlier in her life. She sent her husband to pay off Peg's debts, set her free and find some new apartments for her. Thereafter, Bennett nursed Peg for three weeks, leaving her with enough money for a few months, which helped to tide her over while she wrote the last volume of her memoirs. Other former workers rallied to Peg's side; Miss Love, who had been at Pitt Street on the night of the Duke of Rutland's first visit, was now a kept mistress and offered Peg a home with her but Peg declined, fearing that 'it would be immediately imagined' that she had returned to her 'old vicious course of life'.[41] Miss Love's kindness, however, persisted, and when Peg died, she was among the many friends who offered assistance to pay for her burial. Yet female devotion, however sincere, was not sufficient to settle her affairs. Miss Love's efforts were supplemented, not by genteel and noble patrons, but by unpretentious tradesmen, such as Mr Peter Henegan, her grocer, and 'little M[urra]y the cheese-man'.[42] The fact that these men had to meet Peg's posthumous expenses is a reminder of women's comparatively precarious financial and social status, in every rank of life, and how important it was for women to take what precautions they could by combining their forces.

Women's Groups

The establishment of female friendship groups shows the need for support, not just emotionally but also in a professional context, while developing a career or protection in pursuit of that career. This encouragement to women over the years is an attribute of the Women's Studies Group which I value. Women from all stages of their careers have come together for work, meetings and leisure trips; all activities, incidentally, shared by the women who have been the focus of my research. As well as supporting each other, the world inhabited by eighteenth-century prostitutes was not so different from our women's studies group regarding their own erudition. They watched plays at the theatre, gave each other books to read, watched opera and enjoyed visiting splendid estates and gardens.

Peg's recourse to prostitution might look like the result of a habit of making bad choices, but with few alternative opportunities open to most women regarding earning a living, she had little alternative. However, she would never have considered herself a victim, despite her unsuccessful choice in men. Running a brothel was one way in which she could take control of her life. The more we know about that environment, the harder it is to contradict her statement that her only other option was death by starvation.[43] Chillingly, after a life rich in direct and vicarious experiences, Peg writes: 'Nor do I even now, know one single line, which, situated as I was, I could have embraced for support.'[44]

Some eighteenth-century prostitutes had the sense to seek protection by forming groups that acted rather like unions. This not only gave women the female companionship they needed, but also acted as financial fortification. Satirical squibs in newspapers and articles reported the whores' activities at their regular meetings. At a time when the introduction of free trade was the focus of political debate, the *Dublin Evening Post* of 24 December 1779 displayed on its front page '*The* HUMBLE PETITION *of the* SISTERHOOD', a squib in which a group of whores are supposed to request that they may trade free of tax, since 'The *commodities* we bring to market, and offer to sale, are generally of *Irish manufacture*.' This is typical of the *double entendres* that characterize the whole article: for example, lexicographer Francis Grose (1731–91) defines 'COMMODITY' as 'the private parts of a modest woman, and the public parts of a prostitute'.[45] The name of the first signatory is given as 'P. PLUNKET, *Abbess of Drogheda-street nunnery*', and the first witness is, allegedly, her faithful friend 'S. Hayes'.

Ned Ward (1667-1731), the journalist who wrote *The London Spy*, and former publican at the King's Head tavern, was well placed to write his attack on procuresses who enticed young women into prostitution. He had no doubt witnessed their activities from his position at the bar; he gives a description of the 'BAWDS INITIATING *Club*', an association organised by a bawd who pays her 'Experienc'd Covy of Salacious Wagtails' to recruit young virgins to their ranks.[46] She targets

> Young Girls out of Service; Forward Wenches without Parents, and such who, thro' the ripeness of their Years, their natural propensity to Lewdness, and the want of Vertuous Education, might be decoy'd by their own Sex to take those vicious Liberties, which too many Young Creatures, in the Salacity of their Youth, are very apt to be inclin'd to.[47]

The whores meet at her brothel 'upon *Mondays*, *Thursdays*, and *Saturdays*, to spend their Twelve-pence a piece in *Brandy*, *Ratefea*, and such sort of Liquors'.[48] At the initiation ceremony, a 'new Convert' treats the society with a bowl of punch, 'of which herself is to drink the first Cup, toss the empty Vehicle over her unmaiden'd Head, and to cry *Farwell Modesty*'.[49] She will learn the 'dark Misteries of Harlotry', enabling her to maximize her earnings and deal efficiently with contingencies such as debt, 'a Great-Belly' [pregnancy] and the danger of arrest.[50] Nevertheless, she will inevitably decline to a state of 'Pox and Poverty': Ward depicts the whores and their clients as victims of the 'Old Diabolical Jezabel' who runs the club, and is ultimately its sole beneficiary.[51]

Such networks of women, or whores' clubs, were also depicted in whores' memoirs. According to the narrator of *Memoirs of the Celebrated Miss Fanny Murray* (1759), the celebrated Fanny Murray, née Rudman (1729-1778), joined the club that met in a tavern in Covent Garden 'to talk over their various successes, compare notes, and canvass the most profitable means of improving them the week following.'[52] Rules were made to protect the common interests of the group and a fund was set up to act as a back-up in times of distress. A member who managed to 'become a modest woman by going into keeping', thus extricating herself from the business, was obliged to donate a large sum to the fund for those in more precarious positions.[53] Peg Plunkett's autobiography also mentions a whores' 'sisterhood' where the women supported each other financially; it allowed for a 'subscription or kitty, from which women could withdraw funds in hard times'.[54] My favourite rule from the Covent Garden club (one that the WSG might like to consider taking on) ensured the protection of drunken friends who had imbibed so much alcohol that they were unable to make their way home: 'Any member who shall get so intoxicated as not to be able to walk, shall be immediately sent home in a coach or chair, at the expense of the society, to be refunded by her at the ensuing meeting.'[55]

Chapter Ten

Rivalry, Camaraderie and the Prima Donnas: Elizabeth Billington and Gertrude Mara

by Brianna E. Robertson-Kirkland

Suzanne Aspden's 2013 book *The Rival Sirens* highlighted the cultural significance of rivalries between eighteenth-century operatic prima donnas, commenting that these were not 'superficial' conflicts but tell us much about the circumstances of the singers and the public's approach to opera.[1] Discussion of rivalries between famous prima donnas was common within the press and continued throughout the eighteenth century, forming a discourse where the two leading ladies were not assessed by their individual talents, but were constantly compared. In *Rival Queens*, Felicity Nussbaum examines how the second and third wave of actresses appearing on the British stage between 1700 and 1780 exploited their rivalries for commercial gain and were able to move away from the realm of 'novelty' to become celebrated individuals in their own right.[2] However, celebrity came at a price and, much like operatic entertainment, was not confined to the stage but reappeared as soap opera within periodicals that often depicted the rivalry as both professional and personal antagonisms between quarrelling singers.

Yet aspiring leading ladies could be motivated to encourage such rivalries as they generated media attention, enabling them to secure roles and high status within the theatre. Even so, it was not enough for two singers simply to be seen to be rivals: their contention required careful construction in terms of musical and cultural opposition to be of interest to the public. This was the case with two of the most successful prima donnas who performed in Britain in the latter half of the eighteenth century: Gertrude Mara, née Schmeling, and Elizabeth Billington, née Weichsel. This chapter will show how Billington, after her first appearances on the London stage, changed her vocal style, which in turn helped to construct a successful rivalry with the reigning prima donna, Mara. However, unlike other press-driven rivalries, discussion of Billington and Mara centred on their vocal talents rather than personal antagonisms, which I suggest was due to their personal camaraderie. This allowed the two stars to keep the rivalry focused on their professional differences and capitalize on the competition.

Two Opposing Styles: Pathetic and Virtuosic

Mara's rivalry with Billington was not the first that she had experienced within her career, as she had been engaged in a highly-publicized rivalry with Portuguese soprano Luisa Todi (1753–1833) in Paris in 1782. Unfortunately for Mara, it was widely acknowledged that Todi came out on top, being described as 'the nation's singer', and shortly after, Mara left Paris to perform elsewhere.[3] In addition to this rivalry, Mara was involved in at least two others once she arrived in London in 1783. The music scene in this city encouraged musical rivalries as there were two main competing opera houses – the King's Theatre and the Theatre Royal, Covent Garden – but there were also two competing vocal styles: pathos and virtuosity.

Earlier in the century, the pathetic style had represented an older tradition of singing that favoured unaffected, rhetorical expression. However, a new, more ornate virtuosic style was growing in popularity with British audiences. These two opposing vocal styles set the groundwork for a tradition that would encourage a prima donna to demonstrate her skill in one style over the other. Francesca Cuzzoni (1696–1778) and Faustina Bordoni (1697–1781), whose particularly famous rivalry culminated in a dramatic riot on 6 June 1727 during a performance of *Astianatte* by Giovanni Bononcini (1670–1747), embodied the opposition between these vocal styles. Cuzzoni performed in the older pathetic style that exemplified virtue and serenity, while her opposition sang in a new fiery, virtuosic style and depicted volatile and turbulent characters. In the first opera in which they both appeared, Handel's *Alessandro* (1726), their characters were already clearly defined. Cuzzoni played Princess Lisaura, a young woman who pines for the great leader Alessandro, who is torn between her and the spirited Princess Rossane, a woman taken captive by Alessandro's army in a previous campaign. Lisaura's mournful aria '*Che tirannia d'amor!*' ('Tyranny of Love'), in Act II, Scene 3, is breathtakingly sorrowful as she reflects on the pain endured as she clings to the vain hope that he will return her affection. This role contrasts with Bordoni's more cunning and confident character Rossane, whose flirtatious aria '*Alla sua gabbia d'Oro*' ('At his golden cage'), sung in the very next scene, uses fiery coloratura displays, vocally reminiscent of birdsong, to imply that she is unable to escape her golden cage while cleverly insinuating that Alessandro longs to be caught in the cage with her.

While both singers were skilled in virtuosity, Cuzzoni and Bordoni deliberately chose to be vocally distinct, thereby constructing an apparent duality that would allow the two singers to be employed by the same opera company: the Royal Academy of Music. When these two singers came together they offered, as Aspden has suggested, a satisfying whole for the audience, but ensured that neither singer committed the most heinous of musical sins: copying.[4] To copy someone else's ornamentation, otherwise known as 'graces', was completely unacceptable since singers built their careers on developing a unique and individual approach to apparently improvised vocal ornamentation. Singing teacher Pier Francesco Tosi (c.1653–1732), whose treatise *Opinioni de' cantori antichi e moderni* (1723) was widely read and quoted throughout the eighteenth and nineteenth centuries, was quick to chastise singers who copied, stating that graces should 'bear not even so much as a Shadow of a Resemblance of the Original; otherwise, instead of a beautiful Imitation, it will become a despicable Copy.'[5] Tosi, who appeared to prefer Cuzzoni's pathetic style compared to the newly-popular virtuosic style, praised both singers in his treatise.[6] However, though the rivalry was a fictional construct designed to engage audience interest, it had become all too real both financially for the Royal Academy of Music, who struggled to support the growing salaries of the two prima donnas, and the audience, who created such a disturbance in June 1727 that the rest of that performance and the opera season were abandoned.

During Cuzzoni and Bordoni's reign, the more expressive, pathetic style of singing that avoided excessive ornamentation represented the singing of the past, while florid virtuosity was growing in popularity. However, the two styles also represented two different national characters of singing that would compete throughout the century. The pathetic style was associated with English airs, particularly since, as Simon McVeigh points out, the English preferred 'melodic directness and music that "spoke to the heart"'.[7] The Italian virtuosic or bravura style, as it would come to be known, capitalized on vocal agility, allowing singers to demonstrate their proficiency in vocal dexterity and speed, though not expression. The popular Italian castrati had claimed virtuosity as their signature technical accomplishment, solidifying the image of the style as a product of Italy.

Vocal virtuosity and floridity have often been presented as a characteristically castrato technique, with scholars such as John Potter suggesting that 'By the middle of the 18th century the castratos were taking virtuoso singing into realms that we can now barely imagine.'[8] Anecdotes like the story of Farinelli (1705–82) competing with a trumpet player certainly strengthen this idea: it was continuously recounted in periodicals throughout the eighteenth and nineteenth centuries.[9] However, as a result of the operatic castrato's popularity, aspects of his technique, including virtuoso singing, were emulated by other singers including the female soprano who, as Potter suggests, would come 'to equal, and eventually supersede' the castrati.[10]

Mara's virtuosity and proficiency when performing bravura arias were well-known, though she was unable to attain a similar level of aptitude when performing English pathetic airs, as British critics frequently observed: 'Madam Mara's *forte* is *bravura songs*. Her voice has considerable flexibility, extent and power. In Italian songs that demand these requisites, she *must please*; but Handel's pathetic English Airs will only serve to betray her defects.'[11] The *Morning Herald* agreed with this verdict:

> Mara certainly keeps the post of first woman with equal credit to herself, though we must confess that the songs allotted to her abound more with musical difficulties, than with any striking beauties, and are more calculated for a trial of skill, than for the display of the soft and pleasing part of that lady's voice.[12]

Despite these criticisms, Mara quickly established herself as a leading lady, performing regularly in the top London theatres and concert halls including the home of Italian opera, the King's Theatre; the Theatre Royal, Covent Garden; Hanover Square Rooms; and even the home of British opera at Drury Lane, but her reign as prima donna was met with a final challenge by the younger soprano, Billington, in 1791. Though Billington had made her London debut in 1786, it had taken almost five years for the rivalry to build enough interest to warrant a public competition, where a performance of the same opera, on the same night, with Billington and Mara in the same role, would be given. This will be discussed in more detail below; first, however, it is necessary to show how, after a moderately successful London debut, Billington rose to a position where she could be considered a realistic rival to Mara.

Billington had already been performing leading roles in Dublin for three seasons, before playing Rosetta at Covent Garden in *Love in a Village* (1762) by Thomas Arne (1710–78).[13] While reviews praised Billington for her sweetness of tone and compass of register, there were recurring criticisms that she sounded too Italian. According to the *Morning Herald*: 'It may be [alleged], that too much of the *Italian* manner characterizes the singing of this performer: but that charge will be unfair, as it is not the result of affectation, but teaching.' The *General Advertiser* concurred:

> This Lady possesses, indeed, a most extraordinary voice, managed with the accuracy of science, and touched with the graces of taste; and when her tones are somewhat released from the thraldom of Italian fetters, she will justly be considered as the most distinguished, of the vocal tribe, that the English stage ever boasted.[14]

It was common for established professional singers to attend a few lessons with another teacher to improve their vocal technique, but Billington demonstrated an unusual commitment to professional development by regularly engaging in vocal lessons with a number of different teachers. Her husband, James Billington (1756–94), was initially employed as her vocal teacher before the couple eloped in 1783, but by 1786 she was engaged in lessons with the Italian singing master Michele Mortellari (c.1750–1807), and in the summer of 1786 she went to Paris for an intensive session of lessons with Antonio Sacchini (1730–86).[15] The reviews were in agreement that Billington's virtuosic proficiency was undeniable, but her technical feats were a demonstration of her Italian training rather than an expression of her individual style. Furthermore, Billington was not only a native English singer, but made her first appearance in English opera, which made critics less tolerant of her borrowing from the Italian school. If she wished to establish herself in the long term as one of the top prima donnas in London, she needed to adopt a more individual style, fit for an English soprano.

Billington addressed these concerns and made significant changes to her vocal performances very soon after her debut. In March 1786, she performed the role of Clara in *The Duenna*, where she sang an aria composed in a new style unfamiliar to operatic audiences:

> The favourite air of R[au]zzini, 'By Him we Love [offended],' was sung in a style unknown to a British Theatre, and fully merited its great encore. The introduction of the new song, did honour to [Billington's] abilities. To say that it was *divinely* sung, would scarcely be a flattering panegyric. In this song she gave a full scope to her Cantabile and Bravura exertions. Indeed we never met the union of those two qualities so perfect in the same subject.[16]

Venanzio Rauzzini (1746–1810) was a castrato singer, who held the position of *primo uomo* at the King's Theatre from 1774 to 1777. He was also a composer, concert manager and teacher and it is likely Billington came to him for vocal lessons around the time he composed '*By him we love offended*'.

She had already demonstrated accuracy in performing virtuosic, bravura arias but this new fusion style revealed a more expressive, pathetic side to her singing. By effectively combining the two styles, Billington proved that she was as vocally accomplished as any Italian-trained singer but maintained her Britishness by effectively capturing expressive lyricism and pathos void of unnecessary embellishment. She had managed to achieve something no other singer had done quite so successfully before, as she was not afraid to sing with expression and melodic simplicity and then switch to show off the more flamboyant and vocally agile side necessary for any *prima donna seria*.[17] The *prima donna seria* or the leading lady of *opera seria* would be given at least one long and complex bravura aria within the opera to demonstrate her vocal prowess; therefore, vocal flexibility was requisite for obtaining such a status. Anna Selina Storace (1765–1817) had attempted to make the transition from *prima donna buffa* (leading lady of comic opera) to *prima donna seria* prior to her return to England in 1787, but her voice did not have enough flexibility to successfully perform such a role.

The poet Anna Seward made one of the first observations regarding the similarity in Billington and Mara's vocal abilities in a letter in June 1786: 'Mrs Billington's voice is of great sweetness, compass, power, and execution; and her skill cannot be questioned … Already she almost rivals Mara in the s[c]aramouch part of her performance; but has, however, too much sense to gambol like her in the sacred songs.'[18] Seward considered Mara's use of vocal ornamentation excessive, particularly in music from Handel's oratorios, but Billington was able to adopt an appropriately conservative style.[19] Though she was clearly proficient in the bravura style right from her London debut, it was her change in vocal style that prompted Seward to think of Billington as vocally Mara's equal and rival.

These comparisons were taken up by a number of other critics from 1786 onwards, particularly as the two sopranos regularly played the same operatic roles, including Mandane in *Artaxerxes*, Polly in *The Beggar's Opera* and Rosetta in *Love in a Village*. Furthermore, Billington and Mara frequently sang the same suitcase arias, a convention where singers would insert their most popular arias into other operas. These included '*Ah che nel petto io sento*', adapted by Sarti from Paisiello's '*Nel cor più non mi sento*'; 'Angels ever bright and fair' from the opera *Rodelinda*; and 'The Soldier Tir'd'. Though Charles Burney (1726–1814), in 1789, had suggested that Billington's initial performances were 'in emulation' of Mara, she appeared untouched by criticism that she was a mere Mara copyist.[20] Indeed, the rivalry was spurred on by her remarkable likeness to Mara, particularly in the execution of bravura song: 'Nature has gifted [Mrs Billington] with sweet and powerful tones; and she is skilful and modest in the use of them. Except the MARA, the ALLEGRANTI, and the MERCHETTI, there is no better Singer in Europe.'[21] Though Billington could match Mara's vocal virtuosity, she took care to maintain her vocal individuality by upholding a more modest approach to ornamentation: '[Mrs Billington] unites simplicity with execution, as well as the Mezza Bravura, in each of which she is so truly excellent, that it would prove a difficult task to determine in which she most excels.'[22] In the course of the season she had acquired a quality of individuality, and with this the groundwork was set for Billington to be considered a contender in challenging Mara as the most fashionable London-based prima donna.

A Final Contest: Two Prima Donnas and Thomas Arne's *Artaxerxes*

A final contest, presumably organized by the theatre managers, if not Billington and Mara themselves, was set for Saturday, 19 November 1791. The contest would decide which soprano was the superior: the English Billington or the foreign Mara. Though it is unclear who came up with the idea of the contest, it directly played into the desires of both the audience and the British press, particularly since the choice of date favoured the British candidate. Mara had announced her return to the continent immediately after three performances of the opera *Artaxerxes* at the Haymarket Theatre, which culminated on Tuesday, 22 November. Since Mara had planned and publicly announced her departure, it would have been easy for London critics to proclaim Billington the winner and Mara the leaving loser. However, reports of this nature did not appear until weeks after the event had taken place, when a correspondent sent the following account to the *Morning Post and Daily Advertiser*, but without endorsing it:

> Mrs Billington in the late competition with Madame Mara, on her first trial of skill, completely established her title to superiority. On Saturday evening she did much more - she sung the airs with such strength and sweetness, and delivered the recitative with such harmony and power; in short, she performed the character in a style so *musically majestic*, that the idea of Madame Mara ever again attempting to vie with her, and enter the lists as a rival, will most probably be treated with ridicule, and scouted as being absurd.[23]

However, several reports written immediately after the competition declared Mara's performance superior to Billington's. The *Gazetteer and New Daily Advertiser* (henceforth *New Daily*) found it difficult to say any voice was 'more melodious' than Billington's, but their 'praises' were given to Mara alone: her 'superiority consists in the greater sweetness and clearness of voice.' The review also provides an insight into the audience's reaction to such rivalries: 'The town approves such contentions, and both houses were accordingly filled with delighted and applauding audiences.'[24] On the night of the contest, all reports commented that the two opera houses were filled; however, *Artaxerxes* had already been performed the previous night at the Haymarket Theatre with Mara in the leading role. This was perhaps a cunning marketing ploy by the theatre management, who aimed to capitalize on the contest alongside Mara's announced departure. Staging the contest on the second night would encourage an audience to attend at least two of Mara's three final performances in order to assess who was the superior soprano. The plan worked: at Mara's first performance, 'the house overflowed at an early hour'.[25] The Theatre Royal management would also repeat their performance of *Artaxerxes* with Billington in the leading role, but this was not until the following week, after Mara's departure. By that point, the novelty of the competition had worn away and it was reported that 'in no part of the evening could it boast an overflow'.[26] Mara's popularity continued to resonate with London audiences after her departure. Though Billington may have been a native British soprano who could match Mara's virtuosity, it did not immediately make her the nation's favourite prima donna.

Even so, a number of newspapers had given their support to Billington, such as the *Star*: 'If an estimate of the merits of MARA and BILLINGTON be form[ed] by the plaudits given by the audiences, the latter is not inferior to the former – if by the degree of feeling which accompanied their vocal exertions, she is superior.'[27] Billington's emphasis on feeling over virtuosity reaffirmed her individual vocal style, and also her alignment with a more British style of singing. The *London Chronicle* also praised Billington's performance, stating that she 'displayed her great vocal talents to the utmost advantage', though they could not deny that Mara displayed her 'usual' wonderful execution. The *London Chronicle* was careful not to select a winner, but the choice of language when describing the two performances highlighted Mara as the prima donna of the past, while Billington was the prima donna of the present.[28]

Mara was only absent from the London stage for a short time: before her departure, her husband had signed a contract for her return in the spring of 1792.[29] The rivalry, however, did not continue in the form of staged vocal contests but rather in merchandise. Printed single sheet songs intended for amateur music-making, including '*Ah che nel petto io sento*' and 'The Soldier Tir'd', included the statement 'sung by Madame Mara and Mrs. Billington', which allowed the publishing houses to exploit the popularity and the rivalry of the two star prima donnas.[30]

Contest, Collaboration and Camaraderie

In contrast to other rivalries, particularly that of Cuzzoni and Bordoni earlier in the century, the focus of Billington and Mara's rivalry remained on their vocal abilities and did not descend into a dramatic soap opera of warring prima donnas. On a practical level, it was beneficial for Billington and Mara to act cordially towards one another as they shared many of the same contacts and had even attended lessons with the same teacher, Venanzio Rauzzini. Through him, they had both been invited to sing at his Bath concert series and they frequently performed alongside Rauzzini's other vocal students including Anna Storace and John Braham (c.1774–1856).

Billington had already been involved in a public quarrel with Storace in May 1787, and while the exact details of the quarrel do not appear in print, in early May 1787 Billington was reported to have withdrawn from performances at the concerts of Antient Musick on Tottenham Street and the Bath concert series with strong insinuations that it directly related to Storace's presence in both concert series.[31] However, in December 1787 a different interpretation of events appeared: 'The little story of the quarrel between Mrs. Billington and the Storace, turns out, as we supposed it would, a mere *Conte faite a* [sic] *Plaisir* [a piece of light fiction]. They each of them know the other's pretensions, and respect them accordingly.'[32] Throughout the time of the quarrel, Billington and Storace did not appear together in performances and news reports encouraged gossip that focused on the quarrel rather than their vocal abilities. The public announcement that the quarrel was nothing more than a joke appears as an attempt to restore professional unity and quieten gossip.

The absence of any reports of personal antagonisms between Billington and Mara is significant, suggesting that they aimed to keep the rivalry focused on their vocal talents, and in doing so they demonstrated much mutual respect. Billington declared that 'Mara's execution [was] superior to her own', while Mara demonstrated her admiration for Billington when she asked her to be part of her final benefit concert given in 1802.[33] The advertisement for Mara's benefit highlighted Billington as one of the main performers, despite the fact that she sang only in the second half, by stating that the two sopranos would sing 'a new Duet' together.[34] Although rivalry had not been discussed for a decade, it could be suggested that Mara's announcement was specifically aimed to tease the audience into attending with the hope of witnessing another contest between the two prima donnas. Yet Billington's involvement in the concert appears to have been motivated by her personal friendship with Mara. She was only able to appear in the second half of the concert as she had already been performing in *Artaxerxes* earlier in the evening. Billington was already a highly sought-after prima donna both on the Continent and in London, so performing at Mara's concert was not a way to ascend the career ladder. She had previously demonstrated a commitment to musical comrades in times of need: Michael Kelly stated that she frequently renounced 'many profitable engagements in London' to assist Rauzzini, the manager of the Bath concert series.[35] Even Billington's choice of repertoire was adapted to the occasion: she did not include any arias that hinted at the two sopranos' stylistic similarities. In fact, although she had appeared in the advertisement headline, her role in the concert was limited to one solo 'Scena' composed by Haydn and a quartet by Harrison as well as the newly-composed '*Grand Duett*' by Charles Florio (c.1768–1819), who was well known to have been Mara's lover.[36]

In an account of the performance of the duet, Thomas Green described the sopranos 'each smiling on the other', another indication of their camaraderie. However, throughout the review, Green aimed to position soprano against soprano, stating that after Billington's 'Scena', which had 'the house echoing with thunderous applause', Mara came forward and 'burst forth in a most difficult Italian aria, "*Agitata dall' affanno*," with a vehemence of expression and infuriated vigour of stupendous execution quite unparalleled and overpowering.' This was quite a change from the first half of the concert, where she had exhibited 'a frightful decay of powers' while performing 'Pious Orgies'. According to Green the duet was a further test, in which he believed Billington to be victorious as she 'overpowered' her rival.[37] However, another account of the duet given by John Parker stated that it aimed to display their 'mutual accomplishments'.[38]

Looking to the duet itself, the composition was an elaborate display of fiery passages, requiring perfect rhythmic synchronization and precision from two sopranos, who sang in close harmony throughout. While Billington and Mara may have been motivated to perform together to settle some professional curiosity as to who was the better bravura singer, the aria appeared to celebrate their shared excellence in performing the bravura style and was specifically written to showcase their similarities. In this light, the rivalry had turned full circle as their similarities were the original source of contention.

Conclusion

Billington and Mara's mutual respect for one another allowed them to stage a rivalry based on their vocal talents rather than personal quarrels. This allowed them to maintain some amount of control, as the media campaigns could not link the rivalry to any sources of personal antagonisms that would encourage unrelated public gossip. Because of this, the rivalry stands out as a successful venture that increased the popularity of both sopranos and even encouraged them to excel professionally, so as never to be outshone by one another.

Prima donna rivalries played a vital role in the culture of opera, but this chapter has demonstrated that certain singers were not mere pawns in media-driven campaigns. In the case of Billington and Mara, there were clear professional agendas for allowing such a rivalry to be constructed and maintained during the early years of their London-based careers. These rivalries were not superficial squabbles, but were intrinsically part of operatic culture throughout the eighteenth century. Consequently, this cultural phenomenon merits further research, where the main players of the operatic companies, including prima donnas, are considered as stakeholders in the fabrication of such rivalries rather than passive victims.

Chapter Eleven

Eliza O'Neill and the Art of Acting

by Jacqueline Mulhallen

Eliza O'Neill is now almost a forgotten name in English theatre, yet at one time she was considered the successor to the great Sarah Siddons (1755–1831). Indeed, her biographer, publishing under the name of Charles Inigo Jones, said that the manager of Covent Garden, Henry Harris (d. 1839), 'saw it necessary to secure the talents of Miss O'Neill as a successor to the distinguished heroine who had retired.'[1] This engagement was a wonderful accolade for a young and relatively inexperienced actress who had made her London debut in 1814.

O'Neill was born in Ireland, where her father, John O'Neill, was the manager of the Drogheda theatre. Her brother was an actor and she herself appeared on the stage at the age of 12. She performed in Belfast for two years and then in Dublin's Crow Street Theatre, where she played Juliet.[2] In 1814, she took London by storm in that role. To secure her talents, Harris gave her £300 worth of jewels and her own carriage; she earned £6,000 for touring.[3] Despite the theatre in Covent Garden seating about 3,000 in a full house, it was difficult to secure a place for O'Neill's performances as they were always sold out.[4] Despite this astonishing early success, however, her career was to last only five years. At the end of the 1818/19 season, she retired to marry a fellow-Irishman, William Wrixon-Becher (1780–1850), who became MP for Mallow, County Cork, and inherited a baronetcy in 1831.[5]

This chapter explores some of the factors that enabled her to enchant her audiences, with a focus on contemporary reactions to O'Neill's performances and comparisons with Siddons. These critical evaluations provide valuable impressions of O'Neill's acting style for, unlike Siddons, she did not leave any personal memoirs of her career and we know only how she appeared to others. Sarah Siddons had only retired in 1812, two years prior to O'Neill's debut, although she continued to give readings.

She had dominated the London stage since the 1780s, particularly in tragic roles and in Shakespearean roles which she made her own by her intelligent and imaginative close interpretation of the original texts. In response to her performances, audiences swooned, wept and even became hysterical.[6] Tall and statuesque, Siddons had a commanding presence and beauty and was painted as the 'Tragic Muse' by Sir Joshua Reynolds (1723–92).[7] It was largely due to her irreproachable private life that acting became an acceptable profession and that actresses began to lose their identification with prostitutes.[8] To be acclaimed as Siddons' successor so early in her career gives a good indication of O'Neill's talent.

Although O'Neill could and did play comedy, the discussion will focus on the tragic and tragicomic roles played by O'Neill at Covent Garden, since it was for those that she became more renowned.[9] As one typical anonymous review stated: 'In tragedy she at once agitates and delights us; her excellence is uniform, and without alloy. In comedy she pleases and satisfies; but does not so entirely and undividedly possess the heart.'[10]

With the exception of roles created by O'Neill, which will be mentioned at the end of this chapter, all the parts discussed were previously performed by Siddons.[11] Apart from Shakespeare's plays and a few other works, it is unlikely that the drama performed by O'Neill and her contemporaries will be familiar to today's audiences, or to non-specialist readers. These plays, however, repay study, both as literature and as performance history. They are also particularly valuable for the purposes of this book, as they recapitulate history in a repertoire whose earliest examples date from the reign of Elizabeth I, and that was still popular at the accession of Victoria. The play texts, their performance history, and the critical writing they engendered provide a rich source of views on women, both as characters and, after 1663, following Charles II's personal intervention, as legitimate performers on the public stage.[12] They included 'standard pieces', offering 'standard characters' on which performers could found their careers.[13] Yet these standards were curiously unstable, as play texts were open to adaptation. Shakespeare's plays, for example, were subject to major alterations, intended to keep them abreast of changing theatrical and political trends.[14] It is rather disconcerting to realize that O'Neill's Juliet was based on a script that allows Romeo, who has poisoned himself in the belief that Juliet is dead, to recover consciousness in the tomb scene, and engage in passionately regretful dialogue with his bride before the poison finally kills him.[15]

Theatrical Heroines: Stage Roles for Women

Dramatic representations of women also changed over time, though they generally failed to do justice to the variety of their roles in real life. Women's sexual and familial status exercised a power over their destiny that had no equivalent in the lives of men, on or off stage: playwrights tended to exaggerate this concern by creating an abundance of plots that turned on women's behaviour as daughters, brides-to-be, wives and mothers, often engendering painfully divided loyalties in the process. For example, Belvidera, in *Venice Preserv'd* (1682) by Thomas Otway (1652–85), discovers that her husband is involved in a political plot that, if allowed to run its course, will cause the death of her father. Above all, they needed to preserve their chastity. Calista, the heroine of *The Fair Penitent* (1703) by Nicholas Rowe, has lost her virginity to her lover, Lothario, before the play begins; the resultant havoc leads to multiple deaths, including her own suicide. Charles Inigo Jones, author of *Memoirs of Miss O'Neill* (1816), cites as 'the standard English opinion on the subject of female frailty' the heroine's statement, in Rowe's *Jane Shore* (1714), that an adulterous wife is an irredeemable outcast.[16] Jane has openly cuckolded her husband by becoming the mistress of Edward IV; after her lover's death, his successor, Richard III, commands that anybody who gives her food or shelter shall be put to death. Her husband finds her starving in the street, forgives her and offers her food, but she dies anyway, carried off, one feels, by her consciousness that she is unfit to live. Yet things happen very differently in *The Stranger* (1798), adapted by Benjamin Thompson (1776?–1816) from *Menschenhass und Reue* (*Misanthropy and Remorse*) (1790) by August von Kotzebue (1761–1819). At the climax of this highly-popular yet controversial drama the erring but repentant Mrs Haller is forgiven by her husband, the 'Stranger' of the title, and received into the bosom of her reunited family without any ill effects. Jones was alarmed by thoughts of what this might portend: 'A Mrs. Haller and a Mary Wolstancroft [*sic*] are the same; and if their morality is to be the guide and standard of female excellence, virtue will be but an empty name, and guilt lose all its turpitude.'[17] O'Neill played Belvidera, Jane Shore and Mrs Haller in her opening 1814/15 season at Covent Garden and Calista in her second. She performed Jane Shore with 'overwhelming' pathos, and as Mrs Haller generated such a potent mixture of 'extasy' and 'pity' that spectators forgot 'the crime and the breach of morality which it inculcates'.[18] She could ride on waves of emotion over the tectonic shifts that were slowly but surely beginning to transform society.

'The charming picture she presented': O'Neill in Character

William Charles Macready (1793–1873), the greatest of early Victorian actors, worked with O'Neill for most of her career at Covent Garden. His description of her Juliet in the 1814/15 season provides valuable insight into her techniques:

> The charming picture she presented was one that time could not efface from the memory … To her might justly be ascribed the negative praise, in my mind the highest commendation that, as an artist, man or woman can receive, of a total absence of any approach to affectation. There was in her look, voice, and manner an artlessness, an apparent unconsciousness (so foreign to the generality of stage performers) that riveted the spectator's gaze; but when, with altered tones and eager glance, she inquired, as he lingeringly left her, the name of Romeo of the Nurse, and bade her go and learn it, the revolution in her whole being was evident[.]
>
> …
>
> I have heard objections to the warmth of her passionate confessions in the garden scene; but the love of the maid of sunny Italy is not to be measured and judged by the phlegmatic formalist. … Love was to her life; life not valued, if unsustained by love. Such was the impression Miss O'Neill's conception of the character made, rendering its catastrophe the only natural refuge of a guileless passion so irresistible and absorbing … the impatience of the love sick maid to obtain tidings of her lover was delightfully contrasted with the winning playfulness with which she so dexterously lured back to doting fondness the pettish humour of the testy old Nurse … The desperate alternative ... transformed the gentle girl at once into a heroine, and the distracting contention of her fears and resolution rose to a frantic climax of passion, abruptly closed by her exclamation, 'Romeo! I come! This do I drink to thee!' Through my whole experience hers was the only representative of Juliet I have seen.[19]

This very detailed description has been quoted at length since it is a report of the impact of her performance not on a critic, but on a young fellow actor who had recently been a great success as Romeo, at Bath. Macready's account is useful as he provides a professional insight and was known to be intensely critical of himself and other performers. Interestingly he acknowledges O'Neill had her critics when he notes, 'I have heard objections to the warmth of her passionate confessions.' One of those less enthusiastic commentators was the dramatist Frederick Reynolds (1764–1841), though he was aware that few would share his opinion. He claims O'Neill 'possessed no doubt a considerable portion of feeling; but which, in my opinion, was of too boisterous and vehement a nature. In this judgment, however, I was again in the minority; for, by the verdict of the million, Miss O'Neill was pronounced a younger and a better Mrs. Siddons.'[20]

The critic William Hazlitt (1778-1830) also praised her performance: 'In the silent expression of feeling, we have seldom witnessed anything finer than her acting, where she is told of Romeo's death, her listening to the Friar's story of the poison, and her change of manner towards the Nurse, when she advises her to marry Paris.'[21] An account by 'Timothy Crusty' supports these views:

> ...after the masquerade scene, when she had been eagerly enquiring who Romeo is, just as she was preparing to quit the banquet-room, she turned round and stood as if lost in unutterable thought, with her eyes fixed upon the spot where Romeo had lately passed away from her sight; as if her fancy reproduced his form in that very place … Her 'rapt soul was sitting in her eyes' – her whole body spoke – then, with a deep, impatient sigh, she turned away.[22]

Another critic wrote of her, 'It is not Miss O'Neill we see, but the character that she is unfolding.'[23] At the time auditoriums were lit and the actor had to be aware of the audience in a way actors are often not today, yet from these descriptions it would appear that O'Neill was totally involved in her part. So how far was this consistent with contemporary ideas of acting?

Theatrical Handbooks and the Art of Acting

In the eighteenth century, acting was considered an art akin to poetry, involving many of the same faculties, and was granted a respect that it has never had since. There were many talented actors and it was an age of innovation. Handbooks were published on every aspect of the profession, from educational background to facial expression, the management of feet and legs and the art of using hands. For example, a treatise ascribed to Roger Pickering (d. 1755), devoted to the management of the body and voice, recommends drawing back the left leg to express '*Astonishment* and *Surprize*, arising from *Terror*'.[24] Whatever their views on technique, however, one factor was of paramount importance. Despite his focus on the physical elements, Pickering insists 'The *Delicacy* of *Theatrical Expression* can never be expected from an Actor that does not *feel* his Part.'[25]

In 1807, James Henry Leigh Hunt (1784–1859), an eager advocate of feeling on the stage, published his *Critical Essays on the Performers of the London Theatres*. He believed the actor's emotions must be genuine: 'the countenance cannot express a single passion perfectly, unless the passion is first felt: ... a keen observer of human nature and it's [*sic*] effects will easily detect the cheat.'[26] Hunt contrasted the actor John Philip Kemble (1757–1823), who 'studiously meditates a step or an attitude in the midst of passion', with his sister, Siddons, who 'never thinks about either, and therefore is always natural'.[27] Indeed, Hunt could 'hardly imagine, there has been any such thing as a rehearsal for powers so natural and so spirited'.[28] Siddons rehearsed thoroughly but more important to Hunt was that he knew she had

> talked of the real agitation which the performance of some of her characters has made her feel. To see the bewildered melancholy of *Lady Macbeth* walking in her sleep, or the widow's mute stare of perfected misery by the corpse of the gamester *Beverley* ... would argue this point better than a thousand critics.[29]

Given this account, we can consider Eliza O'Neill as following in Siddons' footsteps, as Siddons was clearly an actress who was emotionally involved in her roles.

The turn of the century did not see the handbooks disappear, with at least two new books on gesture published between 1797 and 1807.[30] Gesture was highly important: an international extra-theatrical language that has now been completely lost and that formed an important aspect of ballet. The minor theatres, forbidden to perform spoken drama, employed mime. There were recognized symbolic gestures such as a tableau formed of a pair of reunited brothers or a repentant husband or father. Portraits show actors in those very handbook poses. Hunt appreciated how effective they could be, when used by a great performer. He records how Siddons transformed what he termed an 'insipid tragedy', *The Grecian Daughter* (1772) by Arthur

Murphy (1727–1805), by making a spectacular gesture at a crucial point where she actually had no line.[31] He recalls:

> This heroine has obtained for her aged and imprisoned father some unexpected assistance from the guard *Philotas*: transported with gratitude, but having nothing from the poet to give expression to her feelings, she starts with extended arms and casts herself in mute prostration at his feet. I shall never forget the glow, which rushed to my cheeks at this sublime action.[32]

O'Neill, too, understood the value of a well-chosen pose. Her attitudes 'might have afforded a gallery of statues': as Mrs Haller, 'she sunk upon the floor, and, clasping her knees, let her head fall upon them, so that her "wild-reverted tresses" hung as a veil before her.'[33]

It is also important to consider the construction of the space where the actors and audience were accommodated, and performers' behaviour within it. Hunt believed that actors on stage ought to imagine themselves to be in 'a real room enclosed in four walls', so that they would focus on the world of the play rather than on the audience.[34] This was consistent with the contemporary desire of architects to do away with the forestage, where actors generally performed, and the proscenium doors (as was attempted in the rebuilt Drury Lane theatre in 1812), and oblige actors to perform within the scenery. These changes were to lead to the adoption of the modern box set, as we know it today. The growing taste for realism was highly congenial to an actress like O'Neill, with her talent for losing herself in her character.

O'Neill's Artistry

Yet none of this is the whole story of O'Neill's artistic success and popularity. Three very important elements merit close consideration. Firstly, the actor's own combination of physical characteristics, including appearance and voice: these bring something to a role and, if they are much out of sympathy with the character, can jar on an audience. The second element, already discussed in general terms, is the actor's use of the imagination and emotions. Thirdly, the actor's relationship with the audience and with other actors is perhaps the most important factor during performance, since no one can perform in isolation. All these aspects of O'Neill's technique deserve more detailed discussion, often involving contemporary critics' comparisons with Mrs Siddons, who is reported to have 'always declared the highest opinion of Miss O'NEILL's talents'.[35]

O'Neill's physical appearance worked well for her when she played young women, but not when she attempted to play the heroes' mothers, such as Volumnia in *Coriolanus*, and Lady Randolph in *Douglas* (1756), by John Home (1722–1808). She was, after all, a young woman without children. William Oxberry (1784–1824), actor and critic, considered that her Lady Randolph and Volumnia were 'decided failures', as 'she could not represent maternal affection'; he thought that for O'Neill 'love was all the love of fire, youth, and passion; it beamed in her eyes, and trembled on her tongue, and when she strove to subdue its tone to maternal feeling, she became tame, cold, and insipid.'[36] Theatre historian John Genest (1764–1839) considered her appearance in *King John* as Constance, the widowed mother of the young Prince Arthur, the rightful heir to the throne, 'must have been very unsuitable – and truly ridiculous in Coriolanus [*sic*], when she acted Kemble's mother'.[37] It is not impossible for an actress to play another age successfully, and at the time it was not uncommon to do so, but it seems that O'Neill's performance did not overcome the youthfulness and fragility of her appearance and her brief career did not allow her to mature into them.[38] Jones also felt that she was at a disadvantage in the role of Euphrasia in *The Grecian Daughter*, which 'requires a command of the greatest physical powers, such as the constitution and disposition of Miss O'Neill is not adequately fitted to accomplish.'[39] Consequently, she was 'not so strongly or commandingly impressive as Mrs. Siddons', not through any lack of talent, but because 'nature has cast her in a different mould'.[40] Jones also considered O'Neill too feminine for the part: 'Her's [*sic*] is the empire of the soft emotions, and the character of Euphrasia is one of masculine energies, of pre-eminent courage and virtues; one that, in fact, towers above the delicacy, we shall not say weaknesses, of her sex.'[41] The events of the play reveal this remark as a textbook example of gendered criticism, in which masculinity and femininity are cultural constructs that have little to do with distinctions between male and female. When Euphrasia stabs a tyrant to death, on stage, this could be seen as an instance of masculine strength, but the feature that distinguishes her most sharply from other dramatic heroines is the fact that, when her father is sentenced to starve to death in prison, she breastfeeds him, thus bringing a primal female instinct into conflict with feminine 'delicacy'. Since the episode happens off stage, however, there is no need for the delicacy of the actress to be compromised.

O'Neill's voice, also, was not initially strong. On 4 March 1815, diarist Henry Crabb Robinson (1775–1867) found her voice 'harsh', and complained that 'in moments of great excitement she wants power'.[42]

However, it improved during her second London season, 1815/16, when an anonymous critic praised its 'astonishing sweetness'.[43] Jones' account, however, is rarely negative: his view was that it possessed 'a just melody, with sufficient strength to give utterance to the most violent bursts of stormy action' and that as Belvidera in *Venice Preserv'd* her voice has a 'gentleness and thrill of soft anguish in the tone that goes to the very soul, and far excels the strong shrill cadence of Mrs. Siddons.'[44] Later on, he expresses the difference between their voices in gendered terms like those used in comparing their physical presence: 'Wanting the masculine strength of a Siddons, it never loses the delicate pitch that should characterise the female tone.'[45] Of course, these writers lacked the technology to record something as evanescent as a voice: even if it had occurred to them to transcribe its pitch in musical notation, they had no means of conveying its timbre. O'Neill's fervent admirer 'Timothy Crusty' tried to compensate for this deficiency by appealing to taste and touch, evoking 'the honey of a voice rich as hybla, powerful as Lacryma Christi, piercing as Champaigne, tender as May-dew'.[46] Macready's evocation of vision was even more sensuous; he said he knew no elocution more perfect than that of Miss O'Neill: 'It was a pleasure to watch the movement of her lips.'[47]

O'Neill's greatest power lay in her imagination and ability to access her emotions. Hunt described her as excellent in particular passages requiring sudden emotion: 'Her very best touches perhaps are those in which she deprecates and protests against any thing. Her No, no, no! for instance, is very natural, hurried, and absorbing.'[48] Hazlitt believed her 'great excellence is extreme natural sensibility'; she had no equal 'in truth, in beauty, and in that irresistible pathos, which goes directly to the heart'.[49] When she played Elwina in *Percy* (1777) by Hannah More, he considered her 'expression of mute grief' on hearing of Percy's death 'as fine as possible'; nor did he believe anything could be 'more natural, more beautiful of affecting, than the manner in which she receives his scarf, and hurries out with it, tremulously clasping it to her bosom'.[50] In *Isabella; or, the Fatal Marriage*, a 1757 adaptation by David Garrick (1717–79) of *The Fatal Marriage* (1694) by Thomas Southerne (1660–1746), the heroine is forced by poverty to part with her wedding ring: although several lines of touching blank verse are provided for the occasion, Jones considers that O'Neill's look 'speaks more than language can convey'.[51] When she played Monimia in Thomas Otway's *The Orphan* (1680), he admired 'the plaintive softness also with which she replies, "It was our wedding night;" and the subsequent part, when she burst out into the most poignant exclamation.'[52] This scene certainly requires a virtuoso performance: Monimia cannot understand why Castalio's manner is so hostile, after they have just spent the night rapturously consummating their clandestine marriage; Castalio is consumed with jealous rage because she refused to let him into her bedroom. Only the audience knows that she has unwittingly spent the night with his twin brother. O'Neill was also capable of a 'shocking and convulsive laugh' when being borne off stage as Mrs Beverley at the end of *The Gamester* (1753) by Edward Moore (1712–57). She has just witnessed her husband's agonizing suicide by poison and, as Siddons did in *The Grecian Daughter*, as there was no speech, she supplied another reaction.[53] As Mrs Haller in *The Stranger*, she could produce 'sudden bursts of violence': appropriate responses to her present sufferings and her convulsive attacks of remorse for her past actions.[54]

Clearly O'Neill's abilities to imagine herself the character, to access the emotions of that character and to make others believe that she was the character were great. Her style appears to evoke the method-acting technique that Konstantin Stanislavski (1863–1938) would later famously advise. This idea is corroborated by an account of her in character given by James Boaden (1762–1839) in his biography of John Kemble, published following O'Neill's retirement from the stage:

> Mr. Kemble at times suffered extreme agony from the *gout*; but if the theatre required his aid, and he could in any manner support himself on the stage, he would never keep his room, but with infinite address conceal even his torture from the audience, and sustain the character with real philosophy. On one of these nights he was acting the *Stranger* to the Mrs. Haller of Miss O'Neill. A friend of mine, on entering the green-room, found him literally groaning with pain; and being called to the opposite side of the stage, he entreated that gentleman to lead him to his station. On his way thither his dramatic consort passed him and, sustaining the character, addressed him thus – 'I am very sorry to see my poor husband in such pain.' Tortured as he was, Mr. Kemble replied with equal preservation of character – 'Yes; you are a dear creature, and deserve *forgiveness*.'[55]

This notion is borne out by Macready, who described her as 'a great actress … a remarkable instance of self-abandonment in acting. She forgot everything for the time but her assumed character. She was an entirely modest woman; yet in acting with her I have been nearly smothered by her kisses.'[56]

'A rare and bewitching talent': Critical Responses

These anecdotes reveal O'Neill's relationship with her fellow actors, while her ability to access emotion enabled her to have a strong rapport with her audience, though opinion varied as to the degree of her success. Crabb Robinson compared O'Neill unfavourably to Siddons, believing that 'she did not appear to be a great actress'.[57] Nevertheless, he admired her 'fondness and ingratiating caresses' as Isabella in *The Fatal Marriage*, and thought she 'died well', her last motions 'as if in search of her child'.[58] As Mrs Beverley in *The Gamester*, the 'moments of strong passion in which Miss O'Neill excited interest … were a poor compensation for hours of tedium.'[59] Yet later in the century Crabb Robinson coupled O'Neill with Siddons by comparing newer actresses with them both, and in 1857 he described her as 'the successor of Mrs. Siddons'.[60] Macready remembered her alongside Siddons, Kemble and Edmund Kean (1787–1833), describing her as 'a genius'.[61] Boaden considered O'Neill possessed such a 'rare and bewitching talent, as at once placed her at the summit of her art' but that 'through the whole range of characters common to both these actresses, the mental intelligence of Mrs. Siddons seemed to be unapproached and unapproachable.'[62] Oxberry expressed a similar view: O'Neill 'twined most upon our affections; but Mrs. Siddons made an impression on our minds, that time never eradicated'.[63] Jones, however, while sharing this perception of the difference between Siddons and O'Neill as a contrast between thought and feeling, believed that O'Neill's emotional appeal was more enduring and effective than Siddons' intellectual impact: comparing their versions of Belvidera's agonized appeal to her father to save her husband's life in *Venice Preserv'd*, he says, 'The one [Siddons] literally plays round the head – we admire it, and it is lost; the other goes to the heart, and is rivetted.'[64] 'Timothy Crusty', while conceding 'dramatic *talent* in the highest degree' to Siddons, awarded 'the palm of *genius*' to O'Neill, because, 'In real feeling of the character which she represented, I must think that Miss O'Neill far transcended Mrs Siddons.'[65] As Hunt clearly conveyed, Siddons was highly capable of expressing real feeling, and Crusty's testimony is not included here to assert O'Neill's technical superiority; instead, it offers an unusual opportunity to consider the concept of genius in this era in relation to women.

'Genius' at this period was, of course, a very complex word, capable of extremely diverse meanings. Dr Johnson's definitions included 'The protecting or ruling power of men, places, or things', 'A man endowed with superiour faculties', and, more modestly, 'Mental powers', 'Disposition of nature by which any one is qualified for some peculiar employment', or 'Nature; disposition'.[66] Although people no longer believed in supernatural ruling powers, it was still possible to see a 'genius' as a person (not necessarily a man) possessed by some force beyond conscious control, which might describe a performer in the grip of a self-induced passion. 'Timothy Crusty' sets his concept of intellect, as represented by Siddons, in opposition to O'Neill's ability to feel, and to inspire, emotion: '*Her* style addressed the intellect more exclusively. She was a great actress – but she *was* an actress. Miss O'Neill was a woman – a confiding, tender, passionate, love-inspiring woman.'[67] He compares their backstage demeanour in terms that seem to belittle Siddons' professional detachment in comparison with O'Neill's retention of emotion:

> Stationed behind the scenes, I have watched [Siddons] as she left the stage, after a wondrous burst of dramatic power, – I have seen her arms fall composedly by her side, her face pass in one instant from the extreme of expression to her common look. .... I have observed Miss O'Neill, in similar circumstances, *retaining* the impress of the passion which had really entered into her heart.[68]

Crusty was most impressed by O'Neill's explanation that the tears she shed after her exit were inspired by her artistic response to the theatrical event, not by identification with the character: she says, '"Were they such tears as guilt or agony really shed, I must have been dead long ago."'[69] He argues that this shows 'genius to feel, good sense to disclaim more feeling than was natural, or indeed possible'.[70] While saying O'Neill has both, he seems to be opposing genius to intelligence. In any case, there can be no doubt as to her ability to transmit emotion to the audience, as did Siddons and Kean; according to Oxberry, 'we have seen two (and heard of several) instances of gentlemen fainting from the excess of their emotions, whilst witnessing her performances.'[71]

O'Neill's gifts did not just enable her to interpret the established repertoire: she extended it. Oxberry noted 'the many new tragedies, to which Miss O'Neill's genius gave the Promethean touch.'[72] She created the roles of the heroines in four plays by her fellow countryman and Irish nationalist Richard Lalor Sheil (1791–1851): *Adelaide* (1814), *The Apostate* (1817), *Bellamira* (1818) and *Evadne* (1819). Oxberry considered her performance in the duel scene in *Evadne* 'equally beyond description or commendation', while '*Adelaide* would not have been heard throughout, but for her exertions' and 'the *Apostate* owes her much'.[73] She also created the role of Bianca in *Fazio* (1815), a tragedy by Henry Hart Milman (1791–1868) that required the heroine to portray conjugal love, jealousy, madness and penitence, all with equal intensity and conviction.[74] Percy Bysshe Shelley saw her performance, and so it was that O'Neill had a great part written for her by a major poet. When he wrote his great tragedy, *The Cenci* (1819), he considered that she was the only actress who could play his heroine. This would have been a demanding and controversial role: Shelley's play draws on accounts of Beatrice Cenci (1577–99) who was executed for murdering her violent and sexually abusive father, Count Francesco Cenci (1549–98). Shelley's Beatrice is intelligent, generous, dignified and loving but the murder of her father almost destroys her, although she regains her character in the last scene, facing death with courage and resignation. Shelley would have liked Edmund Kean (1787-1833), the leading male actor of his day, to play Cenci, but he worked at Drury Lane and O'Neill at Covent Garden; Shelley was clearly aware of this since he speaks of the impossibility of Kean playing Cenci. It was, of course, only impossible if the play was to be performed at Covent Garden. Shelley's decision to send the play to Covent Garden indicates that he considered it more important for O'Neill to play Beatrice than it was for Kean to play Cenci. When Shelley heard that O'Neill had retired at the end of the 1819 season, he gave up the idea of its being performed.[75]

Even after O'Neill became Lady Wrixon-Becher, her reputation as an actress lived on in the public memory. The impact of her visit to the House of Lords in 1855, and the sensation it caused among the assembled peers, extended to Australia: she was regarded as 'the only *Juliet* ever seen by any but the mind's eye outside the page of Shakspere [*sic*].'[76] When she died in 1872, aged 81, she was still remembered for this role, as performed nearly sixty years earlier: the *Boston Post* recalled that her first performance at Covent Garden 'brought down the house'.[77] Her short but sensational career was writ large in the Victorian imagination, and is clearly in need of further attention from stage and performance scholars.

Chapter Twelve

Better than the Men: The Uses and Abuses of Women's Strength, Speed, Skill and Endurance in the Long Eighteenth Century

by Peter Radford

Recent scholarship has focused on women's intellectual, literary, artistic, musical and organizational abilities, but still, the physical abilities of women and girls are often overlooked. Across Britain in the long eighteenth century, women and girls engaged in a wide range of sports, in some of which the standard they reached was reported to be very good, perhaps equalling the men's. Participation was often widespread, attracting crowds of spectators and being reported extensively in the press. Their achievements were generally admired and enjoyed, rather than being seen as unsuitable for their sex: in fact, the swiftness, dexterity and stamina on display often overlapped with the qualities that women in the lower classes needed to earn their living. Women and girls learned, however, that their physical abilities could be exploited in other ways, and they sometimes undertook physically demanding, difficult and dangerous occupations that men were unwilling or even unable to perform.[1]

'Any women that chuse to start'

Foremost among women's sports was running. My database of foot-races in Britain lists 68 running races for women and girls at 53 locations in 22 English counties, plus races in Ireland, between 1700 and 1749. From 1750 to 1799 the number increases to 133 events at 68 locations in 20 English counties, giving a total for the whole century of 201 events at 121 locations in 29 English counties, plus events reported in Ireland, Scotland and Wales. No other sporting activity comes close to this number and distribution, but the true figures are likely to be very much higher. For example, newspapers frequently mention the 'annual'[2] event at Old Wives Lees in Kent, and there are reports of them in the seventeenth, eighteenth and nineteenth centuries, but actual details have been found for only ten occurrences in the eighteenth century; the other ninety have to be surmised and are not, therefore, included in the figures above.

Events were advertised for 'wives' and 'pregnant women' as well as 'girls', 'maids' or 'young women', with some providing specific age restrictions. In 1774 there were races at Yattendon for women 'between the Age of seventeen and forty'; in the same year at Gray's Meadow near Henley, Oxfordshire, the age limits were a little tighter, between 16 and 30; at Pignies Green (now Pinkneys Green) near Maidenhead, in 1796, the age limit was 'not exceeding 20 years of age'.[3] However, in August 1789, at the Prince of Wales's Birthday Sports at Brighton, there were *two* age categories, 'Girls, under *Twenty-five* Years of Age', and 'Women, above *Thirty-five* Years of Age': both events had heats.[4] In 1792 in Darlington, County Durham, there were *three* categories: 'not exceeding 15 years of age', 'old women', and one for 'any women that chuse to start'.[5] We might imagine mothers and daughters racing on the same day, or even grandmothers, mothers and daughters.

Despite their widespread occurrence, it is, perhaps, unwise to generalize too widely about these races for women. In addition to the differences in age-grouping and marital status, the events themselves could be very different in character: some were free-standing events, others part of bigger occasions such as fairs, revels, horse races or cricket matches. Many were annual with long, historic traditions, but some had shorter, though still annual, histories, such as celebrations of the king's birthday and, after 1815, the victory at Waterloo. Others were simply commercial opportunities, where an innkeeper arranged events to draw a crowd and so increase his sale of alcohol.

The events often had a quite complex organization, with organizing committees, specific entry requirements, prior advertising, displays of prizes before the event, appointed officials, strict regulations for the races themselves and published appeals procedures in the event of a dispute. We should not think of them, therefore, as impromptu races on the village green, but as relatively sophisticated events with considerable local significance, conferring local renown on the winners. However, we also need to be careful of the notion 'local': some events did specify that only local girls or women could enter, but most did not. Women were sometimes willing to travel several hours to compete and, as many of these competitors would have been young, this suggests a high level of family support and coordination.

Running was also the basis of one of England's first team games: it took place in Kent and was sometimes called 'a running', but usually 'a match of running', with teams of twelve to twenty-four a side. It was played by women as well as by men, and there are records of 'young women' competing in several matches in the 1760s. They were well-organized events of high local status. Advertisements for the match between young women on Monday, 18 July 1768 on Barham Downs began to appear more than two weeks beforehand: 'Great diversion, and much Company' were expected.[6] Little is known about the details of the game but it seems that each team sent out one runner at a time who attempted to make her 'goal'; the opposing team sent out someone to stop her, by touching her. Such a touch was called a 'stroke', and it took the 'stroked' player out. After the first runner had been sent out, others would follow, each matched by a member of the opposite team. You were only permitted to stroke the runner with whom you were matched. When this was over and all the runners had made their goal or been stroked, roles were reversed. Matches were decided by the number of strokes made. Much preparation was involved, so the runners had to make a major commitment to compete. An alternative date was set in case of bad weather, and the young women were required not only to be at a designated meeting-place at a certain time before the match, but also to meet two days earlier to give in their names and agree on other details, such as the size of the goals, the numbers in the teams and the placement of the buoys marking the limits of the playing area. Good crowds were expected and the match, which may have lasted for several hours, gave 'great satisfaction' to a 'vast concourse of people'.[7] Each member of the winning team was also presented with a shift 'given them by the gentry'; these, too, had been advertised well in advance.[8] This was not a solitary phenomenon: even before it took place, advertising for a similar event at the same site on Monday, 1 August 1768 had begun.[9]

Apart from these running team games, we read of large crowds throughout the eighteenth century turning out to see women and girls in foot-races, including 'Vast Numbers' (Barnet Common, London, 1725),[10] 'a great Concourse of People' (Durdham Downs, near Bristol, 1726),[11] a 'numerous Company' (Moorfield, Derby, 1735),[12] 'a great deal of company' (Shoreham, Sussex, 1762)[13] and 'a prodigious concourse of people' (Hendon, Middlesex, 1786).[14] Some commentators tried to be more precise, reporting 'many thousands' (Kersal Moor, Lancashire, 1681),[15] 2,000 'persons of the first fashion' (Tothill Fields, Westminster, 1791),[16] 3,000 (Eastry Downs, Kent, 1772)[17] and 5,000 spectators at Lincoln in 1772.[18] Considering the number of races, their geographical spread, the numbers that turned out to watch and the fact that information about so many of them was to be found in the newspapers, very few people in Britain in the eighteenth century can have been unaware that many girls and women were runners. However, it did not always fit well with the decorum expected of genteel women, as reflected in the words that novelist Oliver Goldsmith (1728–74) gives to the vicar's wife in his novel *The Vicar of Wakefield*:

> you know the church is two miles off, and I protest I don't like to see my daughters trudging up to their pew all blowzed and red with walking, and looking for all the world as if they had been winners at a smock race.[19]

As Good as the Men

It is not so easy to compare the performance of female runners directly with that of men because different criteria were employed. The running cultures for men and women appear to have developed along almost entirely different lines, with men usually running wagers against time or against one other competitor: most were timed. Women, however, very rarely ran wagers but usually ran in races with three to six competitors, and in 'best of three' events in which the winner was the first to win two races with the last race being decisive, and it appears they were seldom timed.[20] The gap between races would usually be thirty minutes' 'breathing time' so, while the series of races would be physically demanding, tactics would play an important part; therefore, even if the races had been timed, they would not reflect a runner's ability in a one-off race. There was, however, one significant wager run in 1795 by a 15-year-old girl in Wrotham, Kent, who engaged to run a mile in five and a half minutes for 2 guineas.[21] She finished in 5m 28s, thus acquiring a prize that would have had a purchasing power of £206 in 2017.[22] If this performance is to be believed, it would be another 137 years before any woman in Britain would run faster: the 27-year-old Ruth Christmas (1904–2001) ran 5m 27.5s on 20 August 1932.[23] Although the 1795 performance is impossible to verify, analysis of many hundreds of eighteenth-century *male* performances shows them to be as internally consistent as those of the nineteenth and twentieth centuries, so the rigours imposed by the scrutiny of principals and umpires on opposite sides of a wager seem to have ensured a good level of accuracy in the measurement of distance and time, thus producing robust data.[24]

Women and girls might also have been seen engaging in other pastimes, however, including hunting, prize-fighting, throwing, playing stoolball, and even football, ensuring that their more general sporting abilities were accepted and recognized throughout society.[25] Where their activities did admit of comparison between the sexes, the results could be startling.[26] There was, perhaps, no other area of human endeavour in which women were adjudged to be as good as any man, unless men did not consider it a man's activity. The game most often called a 'man's game' was cricket, which reached a high point when the cricketers of Kent challenged the rest of England to a match at London's Artillery Ground on Monday, 18 June 1744 and won by a breathtakingly narrow margin. James Dance (1721–74), who wrote under the pseudonym James Love, chronicled the match in *Cricket. An Heroic Poem*, extolling this 'glorious, manly, *British* Game' (Book 1, line 13), and inviting comparison between the cricketers and the heroes of Virgil's *Aeneid* (Book 2, line 63, note).[27] He makes the great Sussex batsman, Richard Newland (1713–78), identify success in the game with mature masculinity: he swears by Hercules and Mercury, 'the Gods of Strength and Swiftness, so very peculiar to the Game of CRICKET' (Book 2, line 25, note), that if he fails to accept the Kentish challenge, 'The Trophies, from this conq'ring Forehead torn, / By Boys and Women shall in Scorn be worn' (Book 2, lines 33-4).[28] So the image of cricket as a male prerogative must have received a nasty dent when the following report appeared in the *St. James's Evening Post* for Thursday 8 to Saturday, 10 August 1745, as well as other newspapers: 'The greatest Cricket Match that ever was played in the South Part of England, was on Friday the 26th of last Month, on Gosden Common near Guildford in Surrey, between eleven Maids of Bramley, and eleven Maids of Hambleton [sic]', who 'bowled, batted, ran, and catched, as well as any Men could do'. Incidentally, *all* the great matches reported up to that date had been in the south of England, so this assertion meant that the maids of Bramley and Hambledon (both villages in Surrey) had played the greatest cricket match anywhere, ever.[29] It was a bold claim, and there are two versions of it, differing only by one word. Some newspapers reported that the 'Girls' played as well as *any* men,[30] and others that they played as well as *most* men;[31] a significant difference, but in both cases they were acknowledged to be very good indeed.

In the years ahead, women found other ways of demonstrating their equality with men, and sometimes their superiority. In 1768, newspapers reported that Mme Bunel had defeated Mr Tomkins at tennis (2 sets to 1) at the Royal Tennis Court in Haymarket, evoking shades of Billie Jean King and Bobby Riggs in 1973.[32] Furthermore, in 1805 Alicia Meynell Thornton (b. 1782) (riding *Louisa*) defeated Francis Buckle (1766–1832), the leading jockey of his day (riding *Allegro*), over a 2-mile course at York.[33] These feats were more than amusing (albeit impressive) exceptions to the rule. To prove her point, eleven days later Bunel defeated Tomkins again, this time in front of a large and select crowd including 'several of the Nobility' and the Comte du Chatelet, the French Ambassador to Great Britain.[34] They went not merely because a woman was playing a man, but because Mr Tomkins was 'the greatest player in England'.[35] Thornton had previously raced at York on Saturday, 25 August 1804 against her brother-in-law, Captain William Flint, generating enormous public excitement, but had lost, partly because her horse 'broke down' in a 'terrible way', and partly because her adversary took advantage of the fact that she was riding side-saddle by adopting a position that deprived her of the '*whip hand*'.[36] So both ladies put their reputations on the line twice. These are not merely examples of outstanding sporting ability, but also of unusual determination, tenacity and self-confidence.

'Exertion in the Art of Spinning'

In the years before the internal combustion engine or electrical power, knowledge of women's physical capabilities was not limited to their sporting achievements: their normal lives gave plenty of opportunities to display them, and we get glimpses of their abilities being recognized from time to time. In 1767, the king's birthday was celebrated at Sedbergh in Westmorland (now Cumbria) with Olympic Games being held in the Market Square. There were prizes for spinning and knitting for the women and girls, and for cudgelling and wrestling for the men and boys.[37] We should not, however, imagine that the men and boys pursued physical and sporting challenges while the women and girls were sedentary; far from it! A large stage was erected in the square and their spinning wheels arranged in a row. The spinners had 'seconds to attend them'. 'Many wagers' depended on the event and each of the contestants was given 2oz of 'fine Worsted'. On the command they all started; the event was timed to last seventeen minutes: the spinner who had the longest yarn at that time was to be the winner. That title went, unexpectedly, to the youngest girl (named Wilkinson) who was reported to have spun 'four Hanks and 38 Threads'. A hank of worsted is 560 yards, so she must have spun 2,240 yards (plus 38 Threads); the report says, 'she ran at full speed as in a Race all the Time, made about one Yard and three Quarters at every Stroke, and had very few Breaks all the while.'

It is useful to reconstruct Miss Wilkinson's actions, as spinning is often considered a sedentary activity. The 'Long-Wheel' she used was sometimes called a Great Wheel with, perhaps, a diameter of 1 yard [0.914m]. To spin the worsted she had to turn the wheel, probably with her right hand, and draw out the wool into yarn with the fingers of her left hand. In drawing out the yarn, she spun the wheel and then ran backwards away from it. She stopped at the point furthest from the wheel where she was still able to reach it with her right hand; she might even have carried a stick in her right hand to maximize her distance from the wheel at this point.[38] Then she stopped the wheel, spun it in the opposite direction and ran back towards it, winding the completed yarn on to the spindle. As it was a competition, she had to take great care not to break the thread while running the two or three steps backwards and forwards from the wheel, a considerable achievement, as 'she appears to have been spinning yarn to approximately 32 count, which was considered fine yarn and required a lot of manual dexterity to ensure the yarn was even and avoid breakages.'[39] So she spun at lightning speed while engaged in a sort of seventeen-minute shuttle-run of two or three steps a time. This was a very impressive demonstration of female skill, especially since one or two others were not far behind. Spinning could also form the basis of endurance events. In 1785, three young women in Skipton, North Yorkshire, spun worsted yarn in a competition lasting twelve hours. The winner spun 33 hanks (18,480 yards, or 10½ miles!) and to do so she walked backwards and forwards a distance of 15¾ miles.[40] As the competition took so long shc did not run, but not surprisingly, the report of the event was headed '*extraordinary Instance of Exertion in the Art of Spinning*'. The other young women were not far behind either, in yarn spun or distance covered.

Clearly, spinning could have a very significant physical component. To illustrate this further, Baines reports that spinners in Yorkshire and Lancashire 'walked the equivalent of 30 miles a week spinning wool'.[41] Colonel William Fullarton (1754–1808) reports that the wool spinners of Ayr, western Scotland, went much further:

> The women, in all the labourers and farmers [*sic*] houses, were likewise in the habit of spinning, on very large wheels, the coarse country wool. They could not gain more by this kind of spinning than 4d. per day, and the work is more severe than the spinning of flax; as, in order to twist the woollen thread, they run out the rolls of carded wool to a great distance from the wheel, pacing backwards and forwards 20 or 30 miles in the course of a day's work.[42]

Making a Living

Perhaps it is not surprising, given the wages reported, that so many women and girls took up foot-racing, using their pedestrian talents and endurance to make money when times were hard. Esther Crozier (c.1817) took part in pedestrian wagers (one was to walk 50 miles a day for twenty consecutive days), and she 'for many years travelled Middlesex, Kent, Surrey and Essex, selling pocket books'.[43] Mary Frith (c.1815) was another participant; she once wagered to go 30 miles a day for twenty days, and had, for many years of hard labour, 'frequently performed from 20 to 25 miles a day, travelling the country with different articles for sale, and afterwards returned home at night to her family.'[44] Both were in their thirties, but females of any age might use their pedestrian prowess to become family breadwinners.

The youngest was Emma Matilda Freeman; at 8 years old, she was managed by her parents. We have records of four of her events in nine weeks (July-September 1823): 30 miles (7h 57m); 30 miles (7h 49m); 30 miles (time unknown); and 40 miles (7h 50m) for £100.[45] One of the older pedestrians, Mary McMullen, was in her sixties and travelled around the country with her sons (also pedestrians, but less successful than their mother). She was originally from Ireland, but based in Yorkshire. We have records of seven of her events in fourteen months (September 1826 to November 1827): 40, 90, 20, 92, 92, 92 and 20 miles.[46] She could draw large crowds: once, 6,000 people saw her led to the finishing line by 'a fiddle and a tambourine'. On other occasions, however, she was obstructed and annoyed by those who had bet against her, by crowds of rowdy boys who deliberately got in her way,[47] and even droves of cattle.[48] There were even older long-distance walkers and runners: Ann Sim was 70 years old when she walked the 174 miles from 'Sanbed Poor-house, Dumfries' to Edinburgh and back in forty hours, a task she was said to do 'often'.[49] Another 70-year-old attempted to walk 96 miles in twenty-four hours at Paisley, but after going 45 miles she was arrested because the large crowd that turned out to see her became unruly and were thought to be a threat to public law and order. She was 5 miles ahead of schedule at the time.[50]

If we can imagine the satisfaction felt by Mme Bunel and Alicia Thornton when they defeated the best men, and if we can detect a spring in the step of the young girl in Sedbergh who literally out-ran the opposition to win her spinning competition, we must detect a heaviness in the tread of the women weavers of Ayr, the women and girls who ran and walked as their families' main breadwinner, and the old Scottish women who attempted such long distances with so little reward.

Hard Labour

Other women and girls faced even bigger physical challenges, performing, on a daily basis, Herculean feats as shocking as they are impressive. In 1812 Robert Bald (1776–1861) made the comparison:

> Astonishing as the feats are which have been performed by [female] pedestrians for high betts [sic], the palm must be yielded to the coal-bearer; for it is certain, if one of them had the prospect of gaining five guineas, by making a great exertion for one day, the work she would perform would far exceed all that is stated [i.e., all that had been performed by the pedestrians].[51]

He describes a day's work by a coal-bearer (a woman who assisted the miner and carried the coal from the coalface):

> we have seen a woman ... take on a load of at least 170lbs. avoirdupois [77.1kg] ... 150yds [137.2m] up the slope of the coal below ground, ascend a pit by stairs 117 feet [35.7m], and travel up the hill 20yds [18.3m] more to where the coals are laid down. All this she will perform no less than twenty-four times as a day's work.[52]

He calculated that in this way she covered a total of 2.3 miles [3,701m] daily, laden, and the same on return, as well as an ascent of 936yds [855.9m] and a descent of the same. This amounted to one such journey every twenty-five minutes or so for ten hours.

> The weight of coals thus brought to the pit top by a woman in a day, amounts to 4,080lbs [1,851kg].
>
> This she would perform, not as the mere effort of a day, after long training, like our celebrated pedestrians, but she would perform the same work, five days each week, and that not for a week, a month or an year, but for years together.[53]

Women and girls were employed in mines all over Britain, and it was sometimes claimed that they were indispensable because men were too large to get into the smaller spaces.[54] In fact, this practice seems to have been implemented, for similar reasons, 4,500 years previously.[55] However, it was not just a matter of size: girls were thought to have something special about them.

One of Her Majesty's Commissioners, R.H. Franks, who was investigating matters in eastern Scotland for the government enquiry into child labour in 1840/1, reported that 'girls are invariably set at an earlier age than boys to their peculiar labour from a notion very generally entertained amongst the parents, that girls are more acute and capable of making themselves useful at an earlier age than boys.'[56] The female of the species was also credited with greater strength, as Peter McNeill (1839–1929) reveals in his review of the work of miners in Tranent (East Lothian, Scotland) in the late eighteenth and early nineteenth centuries: 'as bearers the miner always preferred the girl to the boy, for, strange as it may appear, a woman or girl could always carry about double the weight of coal that a man or boy could scramble out with.'[57] Women were also more amenable: 'Females submit to work in places where no man or even lad could be got to labour in: they work in bad roads, up to their knees in water, in a posture nearly double: they are below till [the] last hour of pregnancy.'[58] Some women had long employment records: 38-year-old Elizabeth McNeill, at Elphinstone Colliery, had first gone down the mines in 1803 and had worked there for twenty-eight years.[59] Jane Peacock Watson, who had started young at Harlaw Muir Colliery in West Linton, Peeblesshire, was 40 and had 'wrought in the bowels of the earth' for thirty-three years.[60]

Indeed, women and girls had been going down the mines in Britain for many centuries, but McNeill could find no evidence of when the practice began as it stretched back into the past beyond anyone's recall or knowledge. He reports, however, that Thomas Cochrane, 10th Earl of Dundonald (1775–1860), a naval hero during the Napoleonic wars and later a radical politician, thought that the employment of females down the mines 'aroused public indignation' even in 1793.[61] The full extent of the work done by the women and girls down the mines did not come to light until a commission was set up in 1839 to investigate it. The details in the Parliamentary Reports were reprinted and widely circulated in monthly magazines,[62] and public opinion resulted in the political action necessary to ban the employment of women and girls (and boys) in the mines.

R.H. Franks' reports in 1842 fall just outside the period covered in this book, but they give us more detail of what the women and girls had already been doing for generations. He gives the specific example of Ellison Jack, an 11-year-old who had to climb down nine 18ft [5.5m] ladders to get to the loose coal:

> she then takes her creel (a basket formed to the back, not unlike a cockle-shell flattened towards the neck, so as to allow lumps of coal to rest on the back of the neck and shoulders), and pursues her journey to the wall-face, or as it is called here, the room of work. She then lays down her basket, into which the coal is rolled, and it is frequently more than one man can do to lift the burden on her back. The tugs or straps are placed over the forehead, and the body bent in a semicircular form, in order to stiffen the arch. Large lumps of coal are then placed on the neck, and she then commences her journey with her burden to the pit bottom, first hanging her lamp to the cloth crossing her head. In this girl's case she has first to travel about 14 fathoms (84 feet, [25.6m]) from wall-face to the first ladder, which is 18 feet high [5.5m]: leaving the first ladder she proceeds along the main road, probably 3 feet 6 inches [1.1m] to 4 feet 6 inches high [1.4m], to the second ladder, 18 feet high, so on to the third and fourth ladders till she reaches the pit-bottom, where she casts her load, varying from 1cwt [50.8kg] to 1½cwt [76.2kg], into the tub. This one journey is designated a rake; the height ascended, and the distance along the roads added together, exceed the height of St. Paul's Cathedral; and it not unfrequently happens that the tugs break, and the load falls upon those females who are following. However incredible it may be, yet I have taken the evidence of fathers who have ruptured themselves from straining to lift coal on their Children's backs.[63]

There were, however, many examples of the endurance and tenacity of the women and girls down the mines. Helen Reid, aged 16, used to carry 'near two cwt' [almost 102kg] on her back.[64] Isabella Read, aged 12, could carry 1¼ cwt [63.5kg] on her back, and on average did so between twenty-five and thirty times a day, always carrying the load *up* 14 fathoms [84ft, (25.6m)].[65] At the Sheriffhall Colliery Janet Cumming, aged 11, reported that she usually carried 1cwt [50.8kg] but, as she did not always work 'on the same wall', the distance varied from 150 fathoms to 250 fathoms [300-500 yards (274-457m)]; the roof was so low that she had to bend her back and legs and was often up to her calves in water.[66] Margaret Leveston, aged just 6, made ten to fourteen rakes (journeys) a day and carried 'full fifty-six' (i.e. 56lb [25.4kg]).[67]

In Parliament it was stated that 'The persons employed in coal-bearing are almost always girls and women.'[68] This was because they were 'cheaper than the men' and 'would do more humiliating drudgery, and in more noxious and slushy places than men'.[69] They had another outstanding feature; despite all their sufferings, 'when the work is done, they return to it with a vigour which is surprising.'[70] The horror that many genteel readers experienced when reading of these girls and women down the mines was so great that it overshadowed any admiration that they might have had for their endurance and fortitude, and perhaps helped to create the atmosphere in which women were to be discouraged or even forbidden to undertake any physically demanding work or sport.

It should be noted that the women involved in mining were not unique in their load-bearing capacity. The fishwives of Fisherrow, Musselburgh, in 1795 and for many years before, would 'do the work of men' and carry loads of fish to Edinburgh, 'Four days in the week', in creels or baskets.[71] They had a way of going in threes and rotating the basket to one another every 100 yards, and covered the 5 miles to Edinburgh in forty-five minutes. The weight of these baskets is not given, but 'it is a well attested fact, that three of them, not many years ago, went from Dunbar to Edinburgh, which is 27 miles, with each of them a load of herrings on her back of 200 lb. [91kg] in 5 hours. They sometimes carry loads of 250 lb. [113kg].'[72] They also enjoyed their sport: 'On holidays they frequently play at *golf*; and on Shrove Tuesday there is a standing match at *foot-ball*, between the married and unmarried women, in which the former are always victors.'[73]

The examples of the Surrey cricketing maids of Bramley and Hambledon, Mme Bunel, Alicia Thornton, the many women and girl pedestrians, the bearers in the mines in England, Scotland and Wales, and the fishwives of Fisherrow serve to remind us that women's skill, strength and persistence have often been overlooked when telling their story. Their achievements in physically matching or out-performing the men of their day should be recognized as landmarks in their history and deserve to be remembered and honoured.

Chapter Thirteen

'Merely butterflies of a season'? The Halls, Ideology and Control in the Early Nineteenth-Century Annuals

by Marion Durnin

In his preface to the 1832 edition of *The Amulet*, Samuel Carter Hall (1800–89) wrote that he wished to avoid 'a very general complaint against the annual works – that they are merely butterflies of a season, and lose their attraction when that season is past.'[1] The immensely influential annuals and gift-books that flourished in Britain between the 1820s and the 1840s are an important though oft-derided genre of print culture. They were prized as much for their innovative and sumptuous bindings as for their literary content. Rudolf Ackermann's *Forget Me Not: A Christmas and New Year's Present for 1823* (published in November 1822), a hybrid of the English pocket book and the German *Taschenbuch*, initiated the craze for annuals as tokens of love and affection, first conceived as Christmas gifts. Displaying their hallmark sentimental titles and lavish presentation, the annuals became a test bed for innovation in design and print technology.

Samuel Carter Hall was both founder and sole editor of *The Amulet*, deemed one of the most beautiful of the annuals, which ran from 1826 to 1837, and simultaneously edited *The Spirit and Manners of the Age*, which ran from 1826 to 1829 and was not solely an annual, since it appeared in weekly, then monthly, numbers. In both these publications his wife Anna Maria Hall, née Fielding, tested public opinion of her earliest writings – chiefly Irish tales and sketches – which were later to seal her reputation when collected as the highly successful *Sketches of Irish Character* (1829). She also provided editorial help with *The Spirit and Manners of the Age*, and edited *The Juvenile Forget-Me-Not* (1829–38). Together the Halls pursued lifelong careers in journal editing and writing.

In this chapter, I wish to address the notion that, rather than being evanescent or vapid creations, the annuals conveyed a serious ideological intent, which can be detected in their content and in the supporting editorial commentary. Carter Hall had lofty ambitions for his publications, both literary and spiritual. His concerns regarding their direction and survival, often voiced in his prefaces, reveal the financial, cultural and ideological battles played out in and around these works. I suggest here that Carter Hall's editorial control regarding the content and embellishment of *The Amulet* and *The Spirit and Manners of the Age*, combined with his wife's contributions, had strategic ideological implications that evidence an essentially political agenda.

The stated aim of *The Amulet* was to blend religious instruction with amusement through the medium of literature. Carter Hall was concerned that readers 'would perhaps shun [Religion] in the severer garb in which she sometimes appears', but hoped they might be 'won to her side by the attractions of a more tasteful attire'.[2] He was also concerned that it should be 'considered as a religious publication only so far as that every article tends to impress some moral lesson'.[3] From the publisher's perspective, the function of *The Amulet* was the same as that of other gift-books: to furnish objects of desire to the lucrative market of a growing readership. Immediately, however, seemingly laudable editorial aims came up against the concerns of 'serious' writers, who were torn between handsome payments and the possibility of reputations being tarnished by association with the popular.

Although the periodical had a broadly religious agenda, Anne Renier claims that 'apart from a more solemn than romantic preoccupation with death, graves, churchyards, infanticide and the sufferings of slaves, and an occasional reference to angel visits, *The Amulet* differs not very much from its more secular companions.'[4] Topics concerned with ethics were often included and famous names in the literary world were courted with the promise of large fees. The illustrations were even more costly: Carter Hall paid the sum of 180 guineas for a print entitled 'The Crucifixion', after John Martin (1789–1854), engraved by Henry Le Keux (1787–1868).[5] Not all the subjects were so edifying. The advent of steel-plate printing, combined with fierce competition between rival annuals, led to the publication of titillating portrayals of unrealistically-proportioned young ladies, often 'reigning beauties', as William Makepeace Thackeray (1811–63) dubbed them in *Pendennis* (1848–50).[6] These developments were increasingly in tension with *The Amulet*'s declared editorial theme of Christian virtue.

Annuals also produced unexpected opportunities for women. As Katherine Harris observes, 'Around 1830, the annuals became so popular that not even the press's vitriolic diatribes could dissuade consumers and readers from participation in the craze. The frenzy occurred at the same instant that women began to take control of the annual's contents as both editors and contributors.'[7] An interesting paradox is manifest here regarding the role of women and the boundaries of allowed behaviour: while women occupied an 'anomalous position in journalism', the annuals did afford them an entrée to a publishing career.[8] Such publications were considered a safe space, as the propriety fostered in their tone offered a certain protection to women's reputations. Thus women like Mrs Hall could earn a living by writing for or editing annuals. Despite her deeply conservative views on the role of women, the life in journalism and writing that she pursued was more radical. Nevertheless, a general antipathy to women in the publishing industry meant that a jaundiced eye was cast on 'certain literary wives, who neglect their husband's shirt buttons': many men would 'look out for a bride who has "no ink on her thumb when they kiss her hand"'.[9] A certain ambivalence accrued not only to the women, but particularly to the men who contributed, for as the annuals increased their female readership, they were perceived more and more as feminine spaces of discourse: 'The guiding aesthetic in annuals was that literature gives voice to desires of the heart.'[10]

Their sentimental tone may have encouraged the giving and receiving of annuals as an important, even necessary element of courtship: some years after the infatuation with annuals had faded, this custom was revisited by George Eliot (1819–80). In *Middlemarch* (1871–72), whose events take place between 1829 and 1832, she writes of Ned Plymdale '(one of the good matches in Middlemarch, though not one of its leading minds)' trying to impress the beautiful Rosamond Vincy with 'the last "Keepsake," the gorgeous watered-silk publication which marked modern progress at that time'.[11] It is then mocked, much to Rosamond's chagrin, by the intellectually superior Lydgate, who condemns one of the engravings as 'a "sugared invention"'.[12] A generation later, C.T. Tallent-Bateman (1852–1927) applied similar imagery when he described annuals as cakes rather than bread, and observed that 'even cakes become distasteful, when they provide only two or three currants each, notwithstanding that the surface is liberally endowed with sugar.'[13] Their instant appeal was dismissed as a sign that they lacked serious intellectual content.

For this reason, the annuals and some of the 'uncanonized' and idiosyncratic periodical works of the early nineteenth century, such as *The Spirit and Manners of the Age*, invited scorn alongside the success that rendered them so lucrative to proprietors and publishers. Yet even such eminent authors as Robert Southey, Thackeray and Alfred, Lord Tennyson (1809–92), vociferous in their derision, did eventually succumb to the lure of a new and wider audience, large remuneration and the attention of reviewers. Tennyson responded to the editor of the *Yorkshire Literary Annual* that he had

> forsworn all annuals provincial or metropolitan. I have been so beGemmed and beAmuletted and be-forget-me-not-ted that I have given all these things up. In consequence of the urgent solicitation of S. C. Hall Esq. I had consented some time ago to make my appearance next year in The Amulet, but vowed at the same time that this concession should be the last.[14]

Tennyson's frustration was echoed by Southey, who dubbed the annuals 'picture-books for grown children' but 'good things for the artists and engravers'.[15] Charles Lamb (1775–1834) in his turn railed: 'For God's sake do not let me be pestered with annuals. They are all rogues who edit them … I get nothing by any of 'em, not even a copy.'[16]

The Spirit and Manners of the Age had a much deeper religious inflection than *The Amulet*. A portrait of William Wilberforce (1759–1833) on the title page of the first issue, and its accompanying dedication declaring that the publication was 'HUMBLY DEVOTED TO THE CAUSE OF LITERATURE, HUMANITY, AND RELIGION', set the evangelical tone and conveyed the belief in a strong moral code that Carter Hall shared.[17] His artistic aims were equally lofty: he was committed to 'the abandonment of all selections and extracts from other works'.[18] The second issue was dedicated to Hannah More: in the dedication, '*The EDITORS*' (the plural presumably acknowledging Mrs Hall's assistance) reveal their own ambitions when they praise her for her efforts '*to purify our literature, to form our manners, and to establish our principles*'.[19] More's known disapproval of 'the resurgence of radical politics and civil unrest accompanying the campaigns for Catholic emancipation and parliamentary reform' would not have been lost on their readers.[20]

Commercial constraints on the annuals and associated periodicals were palpable and insecurity about the very survival of the publications often permeates the editorial comment. Carter Hall's anxiety, and his struggle to keep *The Spirit and Manners of the Age* in business, surface in his hyperbole. He compared the publication to a 'little Bark' that appeared at a season when 'the storm beat furiously, and the strand of literature was covered with many larger wrecks'; he aimed to 'unite the refinements of education with the pure elements of revealed religion' and published in order to counteract the 'moral pollutions of the age'.[21] The intention was to be above party politics, but as Hall was a man of deeply-held Tory views, the reader was left in no doubt as to his political affiliations.

It was within this embattled periodical that Mrs Hall's first Irish stories were published: she began in the 1829 edition with 'Master Ben', 'Independence' and 'Black Dennis'.[22] On initial encounter they perhaps appear incongruous among such items as 'The Evangelical Talmudist' series, brief narratives set by the Revd Robert Philip (1791–1858) in an exotic, oriental setting, remote in time and place: the Holy Land in Biblical times. However, I propose that her stories fitted comfortably with the periodical's ideals and ideology on several levels. The extraordinary habits of the Irish that they describe are related in order to fulfil a need for news on foreign mores from the colonies. Their emphasis on sin, retribution and subsequent forgiveness earned by good deeds accentuated and exemplified the magazine's aims to promote good morality and uphold Christian values. These aims, incidentally, were also shared by the Talmudist: for example, 'Rabbi Asaph and Elzaphan the Scribe' concerns the wisdom of praying neither for poverty nor riches, since the man who devotes himself to acquiring money finds himself 'in *slippery* places'.[23]

Many reasons lay behind the proliferation of stories of Irish interest in the early decades of the nineteenth century. Seamus Deane observes that the growth in production of a sub-genre of Irish sketches, tales and legends, fuelled by technological change, resulted in an increased interest in Ireland and the Irish.[24] The introduction of the cast-iron printing press by Lord Stanhope (1753–1816) and the use of steam power by Friedrich Koenig (1774–1833) and Andreas Bauer (1783–1860) combined to allow greater efficiency and revolutionized book production. Furthermore, a pre-existing mania for antiquarianism created a market for regional Irish material and collided with what Joep Leerssen describes as the nostalgic desire to glimpse the vanishing Ireland of 'the pleasant peasant', to read stories about 'rustic, ahistorical and apolitical community life, the idyllic view of Ireland as a mere province or backwater where timeless quaint characters go about their humble and picturesque ways'.[25] The Halls were well-placed to satisfy this demand: they were both born in Ireland, but settled in England, Anna Maria at 15 and Carter at 21, so they understood both their subject and their market. They undertook regular trips to Ireland with the artists they engaged in order to research their sumptuously-illustrated topographical guide, *Ireland: its Scenery, Character, &c* (1841–3).

The Halls report that steam-boats did more than either 'Time or Legislation' to unite England and Ireland as, formerly, it had been a journey of 'so uncertain a duration that not unfrequently weeks were spent between the opposite Ports'.[26] As Terry Eagleton notes, 'Ireland was indeed in one sense unimaginably remote to some of its proprietors: if a few intrepid British souls set foot there for the odd vacation it was because, so Sir Jonah Barrington considered, the place was as exotically alien to them as Kamchatka.'[27] Readers in England in the 1820s viewed Ireland as 'other'. As Hall himself subsequently stated, 'Ireland was almost as much *terra incognita* to the people of Devon as the Fiji Islands are to them now.'[28] In fact, perceptions had changed little when Thackeray declared on his arrival in Dublin in 1842, 'This then is the chief city of the aliens.'[29] To the English reader there was, therefore, perhaps not much to distinguish between tales from Ireland and those from more exotic regions of the Empire and beyond.

The Iris, an annual with a particularly strong religious tone, edited by the Revd Thomas Dale (1797–1870), is another publication where Mrs Hall's Irish sketches appear in the same volume as works dealing with more obviously exotic material: again, they may initially appear strange companions, but they relate to each other on many levels. In 'Luke O'Brian', which appears in the 1830 edition, the well-intentioned hero finds his long-lost mother starving to death. Since she failed in her maternal duty by abandoning him as a child in order to follow her lover, he does not recognize her, but she knows him by a mark tattooed on his wrist. She became a hardened sinner, first through deliberately committing crimes in order to join her lover, who had been transported to Australia (or, as she puts it, 'that land, which it's a shame to mintion'), and secondly through the concealments she was forced to adopt after her premature return.[30] Nearby, separated only by a short poem by the editor, appears 'The Slave Dealer', a poem by Scots abolitionist Thomas Pringle (1789–1834). Like Mrs Hall, Pringle depicts the meeting of a long-separated mother and son, and an initial failure in recognition caused by the sinful behaviour of one of the parties. In this case, however, the son is to blame: 'So altered were his face and frame / By th'ill course he had run' (lines 5-6).[31] He is haunted by guilt after beating a female slave to death. Both authors leave the reader free to speculate that the sheer size and strangeness of the world to which the travellers have been exposed may have contributed to their moral deterioration.

Although connections between the exotic in general and Ireland in particular are not so clearly signposted in subject matter or positioning in the 1831 edition of *The Iris*, they can still be found. 'The Convert of the Harem' is a poetic dialogue in which Zara tells her beloved husband Selim that a Greek slave-girl has converted her from Islam to Christianity, necessitating their separation unless a further conversion can reconcile domestic with celestial bliss. She concludes: 'Oh, would I so might die, that thou, / Dear Selim, might'st have life in heaven!' (lines 195-6).[32] The poet raises no possibility that Zara might be wrong. Her lifestyle is depicted in terms of traditional oriental splendour, luxurious wealth and warmly reciprocated marital love, expressed in gifts of 'White pearls, rich rubies' (line 27) and 'The rarest birds, the brightest flowers' (line 22), but she is forced to abandon it because of its inferiority to Christianity.[33] She now feels 'Dark dread, and longings undefined' (line 163), and realizes that 'I cannot be what I have been' (line 190).[34] In the same volume we find 'The Curse of Property. A Sketch of Irish Mismanagement', a tale by Mrs Hall in the manner of the influential Anglo-Irish novel *Castle Rackrent* (1800) by Maria Edgeworth (1768–1849). 'The Curse of Property' recounts the ruination of the Barrybrooke estate through disorder in every aspect of life, from budgeting to boat maintenance. The events are observed through the prism of the colonial lens of an Englishman, the 'venerable baronet' Sir Charles Stanley, 'a kind-hearted, garrulous old gentleman', whose sympathy for the characters encourages the English reader to accept his view of Ireland as imprudent and out of kilter.[35] Though considerably less prosperous and comfortable than Zara's world, the Ireland of Mrs Hall's tale is also depicted as exotic and 'other', allowing English readers to experience at a safe distance, in fiction, any underlying anxieties about a possible return to the violence of the French (1789) and Irish (1798) rebellions of recent memory. They are also free to reflect, should they feel sufficiently complacent, that the problems arising in the harem and Barrybrooke could have been obviated by the adoption of such traditionally English characteristics, respectively, as Christianity and common sense.

A dust jacket for the annual *Friendship's Offering* of 1830, in which Mrs Hall's Irish sketch 'Larry Moore' first appeared, was discovered in 2009 at the Bodleian Library, Oxford. Still bearing its original sealing wax and creases, the jacket was designed to protect the delicate binding. Decorated with Egyptian sarcophagi, even this dust jacket emphasizes the preoccupation with the foreign and exotic that abounds in both text and illustrations. Representations of the Orient, often relying on such standard tropes as 'seraglios, despotic rulers, sensuality, superstition [and] untrustworthy Orientals', were typical of annuals.[36] Thackeray displays his awareness of this trend by enquiring mischievously whether a particularly ill-informed and hackneyed description in the anonymous tale 'My Turkish Visit' in *The Keepsake* (1838) was written by Lady Blessington, thus lampooning both the rise of aristocratic editors and the promotion of the foreign as seductive and exotic.[37] This was a shrewd conjecture: there is no proof that the Irish novelist Marguerite Gardiner, Countess of Blessington (1789–1849), actually wrote that story, but she confirmed her affinity with *The Keepsake* by becoming its editor from 1841 to 1849.

In fact, some writings in the 1830 volume of *Friendship's Offering* display what, for its period, was a high standard of respect for 'others': this may have been due to the fact that the editor was Thomas Pringle. For example, an anonymous poem, 'The African', tells the story of a freed slave who acknowledges that 'in generous England / They took away my chain' (lines 61-2), and gratefully seizes the opportunity to work his passage back to the Cape of Good Hope in an English ship, showing more courage than the rest of the crew.[38] The Scottish travel writer James Baillie Fraser (1783–1856) wrote 'Mourad and Euxabeet. A Tale of Koordistan' (219-47), whose exemplary ending portrays an oriental Christian father learning to accept his daughter's marriage to a Muslim. The prolific and versatile Irish author John Banim (1798–1842) provided a poem entitled 'Song – The Irish Mother to her Child', in which she laments that her baby son will bear 'The old hereditary badge of suffering and scorn' (line 12).[39] Her grief is not provoked by the thought of any innate inferiority in the boy; she is worrying about the way he will be perceived by others, simply because of his nationality. In this context, the opening of Mrs Hall's contribution strikes a jarring note: '"Think of tomorrow!" – that is what no Irish peasant ever did yet, with a view to providing for it: at least no one I have had the opportunity of being acquainted with.'[40] At first glance, this looks like exactly the sort of attitude the Irish Mother feared. Still, as Mrs Hall's sketch progresses, her initial observation is modified in various ways. Larry's condition is not inevitable, but acquired from his habitual consumption of whisky. It does not necessarily apply to the female of the species: his wife has demonstrated her desire to prepare for the future, by her attempts to make him send his son to school, and refuse consent for his daughter's imprudent marriage. Sadly, though, he has refused to act on her wise suggestions. As it turns out, the peasantry have no monopoly of improvidence: Larry's employer, the 'generous good-natured landlord', has sacrificed his estates and social standing to the same error.[41] Still, both the authorial persona and Larry agree that improvidence is a specifically Irish fault, not shared by the English; Larry, showing no desire to emulate them, observes, '"that's the way they get rich, and sniff at the world"'.[42] Meanwhile, the beauty and fertility of 'my own pastoral village of Bannow', the inspiration and setting for Mrs Hall's Irish sketches, quietly suggest that Larry may be right in his assumption that tomorrow will somehow take care of itself.[43] The landscape seems to generate an atmosphere of condescendingly patronizing imperialism.

Mrs Hall's contributions to the annuals were consequently in harmony with the more or less deeply submerged imperialist political agenda of the publications, supported by their ubiquitous discourse of improvement. For example, 'Annie Leslie: An Irish Tale' demonstrates that the protagonist Annie, the offspring of an English father and a Scottish mother, with grandparents from Wales, 'stands as a somewhat exotic hybrid imago awaiting metamorphosis into full Irishness'.[44] This appears to be a fairly clumsy attempt by Mrs Hall to impregnate the story with allegorical references to the Acts of Union that came into effect in 1801, coupling the Kingdom of Great Britain, comprising England and Scotland, with the Kingdom of Ireland to form the United Kingdom of Great Britain and Ireland. The Union caused much discontent, but Mrs Hall supported it, believing it would make for closer relations between England and the land of her idyllic childhood. In 'Anne Leslie', Hall uses the tropes of family and marriage to interrogate the notion of the English imperative to reform the Irish people in an age of imperial expansion. Literature thus bears out the frequent 'typing of Ireland as an alternately dependent or unruly daughter, sister, or wife' as a constant and reliable means of delineating 'Irish political incapacity'.[45] Here Annie represents 'daughter' Ireland being pressured into a loveless and unwanted marriage by her anglicized suitor and English father. She is tempted with blandishments of a limited freedom (a new 'jaunting car' in which to drive to church).[46] The political aim of fostering support for the Union suffuses the story. In what is ostensibly a tale about a lovers' tiff, Hall is intent on putting the case against absentee landlords, with the deleterious effect of absenteeism borne out in the predicament of the characters. However, since she allows her characters to teeter on the brink of stereotype, the result is an attack on the unjust consequences of this system but not the root cause, colonization itself.

Mrs Hall also had her say on the political situation in contemporary England. *The Amulet* of 1832 contains 'The Mosspits', a sensational tale set against the backdrop of the recent 'Swing Riots' of 1830, which began in Kent and spread throughout the south of the country. Agricultural workers were driven to desperation because of low wages and high unemployment. The introduction of new technology, particularly the threshing machine, which meant that fewer hands were required on farms, exacerbated the situation: workers took matters into their own hands and burned houses, tithe barns, hayricks and cattle. The heroine, Agnes, is the virtuous and allegedly 'Methodistical' wife of Edward Hoskins, who falls under the influence of a man politically involved in the agrarian unrest, and is suspected of carrying out arson attacks.[47] Despite being relentlessly didactic, the story is quite thrilling; Lynne Vallone claims it as part of the young Princess Victoria's reading material. It includes dramatic scenes of 'class conflict, sexual predation, madness, and sudden death'.[48] The stoic virtue of Agnes is emphasized throughout; her character is the vehicle for Hall's desire to expose the evil of excess, whether through physical passion, political activism or intemperance, all of which prove disastrous to various characters in her Irish sketches.

Interesting parallels to Mrs Hall's attitude to the Irish appear in an anonymous article in the same volume, entitled 'Actual State of the Slave-trade on the Coast of Africa' and 'extracted principally from the journal of a gallant and distinguished naval officer who passed three years on the African coast, from which he has not long since returned'.[49] This piece incorporates a striking description of the inhabitants of 'Munro, on Cape Mesarado', and 'Caldwell, seven miles up the river St. Paul' in Liberia, which has a likeness in tone and content to Mrs Hall's descriptions of the inhabitants of Bannow.[50] Both the Irish of Bannow and the freed slaves of Cape Mesarado are considered to be a special case, the Irish descendants of 'Anglo-Norman' stock and the Africans the offspring of 'African slaves born in America and liberated'.[51] A tone of superior paternalism is conspicuous in the account of 'these industrious colonists': the author considers 'their minds strongly impressed with religious feelings, their manners serious and decorous, and their domestic habits neat and comfortable'.[52] According to Mrs Hall, the Irish of Bannow are also distinct from the general run of Irish people, being mainly 'descendants of the Anglo-Norman settlers, who, in the reign of the second Henry, invaded and conquered – or, rather, subdued – Ireland; and, until very recently, they retained so much of their ancient customs and manners, as actually to speak a language unknown in other districts of the Kingdom.'[53] Their 'English character' appears in 'an air of sturdy independence, which they really feel, and to which they are justly entitled, for it is achieved by their own honest industry.'[54] Elsewhere, they are actually called 'colonists'.[55]

It would seem from these examples that, if Mrs Hall's contributions to *The Spirit and Manners of the Age* and *The Amulet* were really furthering her husband's intentions, then his professed aim to blend religious instruction with literary amusement, without taking sides in polemical questions was, rather, an attempt to disguise the promulgation of a particular worldview that encompassed a deeply Protestant, anti-socialist and imperialist ideology. Similar features can be found in her contributions to *The Iris* and *Friendship's Offering*. All the annuals under discussion managed to instruct *and* entertain by providing the literary content necessary to balance material with an obviously religious message. However, they also provide the English reader with a distanced perspective on the habits and customs of the people in their colonial possession. Furthermore, they enclose these possibly dangerous foreigners within the pages of a book, where anxiety about possible insurrection by real people is rendered less acute. Books can, of course, be very dangerous but these volumes, with their high tone, cultural aspirations and prices, were not designed to be appealing, or even accessible, to insurrectionists of any persuasion.

When Carter Hall addressed the charge that the annuals were 'merely butterflies of a season', his wish was to increase their circulation by extending their life to the whole year and not just Christmas. However, his use of the butterfly analogy was apposite as, like the insect, the annuals as a 'species' were short-lived. Having unwittingly made a 'fatal agreement' and become a partner in the publication of *The Amulet*, Hall was responsible for the debts incurred when its publishers, Westley & Davis, became bankrupt. This 'terrible event', he records, 'utterly ruined me, and I had to begin life again.'[56] Nonetheless, the fashion for annuals had not suddenly ceased. Carter estimated that in their heyday, the public spent £100,000 on the seventeen different Christmas gift-books that he claims were published in 1829: a sum whose purchasing power would be equivalent to at least £8,000,000 today.[57] These publications 'vanished by degrees' and were eventually replaced by the 'tinsel' of the cheaper magazines.[58]

However frivolous some individual contributions may have been, the annuals remain a gilded resource for further research. Within their covers, it is possible to find revealed the tensions between all parties involved in the phenomenon of the annuals – authors, editors, publishers, illustrators and owners – and to discover, in the case of the Halls, a cultural and political agenda to promote Protestantism and to contain a view of Irish national identity within an imperialist ideology.

Conclusion

Queens of Literature: Royals, Role Models and the Construction of Women's History

by Louise Duckling

In 1886, Eva Hope (1834–1909) published *Queens of Literature of the Victorian Era*, a biographical work celebrating the exemplary lives of six women writers, opening with 'The Queen of Science', Mary Somerville (1780–1872), and closing with 'The Poet of Womanhood', Felicia Hemans (1793–1835).[1] By adopting the queenly metaphor, Hope aligned these women, as paragons of their sex, with the ultimate female role model of the age: the royal example of Victoria. The queen was an exceptional woman, simultaneously serving her queendom as imperial monarch and as a national icon of wifely, maternal and domestic virtue. Victoria therefore reigned over both public and private domains, as a figure of power and submission. As this book has demonstrated, the separate spheres ideology, which prescribed the private realm for women, was not a new phenomenon. However, a cult of domesticity became more deeply entrenched during Victoria's reign, epitomized in the passive and docile figure of the Angel in the House.[2] As a consequence, women entering the public sphere would have been wise to follow the queen's example. This final chapter will explore the idea of queens as role models, focusing on the complex ways in which the anomalous power of royal women is represented in nineteenth-century female biographies and anthologies. These publications cast light on women's lives within the period covered by this book, including many of those featured in this volume, revealing how their place in history was constructed. In so doing, they also suggest why the lives of so many women were posthumously neglected and remind us that there are many histories yet to be written.

Increasingly, in the nineteenth century, women writers – regardless of their intellectual achievements – could be ascribed an elevated or canonical status only if they had first succeeded as *women*, by maintaining appropriate gender standards. Naturally, the decorum of male writers was also open to scrutiny, with literary merit being established in biographical publications asserting the moral worth and significance of the author. An appetite for exploring the lives of the famous had grown in the eighteenth century as a result of the newly-emerging celebrity culture, fuelled in turn by the expanding literary market. Edifying lives were celebrated in biographies, literary histories, memoirs and anthologies, and also in the growing genres of elegies and obituaries described by Gillian Williamson in Chapter 5. Women writers often appeared in entirely separate volumes, reflecting gendered assumptions that they were naturally skilled in certain kinds of feminine genres, such as the hyperfeminine, lyrical verse associated with the figure of the poetess.[3] In the early decades of the nineteenth century, as ever more idealized fictions of femininity took hold, these publications became progressively more interested in the 'setting of womanly greatness above poetic genius'.[4]

Writing Queens and Royal Reputations

Queen Victoria was a fitting role model for women writers, not only because she set the bar for 'womanly greatness', but also because she was a highly-educated and prolific writer. She began a private journal in 1832, aged 13, which she maintained until her death in 1901. Four different versions of the journal survive in various original and transcribed forms, comprising 141 volumes and totalling in excess of 43,000 pages.[5] Extracts were published in *Leaves from the Journal of our Life in the Highlands*, which appeared in two private editions before its release on public sale in 1868, with a second volume, *More Leaves*, appearing in 1884. The books were immensely successful, documenting 'homely accounts of excursions' enjoyed in 'the loving companionship of the Prince Consort', while 'studiously' omitting 'all references to political questions, or to the affairs of Government'.[6] Despite the private and domestic tone, the editor makes a claim for the book's importance and historical value. 'What would not the historian give to have similar materials within his reach,' he asks, 'when writing about the reigns of the great Queen Elizabeth or the good Queen Anne?'[7]

Chroniclers may not have had access to bestsellers when writing the histories of earlier queens, but they were happy to supplement the publicly-known facts with speculation regarding the private lives of royal women, which sometimes bordered on fantasy. This is nowhere more evident than in the innumerable cultural and historical representations of Queen Elizabeth I, who arguably remains England's most enigmatic monarch. Even during her reign, Elizabeth's image was 'multiple and contested', as reflected in the myriad names by which she is still remembered, including Eliza, Good Queen Bess, Gloriana and the Virgin Queen.[8] As Carolyn D. Williams has highlighted in the Introduction, when John Knox published *The First Blast of the Trumpet against the Monstruous Regiment of Women* in 1558, the year of Elizabeth's accession, his views would have resonated with many. Beyond her reign, attitudes towards this atypical, unmarried and powerful queen remained complex, with admiration for Elizabeth's status as a national icon at variance with gendered concerns regarding her personal qualities, as a woman who refused to be domesticated. Scandalous anecdotes and episodes, based on little or no reliable evidence, became part of the ever-changing mythology of this profoundly unsettling queen. For example, the Virgin Queen is described in one apocryphal tale as owing her chastity to a physical 'membrana' or 'impediment', 'which made her incapable of man, though for her delight she tryed many', invoking wantonness in place of virtue.[9] At the other extreme, scandalous tales speculated on Elizabeth's love-life and hinted at the presence of a child or children.[10] These sexual controversies plainly owed a great deal to anxieties arising from Elizabeth's refusal to marry, reproduce and confirm the succession.[11] They are also deeply rooted in gendered concerns regarding Elizabeth's intellectual authority and her success in wielding absolute political power.

By the time of Victoria's reign, Elizabeth's reputation was at an all-time low. In her *Lives of the Queens of England*, Agnes Strickland (1796–1874) describes '"Our good queen Anne"', and not Elizabeth, as being 'the most popular female sovereign' up to that point in time.[12] In an extraordinarily back-handed compliment, Strickland describes how Anne's 'feminine helplessness of mind well fitted her for the limits to which an encroaching oligarchy had confined the functions of a British monarch'.[13] Queen Victoria also operated within this new and confined mode of queenship, as the modern constitutional monarchy had rendered Elizabeth's absolute power and executive style of government politically obsolete. The two queens could not, therefore, be judged in the same terms, but they were frequently compared. There was an enduring sense of nostalgia for Good Queen Bess of Merrie England, who was seen to have presided over the birth of science, modernity and empire associated with the splendour of Victoria's Great Britain. It was not too difficult, however, to highlight the irony in eulogizing the 'golden days of Queen Elizabeth'; in 1843, the editor of *The Illuminated Magazine* sardonically extolled the virtues of 'those merry, merry days, when men were whipped, imprisoned, branded, burnt, at little more than the mere will of Majesty'.[14]

Violence, vulgarity and vanity became the negative hallmarks of Elizabeth's queenly career, and even permeated attitudes towards her refined status as a learned lady. As Valerie Schutte has shown in Chapter 1, Elizabeth received one of the finest humanist educations of her day. Like Victoria, she was also an immensely prolific writer from a young age, producing letters, translations, verses, prayers and poems. Despite Elizabeth's historical importance, her body of work has generally been viewed in a fragmentary way and in relation to issues of policy or gender, rather than in literary terms. Aside from the textual difficulties surrounding her verse, with only two poems deemed to have survived in Elizabeth's own hand, they are almost always occasional poems responding to specific political events and are therefore out of step not only with the timeless aesthetics of high-status literature, but also with emerging gender conventions.[15]

This is the case with Elizabeth's most famous poem, 'The Doubt of Future Foes' (c.1571), which is associated with the Northern Rebellion of 1569. The rising was an unsuccessful attempt by Catholic nobles to replace Elizabeth with her cousin Mary, Queen of Scots (1542-87). The poem opens with an admission that 'The doubt of future foes / Exiles my present joy' (lines 1-2), but continues with rhetorical skill, authority and persuasion, and closes with a stark warning to those who may seek to challenge the queen's position:

> My rusty sword through rest
> Shall first his edge employ
> To pull their tops who seek such change
> Or gape for future joy. (lines 29-32)[16]

The violent threat of an imaginary sword appears to predict future events with startling accuracy: when Mary was beheaded in 1587, the poem would take on a new life and darker meaning. In 1589 it was included in *The Arte of English Poesie*, attributed to George Puttenham (1529–90/1), at a time when those events would have still been a very recent memory, and yet the poem is figured as 'passing sweete and harmonicall', coming from the pen of 'the most bewtifull, or rather bewtie of Queenes'.[17] Puttenham is commenting upon Elizabeth's technical writing skills within a wider treatise describing the complex art of '*poeticall Ornament*', but his praise was frequently cited (and often derided) in a more general context in later studies.[18]

The anthologist Alexander Dyce (1798–1869) quotes from *The Arte of English Poesie* in his *Specimens of British Poetesses* (1825), in order to introduce 'The Doubt of Future Foes' and provide critical and historical context.

However, Puttenham's analysis is undermined by Dyce's own preceding summary, which employs a scornful tone to describe Elizabeth's character, her work and the sycophancy of her admirers: 'The desire of shining as a poetess was one of the weaknesses of this illustrious queen, and her vanity, no doubt, made her regard as tributes justly paid, the extravagant praises, which the courtiers, and writers of her age, lavished on her royal ditties.'[19] Neither Elizabeth's poetry nor Elizabeth the woman conformed to the exemplary model of the nineteenth-century poetess, with all 'her sensibility, her tenderness, her grace', which the anthology sought to celebrate.[20] The appropriate qualities were identified by William Wordsworth when he praised the poetry of Anne Finch, whose life and work is discussed by Yvonne Noble in Chapter 4. In personal correspondence with Dyce in 1830, Wordsworth describes Finch's verse as being 'often admirable, chaste, tender, and vigorous; entirely free from sparkle, antithesis, and that over-culture, which reminds one – by its broad glare, its stiffness, and heaviness – of the double daisies of the garden, compared with their modest and sensitive kindred in the fields.'[21] Unsurprisingly, given these attributes, Dyce had already included four of Finch's poems in his *Specimens*.[22]

Dyce devalues Elizabeth's verse while advocating the superior poetic powers of her admittedly imperfect rival, 'that lovely, unfortunate, but surely not guiltless woman', Mary, Queen of Scots, and supplies an example of Mary's sentimental verse to buttress his argument.[23] In 1848, George Bethune (1805–62) also privileges Mary, who is cast in a more sympathetic light as a 'feminine character ill fitted … for the throne of a rude nation' and as a victim of Elizabeth's jealousy and ambition.[24] Bethune is prepared to make some concessions for Elizabeth, portraying her as a 'vain, pedantic, but really accomplished and intellectual' woman.[25] In contrast, Anna Jameson (1794–1860), one of Elizabeth's sternest detractors, casts Puttenham as a 'contemporary flatterer' and describes 'The Doubt of Future Foes', which she considers the queen's 'best poem', as 'contemptible trash'.[26]

While Elizabeth's verse has been relatively neglected and is little known, she is more famous for her remarkable speeches. These also pose challenges for the historian, as they may have been spoken extemporaneously or, if they did begin as written documents, Elizabeth may have delivered them from memory. As the speeches were not gathered for formal publication, there is no single trusted text, but an array of 'textually complicated' documents, which were sometimes written down after the fact, or display evidence of extensive revision or 'complex coproduction'.[27] While it can be difficult to determine the exact words spoken (or composed) by the queen in her political speeches, they were clearly part of a rhetorical strategy that aimed to position her as 'bound unto an husband, which is the kingdom of England' and mother to the nation.[28] This strategic positioning of Elizabeth within a domesticized queenship was generally rejected by nineteenth-century commentators, given her political agency.

The period's attitude towards women and power is illuminated by Anna Jameson's choice of epigraph for her *Memoirs of Celebrated Female Sovereigns* (1831): '*Nous sommes faites pour embellir le monde, plutôt que pour le commander*' ('We are made to embellish the world, rather than command it'). These words are ascribed to Madame Roland (1754–93), who may appear a curious ambassador for female submission given the fact she was at one time, albeit briefly, the most powerful woman in Paris. However, Roland's posthumously-published *Mémoires* (1795) secured her reputation as a virtuous and principled wife, mother and heroine of the French Revolution, who dutifully followed her husband to the guillotine. In contrast, Elizabeth was unmarried, signed death warrants and kept her own head. Jameson believed that Elizabeth was 'destitute of what is called *heart*, that is, of the capacity for all the gentle, generous, and kindly affections proper to her sex', and ruled with 'the most unfeeling despotism'.[29] Given the decorative and limited powers associated with Victoria's constitutional reign, it is therefore unsurprising that she would successfully negotiate the complex boundaries of rank and power, while Elizabeth is seen to fail.

Royal Role Models and Female Biographies

The commanding qualities that made Elizabeth a great queen simultaneously made her a bad woman, and therefore a complicated role model. This book has profiled a variety of women, both real and fictional, whose lives served a moral or instructive purpose with varying degrees of success. For example, the Dowager Countess of Lincoln's *Nurserie*, as discussed by Sara Read, demonstrates the tensions in Elizabethan and Stuart times between being a good aristocratic wife – by giving birth as often as possible – and being a good and godly mother who nursed her own infants, inevitably reducing the number of children from the marriage. *Advice to Unmarried Women*, written by an anonymous clergyman and discussed by Tabitha Kenlon, should provide moral clarity for its readers, as it is designed to provide a cautionary tale about how not to behave, yet the author's description of fallen women sometimes borders on the erotic, emulating the seductive nature of the sentimental novels of the period. Sarah Oliver explores the figure of the sentimental heroine in the eighteenth-century novel, while the principal roles available for actresses on the stage, as daughters, brides-to-be, wives and mothers, are conveyed by Jacqueline Mulhallen. In the eighteenth century, Elizabeth's female identity was increasingly at odds with these cultural representations of women. On the other hand, Mary, Queen of Scots, as wife, mother, lover and tragic victim, could occupy more easily the role of the distressed heroine of sensibility that was taking hold in the popular imagination.

In the nineteenth century, female biographies aimed to supplant these popular images, which were often morally ambiguous, with more edifying examples of womanly excellence. The biographies served as an educational device for girls and young ladies and could function in a similar way to conduct manuals, given their focus on exemplary lives. They could therefore be regarded, alongside the annuals described by Marion Durnin in Chapter 13, as another form of ideological control. The biographies frequently borrowed from earlier editions, and in this respect *A Cyclopaedia of Female Biography* (1866), edited by Henry Gardiner Adams (c.1811–81), is a classic example of the genre. Unlike the sumptuous annuals, and the elaborate American edition upon which it was based, *Female Biography* was designed to be 'a cheap and portable volume' and it purported to contain 'the life and character … of every woman remarkable for mental gifts or acquirements, moral virtues, or Christian graces'.[30] The biographical entry on Queen Victoria reflects her pre-eminent status as 'an accomplished lady, as perfect in her feminine as in her queenly character'.[31] She represents the 'model of female royalty', wielding '"monarch power," yet sweetly modified by the character of wife and mother'.[32] The book includes a decorative frontispiece in which the figure of Queen Victoria, as the woman *par excellence*, is surrounded by four female worthies: the honourable noblewoman Lady Rachel Russell (c.1636–1723), a dedicated wife and wise mother, who pleaded in vain for her husband's life when he was convicted for plotting against Charles II; Felicia Hemans, 'the sweet singer of the hearth, the home, and the affections', whom Eva Hope would later describe as 'The Poet of Womanhood'; the writer and philanthropist Hannah More, whose *Cheap Repository Tracts* on moral and religious topics sold in vast numbers in the 1790s; and the woman whose story opens this volume in Chapter 1, Lady Jane Grey.[33]

Lady Jane Grey ruled England for just nine days, but in the centuries that followed a variety of popular myths and legends developed around her name. She has been represented as a Protestant martyr, a pure young victim of adult ambition and a tragic lover. In *Female Biography*, Jane earns her place alongside Victoria as a young woman of astonishingly precocious intellect, to which 'were added the loveliest graces of woman, mildness, humility, and modesty'.[34] Jane's truly exceptional talent as a scholar is a known fact and becomes a central theme in her biographical entry, where it is carefully framed within a domestic context using anecdotes of varying reliability.

In the first of these stories, Jane is discovered in her apartment by the famous scholar Roger Ascham 'reading Plato's Phaedon, in the original Greek', a pursuit she had chosen in favour of a family hunting trip: '"I wist all their sport in the park is but a shadow to that pleasure that I find in Plato."'[35] An account of this episode was documented by Ascham himself, who believed Jane's preference reflected great credit on the lady and her tutor; in the context of a Victorian biography, it also conforms perfectly with ideals of private, female refinement.[36] In the second episode, Jane is confined once again; imprisoned in the Tower, she is reported to have written 'four epistles in Latin' and several letters, 'one to her sister, in Greek, exhorting her to maintain, in every trial, that fortitude and perseverance of which she trusted to give her the example.'[37] The historian David Hume (1711–76) believed that, with three days to live, this act of sublime scholarship was a sign of Jane's composure and 'presence of mind'; however, original sources are ambiguous and it seems unlikely that the letter was written in Greek.[38] Whichever language Jane used, the story clearly positions her as an impeccable role model, ideally qualified to write her sister a conduct book in epistolary form. The final tale of academic achievement occurs immediately prior to Jane's execution, when she presents the constable of the Tower with 'her tablets, in which she had just written three sentences in Greek, Latin, and English, suggested by seeing the dead body of her husband'.[39] These tablets, often described as table-books, do not survive; nevertheless, despite the lack of material evidence the story became an integral component in Jane's oft-repeated story.

The 'Constancy of Lady Jane Grey', appearing in the *Religious Magazine* in 1829, reports the three epigrams as having said 'that human justice was against his body, but divine mercy would be favourable to his soul'.[40] In many accounts such as these, Jane's conduct is described in terms bordering on hagiographic; elsewhere, chroniclers find it improbable that a 'young and amiable girl' could have 'written epigrams on the mutilated corpse of her husband'.[41] One of Jane's most famous detractors was Jane Austen, who famously mocked the episode in her juvenile work *The History of England*. Austen is sceptical regarding Jane Grey's knowledge of Greek:

> Whether she really understood that language or whether such a Study proceeded only from an excess of vanity for which I believe

> she was always rather remarkable, is uncertain. Whatever might be the cause, she preserved the same appearance of knowledge, and contempt of what was generally esteemed pleasure, during the whole of her Life, for she declared herself displeased with being appointed Queen, and while conducting to the Scaffold, she wrote a Sentence in Latin & another in Greek on seeing the dead Body of her Husband accidentally passing that way.[42]

Austen's cynical barbs remind us of an important fact: young women would not always have accepted with deference or admiration the idealized role models of women that were presented to them. Indeed, Austen wrote in one of her letters that 'pictures of perfection … make me sick and wicked'.[43] Her witty critique challenges the level of perfection accredited to Lady Jane Grey, not only as an unattainable virtue, but also – unlike Austen's own history writing – as rather humourless, pitiful and dull.

Exploring the Lives of Women: Writing History

The female memoirs, popular biographies and anthologies published in the nineteenth century were an attempt to construct a historical record of women's achievements, but their tendency to idealize exemplary women failed to capture the diverse experience of real women's lives. According to *Female Biography*, 'Elizabeth was rather noble as a queen, than amiable as a woman', but as a queen, her history could not be elided, regardless of her womanly status.[44] Yet the lives of countless other women could only be recorded if subversive elements were carefully disclaimed, negotiated or concealed. A case in point is Elizabeth Billington, the talented English opera singer featured in Chapter 10 by Brianna E. Robertson-Kirkland: her celebrated public talent secures her a mention in *Female Biography*, despite her private character, which is carefully put on record as being 'very bad'.[45] In the majority of cases difficult women's stories would be completely excluded from the pages of history.

It is important to recognize that the living reputation and posthumous fame of men, as well as women, could suffer as a consequence of many factors, including political, religious or class affiliation. However, in a patriarchal society, the question of gender decorum was an additional liability for unconventional women. The powerful paradigm of the Victorian angel – desexed, refined and confined – has played a dominant cultural role in the historical interpretation of women, both then and now, to the extent that it has obscured authentic accounts of female action and physicality, such as the incredible feats of skill and strength displayed by female athletes in the eighteenth century, revealed by Peter Radford in Chapter 12, or the concept of female sexual desire expounded in early modern England, discussed by Jennifer Evans in Chapter 3. In an age of sexual double standards, prostitutes could still be discovered in the pages of erotic memoirs, but they had no place in the official popular biographies; in any case, the mainstream female histories favoured conflict – exemplified in the rival queens Mary and Elizabeth – over the prostitute friendships explored by Julie Peakman in Chapter 9. The radical women writers presented in Chapter 6 by Marie Mulvey-Roberts were not only political and religious dissenters, but also had questionable love lives: unsurprisingly, they are generally omitted from the biographical record, despite the fact that one of these women – Mary Hays – contributed to the genre of female biographies by authoring two volumes herself.[46]

While the female histories explored in this chapter may seem deeply conventional, they nevertheless represent an attempt to record women's lives for posterity, however imperfectly, and women writers were increasingly invested, as critics, biographers and historians, in shaping a female historical and literary tradition. Towards the end of Victoria's reign, Eva Hope's *Queens of Literature* therefore takes its place in a long line of female biographies. Hope's rhetorical strategy is particularly interesting because, while she bestows symbolic crowns of womanhood upon her literary queens, the metaphor is also neatly employed to argue for their pre-eminence, power and influence. Indeed, in her opening chapter she claims that the science writer and astronomer Mary Somerville has 'demolished, once for all, the idea that a woman's brain is less strong than that of a man's'.[47] Women had in fact been demonstrating their intellectual parity with men for centuries, and with no greater visibility than the queens of England, yet even their intellectual achievements were subsumed into a narrative of pious domesticity. The biographical narratives explored in this chapter reveal how women's place in history was constructed according to societal norms, was prejudiced and partial, and was often disparaging. In 1832, Anna Jameson complained that history 'may make a pleasant companion but a most fallacious guide'; while this statement could be made at any time, about all history, Jameson believed this to be especially true in regard to women.[48] Members of the Women's Studies Group for the last three decades can attest that recovering women's history has indeed been a most pleasant, if sometimes frustrating, occupation, and will doubtless continue in the same fashion for many years to come.

Endnotes

Preface: Women's Studies Group, 1558–1837: Exploring the Lives of Women Since 1987

1. *Women's Writing* Special Issue 'Women Out Loud', eds Louise Duckling, Angela Escott, Daniel J.R. Grey, Victoria Joule, Sarah Oliver and Carolyn D. Williams, 17.1 (2010).
2. *Woman to Woman: Female Negotiations During the Long Eighteenth Century*, eds Carolyn D. Williams, Angela Escott and Louise Duckling (Newark: University of Delaware Press, 2010).

Introduction

1. [John Knox], *The First Blast of the Trumpet against the Monstruous Regiment of Women* ([Geneva: J. Poullain and A. Rebul], 1558), 47v.
2. *Ibid.*, 48r.
3. See E.W. Ives, 'Tudor Dynastic Problems Revisited', *Historical Review* 81, Issue 212 (2007), 255-79.
4. See Suzannah Lipscomb, *The King is Dead: The Last Will and Testament of Henry VIII* (London: Head of Zeus, 2015), 117-120, 183.
5. Primogeniture, or the law which meant males automatically took precedence over their female siblings, in the case of royal succession ended with The Succession to the Crown Act 2013 c. 20. The practical effect of this Act meant that when Prince Louis of Cambridge was born on 23 April 2018, his elder sister Princess Charlotte (b. 2 May 2015) retained her place as fourth in line to the throne. See <http://www.legislation.gov.uk/ukpga/2013/20/contents/enacted> (accessed May 2018).
6. L.G. Schwoerer, *The Revolution of 1688–89: Changing Perspectives* (Cambridge: Cambridge University Press, 2004), 3. See also James R. Hertzler, 'Who Dubbed It "The Glorious Revolution?"', *Albion: A Quarterly Journal Concerned with British Studies* (1987), 19:579-585.
7. See Tim Harris, *Revolution: The Great Crisis of the British Monarchy, 1685–1720* (Harmondsworth: Penguin, 2006).
8. 'An Act for the further Limitation of the Crown and better securing the Rights and Liberties of the Subject', 12º and 13º Gul. III c.2, 1700 & 1701, *Statutes*

of the Realm, ed. Alexander Luders and others, 11 vols (London: Dawsons, 1810–28), 7:636-7.

9. Anon., *An Account of the interment of her Royal Highness the Princess Charlotte, in St. George's Chapel, Windsor, on Wednesday, Nov. 19, 1817* (Newcastle: J. S., 1817), 3.
10. Anon., *Cabala, Mysteries of State* (London: M.M.G. Bedell and T. Collins, 1653), 260.
11. Knox, *First Blast*, 28r.
12. See Carolyn D. Williams, '"Difficulties, in no Degree Clear'd up": The Controversial Mother, 1600–1800', in *The Female Body in Medicine and Literature*, eds A.S. Mangham and Greta Depledge (Liverpool: Liverpool University Press, 2010), 16-33.
13. James Boswell, *The Journal of a Tour to the Hebrides, with Samuel Johnson, L.L.D.* (London: Charles Dilly, 1785), 250.
14. Loss of chastity, however, did not always lead to social ostracism. See Soile Ylivuori, 'Rethinking Female Chastity and Gentlewomen's Honour in Eighteenth-Century England', *Historical Journal*, (2016), 59, 1:71-97. Lower-class women often sought to supplement their earnings by prostitution, and gave it up after a few years for low-status jobs or marriage. See Tony Henderson, *Disorderly Women in Eighteenth-Century London: Prostitution and Control in the Metropolis, 1730–1830* (London: Longman, 1999), 14-15, 50.
15. See Martin Madan, *Thelyphthora; or, A Treatise on Female Ruin, in its Causes, Effects, Consequences, Prevention, and Remedy*, 2 vols (London: J. Dodsley, 1780), 2:329.
16. *Ibid.*, 1:200-1, n.
17. *Ibid.*, 1:298-9.
18. James Henry Lawrence, introduction to *The Empire of the Nairs: Or, the Rights of Women. An Utopian Romance*, 4 vols (London: T. Hookham. Jun., and E.T. Hookham, 1811), 1:ii.
19. *Ibid.*, 3:4.

Chapter One: Michelangelo Florio and Lady Jane Grey: A Case Study of a Book Dedication to a Royal Tudor Lady

1. See Tara Wood, '"To the most godlye, virtuos, and myghtye Princess Elizabeth": Identity and Gender in the Dedications to Elizabeth I' (PhD thesis, Arizona State University, 2008); Valerie Schutte, *Mary I and the Art of Book Dedications: Royal Women, Power, and Persuasion* (New York: Palgrave Macmillan, 2015); Valerie Schutte, 'Perceptions of Princesses: Pre-accession Book Dedications to Mary and Elizabeth Tudor', in *Unexpected Heirs in Early*

Modern Europe: Potential Kings and Queens, ed. Valerie Schutte (New York: Palgrave Macmillan, 2017), 63-83.

2. For the study of all printed book dedications in the period covered by this chapter, see Franklin B. Williams, Jr., *Index of Dedications and Commendatory Verses in English Books before 1641* (London: Bibliographical Society, 1962), in conjunction with the Electronic English Short Title Catalogue (STC) and Early English Books Online (EEBO). See also Suzanne W. Hull, *Chaste, Silent & Obedient: English books for women, 1475–1640* (San Marino, California: Huntington Library, 1982).
3. BL Sloane MS 3011. It is undated, but could not have been written any later than 1553, when Jane was imprisoned.
4. See Cambridge University Library, Dd.XI.46, 3r. For a printed edition, see Giuliano Pellegrini, 'Michelangelo Florio e le sue "Regole de la Lingua Thoscana"', *Studi di Filologia Italiana*, 12 (1954), 77-204.
5. See Judith Richard, *Elizabeth I* (Oxon: Routledge, 2012), 16; Aysha Pollnitz, *Princely Education in Early Modern Britain* (Cambridge: Cambridge University Press, 2015), 219.
6. See 25° Hen. VIII c. 22, 1533; 28° Hen. VIII c. 7, 1536; 35° Hen. VIII c. 1, 1543, in *Statutes of the Realm*, ed. Alexander Luders and others, 11 vols (London: Dawsons, 1810-28), 3:471-4, 655-62, 955-8.
7. See National Archives, Kew, E/23/4, f. 13.
8. For testimony on her father's attempt to marry Jane to the king, see '*The Lord Marques of* Dorsett. Numb. 4' in Samuel Haynes, ed., *A Collection of State Papers Relating to Affairs in the Reigns of King Henry VIII. King Edward VI. Queen Mary, and Queen Elizabeth, From the Year 1542 to 1570. Left by William Cecill Lord Burghley* (London: William Bowyer, 1740), 76-7.
9. Inner Temple Library, MS Petyt 47, f. 317. For a transcript, see John Gough Nichols, ed., *The Chronicle of Queen Jane, and of Two Years of Queen Mary, and especially of the Rebellion of Sir Thomas Wyat* (London: Camden Society, 1850), Appendix I, 89.
10. *Chronicle*, 94.
11. *Ibid.*, 1.
12. *Ibid.*, 3.
13. *Ibid.*, 10.
14. *Ibid.*, 54-9.
15. See David R. Carlson, 'Royal Tutors in the Reign of Henry VII', *The Sixteenth Century Journal*, 22 (1991), 253-279, and Pollnitz, *Princely Education*, 228-50.
16. Pollnitz, *Princely Education*, 228.
17. See Eric Ives, *Lady Jane Grey: A Tudor Mystery* 2nd ed. (Oxford: Wiley-Blackwell, 2011), 60.

18. Leanda de Lisle, *The Sisters who would be Queen: The Tragedy of Mary, Katherine & Lady Jane Grey* (London: HarperPress, 2009), 30.
19. Letter 110, to Johann Sturm, [Augsburg], 14 December 1550 in *The Whole Works of Roger Ascham, now first Collected and Revised, with a Life of the Author*, ed. J.A. Giles, 3 vols (London: John Russell Smith, 1864–1865), 1.2:227.
20. *Ibid.*, 228.
21. National Archives, Kew, SP10/15 (numbers 79, 79(i), 79 (ii), EXT 9/51). For a nineteenth-century translation by H. Claud Hamilton, see Agnes Strickland, *Lives of the Tudor Princesses Including Lady Jane Grey and Her Sisters* (London: Longmans, Green and Co., 1868), 133-134. The chapter on 'Lady Jane Gray' [*sic*] was written by Agnes Strickland's sister, Elizabeth Strickland (1794–1875). See Rosemary Mitchell, 'Agnes Strickland', *Oxford Dictionary of National Biography* (Oxford: Oxford University Press, 2004).
22. According to *Lives of the Tudor Princesses*, 133, n. 2, 'Mr. Hamilton found it was a lady by the pronouns'. This seems unlikely, since the pronouns used are either gender neutral (e.g. σοὶ [soi] 'to you') or governed by the gender of the noun to which they refer (e.g. ἐμῆς …εὐνοίας [emes eunoias] 'my affection'). Mr Hamilton's case is, however, proved by the writer's use of a present participle in the feminine gender (ἐλπίζουσα [elpizousa] 'hoping') applied to herself.
23. See Gemma Allen, *The Cooke Sisters: Education, Piety and Politics in Early Modern England* (Manchester: Manchester University Press, 2013), 33.
24. British Library, Royal MS 2 D. XXVIII, fol. 1b.
25. *A Godly Medytacyon of the christen sowle, concerninge a love towardes God and hys Christe, compyled in frenche by Lady Margarete quene of Naverr, and aptely translated into Englysh by the right vertuouse lady Elyzabeth doughter to our late soverayne Kynge Henri the viii* [Wesel: Dirk van der Straten, 1548], 9r. The original is Bodleian Library, Oxford, MS. Cherry 36.
26. John Foxe, *The seconde Volume of the Ecclesiasticall Historie, conteining the Acts and Monuments of Martyrs* (London: John Day, 1583), 1422.
27. From *The Byble which is all the holy Scripture: in which are contained the Olde and Newe Testament truly and purely translated into Englysh by Thomas Matthew* [Antwerp: Printed by Matthew Crom for Richard Grafton and Edward Whitchurch, London], 1537.
28. Foxe, *The seconde Volume*, 1422.
29. Letter 204, Conrad ab Ulmis to Conrad Pellican, [Bradgate], 29 May 1551 in *Original Letters Relative to the English Reformation, Written During the Reigns of King Henry VIII., King Edward VI., and Queen Mary: Chiefly from the Archives of Zurich. Translated from Authenticated Copies of the Autographs, and Edited by*

the Parker Society, ed. Hastings Robinson, The Second Portion. (Cambridge: Cambridge University Press, 1847), 432.

30. *Loc. cit.*
31. See Benjamin Pohl and Leah Tether, 'Books Fit for a King: The Presentation Copies of Martin Bucer's *De regno Christi* (London, British Library, Royal MS. 8 B. VII) and Johannes Sturm's *De periodis* (Cambridge, Trinity College, II.12.21 and London, British Library, C.24.e.5)', *Electronic British Library Journal* (2015), Article 7, 1-35.
32. Letter 128, to Sturm, Augsburg, 21 August 1551 in Ascham, *Whole Works*, 1.2:297. The book in question was *Aeschinis et Demosthenis orationes duae contrariae. Commentariolum J. Sturmii in easdem Hecatommeres* (Argentorati [Strasbourg]: W. Rihelius, 1550).
33. See *ibid.*, 298.
34. *Calendar of the Patent Rolls, Philip and Mary*, 1 (London: Public Records Office, 1970), 53.
35. Michael Wyatt, *The Italian Encounter with Tudor England: A Cultural Politics of Translation* (Cambridge: Cambridge University Press, 2005), 99.
36. See Michelangelo Florio, *Historia de la vita e de la morte de l'Illustriss. Signora Giovanna Graia, gia Regina eletta e publicata d'Inghilterra: e de le cose accadute in quel regno dopo la morte del Re Edoardo VI* ([Middelburg]: Richardo Pittore [i.e. Schilders], 1607), 28. Written in 1561, this is the most contemporary biography of Jane Grey.
37. BL Sloane MS 3011, 1r.
38. *Loc. cit.*
39. *Loc. cit.*
40. *Ibid.*, 1v.
41. Florio, *Historia*, 26.
42. BL Sloane MS 3011, 1v.
43. *Ibid.*, 1v.
44. See *ibid.*, 2r.
45. *Loc. cit.*
46. Wyatt, *The Italian Encounter*, 213.
47. BL Sloane MS 3011, 24v.
48. See 25r, 30v.
49. 84v.
50. 93v.
51. BL, Royal MS 2 D XXVIII, 2a. The dating of this manuscript is unclear, but it was most likely given to Mary at a point in which her father was married, which is why Morley anticipated more royal children.

52. See Schutte, *Mary I*, 47-8.
53. See Julie Crawford, *Mediatrix: Women, Politics, and Literary Production in Early Modern England* (Oxford: Oxford University Press, 2014), 3.
54. *A Godly Medytacyon*, A2r.
55. See Disertissimi Viri Rogeri Aschami, *Familiarium Epistolarum Libri Tres* (London: Francis Coldock [1576]), 7-8.
56. See Pellegrini, 'Michelangelo Florio e le sue "Regole de la Lingua Thoscana"', 90, 100.
57. Cambridge University Library, Dd.XI.46, 3r.
58. *Ibid.*, 2r.
59. *Ibid.*, 2r.
60. *Ibid.*, 2v.
61. *Ibid.*, 3r.
62. *Ibid.*, 2v.
63. *Ibid.*,105v.
64. See De Lisle, *The Sisters*, 122, 128.
65. Wyatt, *Italian Encounter*, 100.
66. See Valerie Schutte, 'Perceptions of Sister Queens: A Comparison of Printed Book Dedications to Mary and Elizabeth Tudor', *Sederi Yearbook* (2017), 149-66.

Chapter Two: '*The* Wine *much better then the* Bush': Thomas Lodge's Address to the Reader in *The Countesse of Lincolnes Nurserie*

The writer's thanks go to Carolyn D. Williams for her input and research into this chapter.

1. 'Mother's legacy' texts include *The Mothers Blessing* (1616) by Dorothy Leigh (d. c.1616), *The Mothers Legacie, To her unborne childe* (1624) by Elizabeth Jocelin (1596–1622), and *A Ladies Legacie to her Daughters* by Elizabeth Richardson, Baroness Cramond (1576/77–1651), first written in 1625 but not published until 1645. For modern critical editions, see Sylvia Brown, ed., *Women's Writing in Stuart England: The Mothers' Legacies of Dorothy Leigh, Elizabeth Joscelin and Elizabeth Richardson* (Stroud: Sutton Publishing, 1999). On the Puritan connection, see Rachel Trubowitz, '"Nourish-Milke": breast-feeding and the crisis of Englishness, 1600–1660', *JEGP*, 99, 1 (2000), 29-49.
2. Alice Walker, 'The life of Thomas Lodge', *Review of English Studies*, 10 (1934), 46-54, 46.
3. Thomas Lodge, '*Protogenes* can know *Apelles*' (title page missing), [London: H. Singleton?, 1579], 6.
4. See *The Complete Works of Thomas Lodge*, 4 vols, ed. Edmund Gosse (Glasgow: Hunterian Society, 1883); Thomas Lodge, trans., *The Famous and Memorable*

Workes of Josephus ([London]: G. Bishop, S. Waterson, P. Short, and Tho. Adams, 1602); Thomas Lodge, trans., *The Workes of Lucius Annaeus Seneca* (London: William Stansby, 1614); and Thomas Lodge, trans., Simon Goulart's *Learned Summary upon the famous Poeme of William Saluste Lord of Bartas* (London: John Grismand, 1621).

5. Thomas Lodge, *A Margarite of America* (London: John Busbie, 1596), A2r.
6. *Ibid.*, A2v.
7. *The Dictionary of syr Thomas Eliot knyght* (London: Thomas Berthelet, 1538), sub 'Momus'.
8. See 'To F.M. *Satyre*. 3.' In T[homas] L[odge], *A fig for Momus: Containing Pleasant varietie, included in Satyres, Eclogues, and Epistles* (London: Clement Knight, 1595), E1v-E3v.
9. Lodge, *A fig for Momus*, G2v.
10. *Ibid.*, H1r.
11. J.F.D. Shrewsbury, *A History of the Bubonic Plague in the British Isles* (Cambridge: Cambridge University Press, 1970), 284.
12. C.D. O'Malley, 'Tudor Medicine and Biology', *Huntingdon Library Quarterly* 32 (1968), 1-27, 11.
13. Thomas Lodge, *A Treatise of the Plague* (London: Edward White and N[icholas] L[ing], 1603), A2r.
14. *Ibid.*, A3v.
15. See Eliane Cuvelier, '"A treatise of the plague" de Thomas Lodge (1603): traduction d'un ouvrage médical français', *Études Anglaises* 21 (1968), 395-403.
16. Alexandra Halasz, 'Thomas Lodge', *Oxford Dictionary of National Biography* (Oxford: Oxford University Press, 2004).
17. *Ibid.*
18. *Ibid.*
19. See David Lindley, *The Trials of Frances Howard: Fact and Fiction at the Court of King James* (London: Routledge, 1993).
20. For dedications see Schutte, *supra*, nn. 1-2; a useful introduction to paratext in general is Gérard Genette, translated by Marie Maclean, 'Introduction to the Paratext', *New Literary History*, 22.2 (1991), 261-72. For early modern paratext, see Heidi Brayman Hackel, *Reading Material in Early Modern England: Print, Gender, and Literacy* (Cambridge: Cambridge University Press, 2005), 69-136.
21. Brayman Hackel, *Reading Material*, 104.
22. [Elizabeth Clinton, Dowager Countess of Lincoln], *The Countesse of Lincolnes Nurserie* (Oxford: John Lichfield and James Short, 1622), A4r.
23. Thomas Lodge, trans., *The Workes of Lucius Annaeus Seneca* (London: William Stansby, 1614), *b*5r.

24. [Thomas Lodge], *Catharos. Diogenes in his Singularitie* (London: John Busbie, 1591), A2v.
25. [Thomas Lodge], *Wits Miserie, and the Worlds Madnesse: Discovering the Devils Incarnat of this Age* (London: Cuthbert Burby, 1596), Aivr, Aivv.
26. William Shakespeare, *Comedies, Histories, & Tragedies*, eds John Heminge and Henry Condell (London: W. Jaggard, Ed. Blount, I. Smithweeke and W. Aspley, 1623), A3r.
27. *Countesse of Lincolnes Nurserie*, A4v.
28. See *ibid.*, 16, for Clinton's failure to nurse her own children.
29. Bridget Clinton, née Fiennes, was the daughter of William Fiennes, first Viscount Saye and Sele (1582–1662), so a cousin of her husband Theophilus, whom she married in 1620. The couple had nine children, but could only just have started their family at the time Clinton was inspired to write her book. Her date of death is unknown, but the 4th earl remarried to Elizabeth Gorges (1604–75) in c.1644. Gorges was also his cousin, her mother being born Lady Elizabeth Clinton.
30. *Ibid.*, A2v.
31. *Ibid.*, A4r.
32. *Loc. cit.*
33. *Loc. cit.*
34. *Ibid.*, 11.
35. *Ibid.*, A4v.
36. Shakespeare, *Comedies, Histories, & Tragedies*, 207. See also Morris Palmer Tilley, *A Dictionary of the Proverbs in England in the Sixteenth and Seventeenth Centuries* (Ann Arbor: University of Michigan Press, 1950), 730-1, W462, sub 'Good WINE needs no bush (ivy bush, sign)'.
37. 'The censure of *Thomas Lodge* Gent: upon the *Authors Booke*', in Peter Bales, *The Writing Schoolemaster: Conteining three Bookes in one; The first, teaching Swift writing; The second, True writing; The third, Faire writing* (London: Thomas Orwin, 1590), B1r.
38. *Countesse of Lincolnes Nurserie*, A4v.
39. All biblical texts are from *The Holy Bible, Conteyning the Old Testament, and the New* (London: Robert Barker, 1612).
40. *Ibid.*, 'The Translators to the Reader', A3v.
41. *Countesse of Lincolnes Nurserie*, 17.
42. *Ibid.*, A4v.
43. *Ibid.*, A2v–A3r.
44. *Ibid.*, 6.
45. See *Canones et Decreta Sacrosancti Oecumenici Concilii Tridentini sub Paulo III. Julio III. Et Pio IV* (Dillingen: Sebald Mayer, 1564), 58r-63r.

46. John Foxe, *The seconde Volume of the Ecclesticall Historie, conteining the Acts and Monuments of Martyrs* (London: John Day, 1583), 1419.
47. *Countesse of Lincolnes Nurserie*, 5; Rachel Trubowitz, *Nation and Nurture in Seventeenth-Century English Literature* (Oxford: Oxford University Press, 2012), 19, 46.
48. *Countesse of Lincolnes Nurserie*, 5.
49. [Thomas Lodge], *Prosopopeia, Containing the Tears of the holy, blessed, and sanctified Marie, the Mother of God* (London: E. White, 1596), A5r.
50. *Ibid.*, G7v.
51. John Bale, ed., *A Godly Medytacyon of the christen sowle, concerninge a love towardes God and hys Christe, compyled in frenche by Lady Margarete quene of Naverr, and aptely translated into Englysh by the right vertuouse lady Elyzabeth doughter to our late soverayne Kynge Henri the viii* [Wesel: Dirk van der Straten, 1548], 9v.
52. [John Ponet], *A Short Catechisme, or playne instruction, conteynynge the summe of Christian learninge, sett fourth by the Kings majesties authoritie, for all Scholemaisters to teache* (London: John Day, 1553), Aiiv-Aiiir.
53. *Ibid.*, Fol. XXr.
54. John Earle, *Micro-cosmographie. Or, a Peece of the World Discovered; In Essayes and Characters* (London: Robert Allot, 1628), H6v-H7r.
55. See Valerie Wayne, 'Advice for Women from Mothers and Patriarchs', in *Women and Literature in Britain 1500–1700*, ed. Helen Wilcox (Cambridge: Cambridge University Press, 1996), 56-79, 60. For 'Puerpera' in the original Latin, see Desiderius Erasmus, *Familiarium colloquiorum opus* (London: Henry Bynneman, 1571), 379-401. For a scholarly modern English translation, see Desiderius Erasmus, *Colloquies, in Collected Works of Erasmus*, vol. 39, collected and annotated by Craig R. Thompson (Toronto: University of Toronto Press, 1997), 590-617.
56. 'A Dialogue of a Woman in Childe-bed' in [Erasmus], trans. W[illiam] B[urton], *Seven Dialogues both Pithie and Profitable* (London: Nicholas Ling, 1606), N4v, O1r.
57. See Margo Todd, 'Humanists, Puritans and the Spiritualized Household', *Church History*, 49, 1 (1980), 18-34.
58. Edward Andrews Tenney, *Thomas Lodge* (Ithaca: Cornell University Press, 1935), 186.
59. Brayman Hackel, *Reading Material*, 103.
60. Thomas Lodge, *Euphues Shadow* (London: John Busbie, 1592), A4r.
61. Earle, *Micro-cosmographie*, A3r; see Ponet, *Catechisme*, Aiir.
62. Dorothy Leigh, *The Mothers Blessing: Or, the godly Counsaile of a Gentlewoman, not long since deceased, left behind for her Children* (London: John Budge, 1621), A5r.

63. Elizabeth Jocelin, *The Mothers Legacie, To her unborne Childe* (London: William Barret, 1624), a4r, B1r, B1v-B2r.
64. *Ibid.*, A3r, A4v.
65. *Countesse of Lincolnes Nurserie*, 12.
66. See Catherine Parr, *The lamentacion of a sinner, made by the most vertuous Ladie, Quene Caterin, bewayling the ignoraunce of her blind life: set furth and put in print at the instaunt desire of the righte gracious ladie Caterin Duchesse of Suffolke, & the earnest requeste of the right honourable Lord, William Parre, Marquesse of North Hampton* (London: Edwarde Whitchurche, 1547).

Chapter Three: God-Given Pleasure: Aphrodisiacs, Fertility and Sexual Pleasure in Early Modern England

1. *The Diary of Samuel Pepys*, eds Robert Latham and William Matthews, 11 vols (London: Bell, 1970–1983), 5(1971):222.
2. *The Autobiography and Correspondence of Sir Simonds D'Ewes, Bart., during the Reigns of James I and Charles I*, ed. James Orchard Halliwell, 2 vols (London: Richard Bentley, 1845), 1:2.
3. *Ibid.*, 1:416.
4. *Ibid.*, 1:419-20.
5. See A. Marsh, *The Ten Pleasures of Marriage, Relating All the delights and contentments that are mask'd under the bands of Matrimony* (London: s.n., 1682), 76.
6. *Ibid.*, 77.
7. All biblical texts are from *The Holy Bible, Conteyning the Old Testament, and the New* (London: Robert Barker, 1612). See also Genesis 1:28 for similar instructions to the first humans.
8. Jane Sharp, *The Midwives Book. Or the whole Art of Midwifry discovered* (London: Simon Miller, 1671), 177.
9. Robert Johnson, *Praxis Medicinae Reformata: or, the Practice of Physick Reformed* (London: Brabazon Aylmer, 1700), 245.
10. For barren women, see: Genesis 11:30, Genesis 25:21 and Judges 13:2; for barren land, see: 2 Kings 2:19 and Psalm 107:34.
11. Jakob Rueff, *The Expert Midwife, Or An Excellent and most necessary Treatise of the generation and birth of Man* (London: S. B[urton], 1637), Book 6, Chapter 1, 11-12 (separately paginated). Foliation Bb2r-Bb2v.
12. See James T. Johnson, 'English puritan thought on the ends of marriage', *Church History* 38, 4 (1969), 429-36, 429.
13. See Susan C. Karant-Nunn and Merry E. Wiesner-Hanks, eds, *Luther on Women: A Sourcebook* (Cambridge: Cambridge University Press, 2003), 137.

14. See Erik R. Seeman, '"It is better to marry than to burn": Anglo-American attitudes towards celibacy, 1600-1800', *Journal of Family History*, 24, 4 (1999), 397-419, 400.
15. Patricia Crawford, *Blood, Bodies and Families in Early Modern England* (Abingdon: Routledge, 2014), 56.
16. See William Perkins, trans. Thomas Pickering, *Christian Oeconomie* (London: Felix Kyngston, 1609), 54, 111, 115; William Gouge, *Domesticall Duties* in *The Workes of William Gouge In Two Volumes: The First, Domesticall Duties. The Second, The Whole Armour of God* (London: John Grismond, 1627), STC (2nd ed.) 12109a, 106, 130-131, separately paginated. (*Domesticall Duties* is bound second).
17. See Alan Macfarlane, *Marriage and Love in England: Modes of Reproduction, 1300–1840* (Oxford: Basil Blackwell, 1986), 51.
18. See *ibid.*, 60.
19. Cissie C. Fairchilds, *Women in Early Modern Europe, 1500–1700* (Harlow: Pearson Longman, 2007), 91.
20. See Angus McLaren, *Reproductive Rituals: the Perception of Fertility in England from the Sixteenth Century to the Nineteenth Century* (London and New York: Methuen, 1984), 32.
21. See Daphna Oren-Magidor, '"Make me a fruitfull vine": dealing with infertility in early modern England' (PhD thesis, Brown University, 2012), Introduction.
22. Anonymous, *Fumblers-Hall, Kept And holden in Feeble-Court, at the sign of the Labour-in-vain, in Doe-little-Lane* ([London?]: J. Clarke, W. Thackeray and T. Passinger, [1675]), 7.
23. Anonymous, *The Mistaken Mid-wife* ([London]: F. Coles, T. Vere, J. Wright and J. Clarke, [1674-9]).
24. Sharp, *The Midwives Book*, 167. See Genesis 3:16.
25. See Anonymous, *The Mistaken Mid-wife*.
26. Anonymous, *The English Midwife Enlarged* (London: Thomas Sawbridge, 1682), 183.
27. *Oxford English Dictionary Online*, s.v. 'exquisite', A.1.a, <http://www.oed.com> (accessed October 2017).
28. Robert Barret, *A Companion for Midwives, Child-bearing Women, and Nurses* (London: Thomas Ax, 1699), 59.
29. Robert Pierce, *Bath Memoirs: or, Observations in Three and Forty Years Practice, at the Bath* (Bristol: H. Hammond, 1697), 195.
30. *Ibid.*, 197.
31. See Sharp, *The Midwives Book*, 178.

32. Laevinus Lemnius, *The Secret Miracles of Nature* (London: Humphrey Moseley, John Sweeting, John Clark and George Sawbridge, 1658), 26.
33. See Philippa Pullar, *Consuming Passions: a History of English Food and Appetites* (London: Hamish Hamilton, 1970), 235-40.
34. See McLaren, *Reproductive Rituals*, 31.
35. See *ibid.*, 38.
36. For a full discussion of early modern aphrodisiacs and their qualities see Jennifer Evans, *Aphrodisiacs, Fertility and Medicine in Early Modern England* (Woodbridge: The Boydell Press, 2014), 87-130.
37. For rocket see William Turner, *The First and Seconde Partes of the Herbal of William Turner* (Cologne: [the heirs of] Arnold Birckman, 1568), 212; for ginger Thomas Newton, *Approoved Medicines and Cordiall Receiptes* (London: Thomas Marshe, 1580), 46v-47r.
38. For capons, parsnips and eryngo see Anonymous, *Aristoteles Master-Piece* (London: J. How, 1684), 12.
39. For borax, see Théophile Bonet, *Mercurius Compitalitius: or, a Guide to the Practical Physician* (London: Thomas Flesher, 1684), 694; for salt meats, see Jacques Ferrand, *Erotomania* (Oxford: Edward Forrest, 1645), 245.
40. Evans, *Aphrodisiacs, Fertility and Medicine*, *loc. cit.*
41. Lemnius, *Secret Miracles*, 27.
42. Bonet, *Mercurius compitalitius*, 694-5.
43. Isbrand van Diemerbroeck, *The Anatomy of Human Bodies* (London: W. Whitwood, 1694), 191.
44. Lemnius, *Secret Miracles*, 152-3.
45. John Sadler, *The Sick Womans Private Looking-glasse (Wherein methodicaly are handled all uterine affects, or diseases arising from the Wombe)* (London: Philemon Stephens and Christopher Meredith, 1636), 118–9.
46. J.S., *A Short Compendium of Chirurgery: Containing its Grounds & Principles* (London: Charles Blount, 1678), 100.
47. Lazarus Riverius (Lazare Rivière), trans. Nicholas Culpeper et al., *The Practice of Physick, in Seventeen several Books. Wherein is plainly set forth, The Nature, Cause, Differences, and Several Sorts of Signs; Together with the Cure of all Diseases in the Body of Man* (London: George Sawbridge, 1678), 503.
48. John Marten, *Gonosologium Novum* (London: N. Crouch et al., 1709), 50.
49. *Ibid.*, 1-2.
50. Helkiah Crooke, *Mikrokosmographia: A Description of the Body of Man* (London: William Jaggard, 1615), 200.
51. Lemnius, *Secret Miracles*, 8.

Stilts

1. *A Most Certain, Strange, and true Discovery of a Witch* (London: John Hammond, 1643), 4. A reproduction of the cover image can be found in the plates section.
2. *Ibid.*, 5.
3. *Ibid.*, 7.

Chapter Four: Tweaking the Biography of Anne Finch

1. *The Poems of Anne Countess of Winchilsea from the original edition of 1713 and from unpublished manuscripts*, ed. Myra Reynolds (Chicago: The University of Chicago Press, 1903), 4-5.
2. *Poems of Anne Countess of Winchilsea*, 192-3.
3. See *The Anne Finch Wellesley Manuscript Poems: A Critical Edition*, ed. Barbara McGovern and Charles H. Hinnant (Athens and London: The University of Georgia Press, 1998); Barbara McGovern, *Anne Finch and Her Poetry: A Critical Biography* (Athens and London: The University of Georgia Press, 1992); Charles H. Hinnant, *The Poetry of Anne Finch: An Essay in Interpretation* (Newark: University of Delaware Press; London and Toronto: Associated University Presses, 1994).
4. See Paula R. Backscheider, *Eighteenth-Century Women Poets and Their Poetry: Inventing Agency, Inventing Genre* (Baltimore: The Johns Hopkins University Press, 2005), 39; Susan Staves, *A Literary History of Women's Writing in Britain, 1660–1789* (Cambridge: Cambridge University Press, 2006), 138-9.
5. See Charles Dalton, *English Army Lists and Commission Registers 1661–1714*, 6 vols (London: Eyre and Spottiswoode, 1892–1904), 1:299. See also Edward Chamberlayne, *Angliae Notitia or the Present State of England*, 2 parts in 1 (London: R. Bently, 1684), 1:228, 233.
6. McGovern, *Anne Finch*, 30.
7. W.J. Cameron, 'Anne Countess of Winchilsea: A Guide for the Future Biographer', 2 vols, (Unpublished MA dissertation, Victoria University College, New Zealand, 1951), 1:50.
8. *Poems of Anne Countess of Winchilsea*, 417.
9. Dalton, *English Army Lists*, 1:299.
10. For further details, see the Introduction.
11. See Sonia P. Anderson, 'Heneage Finch, third earl of Winchilsea', *Oxford Dictionary of National Biography* (Oxford: Oxford University Press, 2004).
12. *Poems of Anne Countess of Winchilsea*, 411.
13. McGovern, *Anne Finch and her Poetry*, 68; Wright, *Producing Women's Poetry*, 154.
14. Michael Gavin, 'Critics and Criticism in the Poetry of Anne Finch', *ELH* 78 (2011), 633-55, 640.

15. 'AN ACT for the Abrogating of the Oathes of Supremacy and Allegiance and Appointing other Oathes', I° GUL. & MAR. c. 8, 1688, *Statutes of the Realm*, eds Alexander Luders and others, 11 vols (London: Dawsons, 1810–28), 6:59.
16. I° GUL. & MAR. c. 9, 1688, *ibid.*, 6:60.
17. *Ibid.*, c. 8, 6:60; c. 9, 6:61.
18. Jeong-Oh Kim, 'Anne Finch's Strategic Retreat into the Country House' in Mona Narain and Karen Bloom Gevirtz, eds, *Gender and Space in British Literature, 1660–1820* (London: Routledge, 2014), 147-63, 163.
19. 'The Preface', *Poems of Anne Countess of Winchilsea*, 8.
20. See *loc. cit.*
21. Anne Kingsmill Finch, *Poems*, Wellesley College manuscript, Wellesley College Digital Scholarship and Archive, English Poetry Collection 43, Image 57, f. 99.
22. Thynne Papers 904/9 (Vols 16-18): Vol. 17 No. 282. See *Poems of Anne Countess of Winchilsea*, 252-62.
23. Deborah Kennedy, *Poetic Sisters: Early Eighteenth-Century Women Poets* (Lewisburg: Bucknell University Press, 2013), 51.
24. Edward Hasted, *The History and Topographical Survey of the County of Kent*, 2nd ed., 12 vols in 13 (Canterbury: W. Bristow, 1797–1801), 11:150-1, note x.
25. Wellesley College manuscript, Wellesley College Digital Scholarship and Archive, English Poetry Collection 43, Images 103-4, ff. 145-6.
26. Hasted, *Kent*, 11:151, n.x.
27. See J.H. Overton, *The Nonjurors: Their Lives, Principles, and Writings* (London: Smith, Elder & Co., 1902), 119, 274.
28. 'Pindarick Poem Upon the Hurricane in November 1703', *Poems of Anne Countess of Winchilsea*, 255-6.
29. See W.D. Macray, 'Nonjuring Consecrations and Ordinations', *Notes & Queries*, 3rd. S. (22 March, 1862), 1:225.
30. Wellesley College manuscript, Wellesley College Digital Scholarship and Archive, English Poetry Collection 43, Images 36-37, ff. 78, 79.
31. See *Poems of Anne Countess of Winchilsea*, 68.
32. *Ibid.*, 269.
33. Hugh Jenkins, *Feigned Commonwealths: The Country-House Poem and the Fashioning of the Ideal Community* (Pittsburgh: Duquesne University Press, 1998), 146-73, 237, n. 24.
34. Personal communication, 18-19 January 2018.
35. See *The Diaries of Lady Anne Clifford*, ed. D.J.H. Clifford (Phoenix Mill: Alan Sutton, 1990), 205.

36. *Secret Memoirs and Manners Of several Persons of Quality, of Both Sexes. From the New Atalantis, an Island in the Mediteranean, Written Originally in Italian*, 2 vols (London: John Morphew and J. Woodward, 1709), 1:167–8.
37. Carol Barash, *English Women's Poetry, 1649–1714: Politics, Community, and Linguistic Authority* (Oxford: Clarendon Press, 1996), 261; Roger Lonsdale, *Eighteenth-Century Women Poets: An Oxford Anthology* (Oxford: Oxford University Press, 1989), 5.
38. D.G. Neill, 'Studies for an Edition of the Poems of Anne, Countess of Winchilsea' (unpublished B. Litt. Thesis, University of Oxford, 1954). See Lonsdale, *Eighteenth-Century Women Poets*, 516.
39. See *The Database of Court Officers 1660–1837*, <http://www.courtofficers.ctsdh.luc.edu> (accessed May 2018).
40. Bucholz cites British Library Add. Mss 38863, 75688 and 75389.

Chapter Five: 'For ever shaded by oblivion's veil': Obituarizing Women in the Eighteenth-Century *Gentleman's Magazine*

1. See Gillian Williamson, *British Masculinity in the 'Gentleman's Magazine', 1731–1815* (Basingstoke: Palgrave Macmillan, 2016).
2. There are several studies of the construction of femininity through periodical literature, for example: Kathryn Shevelow, *Women and Print Culture: The Construction of Femininity in the Early Periodical* (London: Routledge, 1989) and, most recently, Jennie Batchelor and Manushag Powell, eds, *Women's Periodicals and Print Culture in Britain, 1690–1820s: The Long Eighteenth Century* (Edinburgh: Edinburgh University Press, 2018).
3. The development in the eighteenth century of separate public and private 'spheres' was theorized by German sociologist Jürgen Habermas in the 1960s and published in England as Jürgen Habermas, *The Structural Transformation of the Public Sphere: An Inquiry into a Category of Bourgeois Society*, trans. Thomas Burger and Frederick Lawrence (Cambridge: Polity, 1989). The initial adoption of Habermas' theory (which was primarily concerned with the rise of a public world of print and politics outside the confines of the court and government) by historians working on gender has been much modified as research has revealed the formerly hidden role of women in work and public life: see, for example, Leonore Davidoff and Catherine Hall, *Family Fortunes: Men and Women of the English Middle Class, 1780–1850* (London: Hutchinson, 1987), Clare Midgley, *Women Against Slavery: The British Campaigns, 1780–1870* (London: Routledge, 1992) and Kathryn Gleadle, *Borderline Citizens: Women, Gender, and Political Culture in Britain, 1815–67* (Oxford: Oxford University Press, 2009). For men, women and the eighteenth-century cult of

domesticity see Amanda Vickery, *Behind Closed Doors: At Home in Georgian England* (Newhaven, CT: Yale University Press, 2009) and Joanne Bailey, *Parenting in England 1760–1830: Emotion, Identity, and Generation* (Oxford: Oxford University Press, 2012).

4. 'Sylvanus Urban', introduction to the *Gentleman's Magazine* (*GM*), January 1731. ('Sylvanus Urban' was the fictional editorial persona of the *Gentleman's Magazine*.)
5. For a fuller discussion of its history, and details of sales figures and readership (including women readers and correspondents), see Williamson, *British Masculinity*, Chapter 2, 'The History of the *Gentleman's Magazine*, 1731–1815', 14-32 and Chapter 3, 'Readers and Contributors', 33-70.
6. William Hazlitt, *Edinburgh Review, or Critical Journal*, 38 (May 1823), 369-70.
7. Williamson, *British Masculinity*, 62.
8. John Nichols, 'A Prefatory Introduction Descriptive of the Rise and Progress of the Magazine, with Anecdotes of the Projector and his Early Associates', in Samuel Ayscough and John Nichols, *General Index to the Gentleman's Magazine, 1787–1818*, 5 vols (London: J. Nichols & Son, 1818–21), 3:iii-lxxx, lxxiv-lxxviii. Several of these women were participants in the loose networks of the 'bluestockings', on which there is an expanding literature. For an overview see Deborah Heller, 'Bluestocking Studies: the State of the Field – and into the Future', *Literature Compass*, 8,4 (2011), 154-63.
9. See Nigel Starck, *Life After Death: The Art of the Obituary* (Carlton, Vic., Australia: Melbourne University Press, 2006), 1-2, 18-22. Starck gives the earliest extant newspaper obituary (of Captain Andrew Shilling, master of the ship *London*, who died in battle with the Portuguese) as 2 July 1622 in a 'newsbook' published by Nathaniel Newbery and William Sheffard.
10. *GM*, July 1732, 876.
11. Williamson, *British Masculinity*, Appendix 1, Table 1 'Births, marriages and deaths, 1731–56', 187-8. The numbers are based on a sampling of the magazine: the January and July issues for each year to 1815.
12. *GM*, January 1731, 33 and July 1743, 389.
13. Stephen Howard, '"A bright pattern to all her sex": Representations of Women in Periodical and Newspaper Biography' in *Gender in Eighteenth-Century England: Roles, Representations and Responsibilities*, eds Hannah Barker and Elaine Chalus (Harlow: Longman, 1997), 230-49.
14. Nichols Correspondence, MS.Eng.Lett.b.11-19, c.354-72, Bodleian Library, Oxford.
15. Nichols Correspondence, MS.Eng.Lett.b.17, ff.134-5; *GM*, March 1800, 283-4.
16. *GM*, July 1755, 303.

17. Peter Pindar, *A Benevolent Epistle to Sylvanus Urban* (London: G. Kearsley, 1790), 15.
18. *GM*, July 1785, 570-1.
19. *GM*, July 1800, 633-5.
20. Nichols Correspondence, MS.Eng.Lett.b.16, ff. 167–8 (27 November 1799) and c.365, ff.90-1 (6 September 1809).
21. *'On the Death of the Rev. Mr* Chalie, *late Rector of* Winsley [i.e. Wensley] *in the County of York; by his Friend residing in* London', *GM*, January 1750, 39.
22. *GM*, January 1788, 63-4. The incorrectly attributed quotation at the end is line 160 of Alexander Pope, *An Essay on Man. In epistles to a friend, Epistle II* (Dublin: George Faulkner, 1733), 17.
23. *The Plays of William Shakespeare*, ed. Samuel Johnson, 8 vols (London: J. and R. Tonson et al., 1765), 1:297.
24. For Vyse as a poet see <http://spenserians.cath.vt.edu/AuthorRecord.php?action=GET&recordid=1170> (accessed April 2018).
25. I am grateful to my fellow WSG member Carolyn D. Williams for these thoughts.
26. *GM*, March 1786, 267; for Lady Smith and the Vyse family of Lichfield see Pat Rogers, *The Samuel Johnson Encyclopaedia* (Westport, CT: Greenwood Press, 1996), 373. Lady Smith and the Vyse family were friends of Samuel Johnson, also born in Lichfield, and a collaborator with Cave on the *Gentleman's Magazine*. See <http://www.thepeerage.com/p17913.htm#c179121.2> (accessed April 2018).
27. *GM*, March 1786, 266. Clive Wilkinson describes him as born c.1738 in Hull, a merchant's son, and educated in Beverley and Hampstead. He had edited both the *Westminster* and *London* magazines and was an author of poetry and plays. See 'Thompson, Edward (1738?–86). Naval officer and author', *Oxford Dictionary of National Biography* (Oxford: Oxford University Press, 2004). <https://doi.org/10.1093/ref:odnb/27260> (accessed April 2018).
28. *GM*, March 1786, 267.
29. *Loc. cit.*; see also John Gascoigne, 'Jebb, John (1736–86)', *Oxford Dictionary of National Biography* (Oxford: Oxford University Press, 2004), <https://doi.org/10.1093/ref:odnb/14680> (accessed April 2018).
30. Alexander Pope, *Of the Characters of Women: An Epistle to a Lady* (London: Lawton Gilliver, 1735), 5.
31. *GM*, January 1770, 16 (under pseudonym 'T. Row').
32. *GM*, January 1789, 89.
33. *GM*, January 1787, 94.
34. See Williamson, *British Masculinity*, 146-8.

35. See Amy Erickson, 'Married Women's Occupations in Eighteenth-Century London', *Continuity & Change*, 23:2 (2008), 267-307; Bridget Hill, *Women, Work, and Sexual Politics in Eighteenth-Century England* (Oxford: Basil Blackwell, 1989) and Margaret Hunt, *The Middling Sort: Commerce, Gender, and the Family in England, 1680–1780* (Berkeley, CA: University of California Press, 1996), Chapter 5, 'Eighteenth-Century Middling Women and Trade', 125-46.
36. *GM*, March 1786, 267.
37. *Ibid.*, 269-70.
38. See note 8, above.
39. *GM*, March 1809, 285, 286.
40. *GM*, April 1809, 377.
41. *Ibid.*, 378.
42. These calculations are based on all obituarized deaths between 1 and 31 March in *GM*, March 1809, 284-96 and *GM*, April 1809, 385-8.
43. The most fully-developed exploration of women's contribution in the late eighteenth and nineteenth centuries remains Davidoff and Hall, *Family Fortunes*.

Chapter Six: Female Radicals in Bristol: The Three Marys and Mary Wollstonecraft's 'The Cave of Fancy'

The writer would like to thank Peter Cochran, Gina Luria Walker, Joan Wilkinson, the Revd Lindy Latham and Bauhaus in Bristol.

1. See Peter J. Kitson, 'Coleridge's Bristol and West Country Radicalism', in *English Romantic Writers and the West Country*, ed. Nicholas Roe (Houndmills: Palgrave Macmillan, 2010), 115-28.
2. This neglect has been partially remedied in *Women and the City: Bristol 1373–2000*, ed. Madge Dresser (Bristol: Redcliffe Press, 2016), though the particular women discussed here are not included, apart from brief mentions of Mary Robinson (11, 76). Jane Duffus' *The Women Who Built Bristol 1184–2018* (Bristol: Tangent Press, 2018) has entries on Mary Robinson (294-96) and Mary Wollstonecraft (401), but not on Mary Hays.
3. Richard Polewhele [*sic*], *The Unsex'd Females* (New York: Wm. Cobbett, 1800), 16 [*sic*: should be 18].
4. Mary Robinson [Anne Frances Randall], *A Letter to the Women of England on the Injustice of Mental Subordination* (London: T.N. Longman and O. Rees, 1799), 2, n. See *The Radicals*, eds Marie Mulvey-Roberts and Tamae Mizuta (London and Bristol: Routledge/Thoemmes Press, 1994), and Andrew McInnes, 'Wollstonecraft's Legion: Feminism in Crisis, 1799', *Women's Writing* 20,4 (2013), 479-95.

5. See Barbara Taylor, *Eve and the New Jerusalem: Socialism and Feminism in the Nineteenth Century* (London: Virago Press, 1983), 132.
6. A speech she gave in Nottingham drew an audience of 5,000. See *The Movement, Anti-persecution Gazette, and Register of Progress: A Weekly Journal of Republican Politics, Anti-Theology, & Utilitarian Morals*, ed. G. Jacob Holyoake, assisted by M.Q. Ryall, 2 vols in 1 (London: G. Jacob Holyoake, [1843–5]), 1:315.
7. See *Women and Radicalism in the Nineteenth Century: Specific Controversies*, ed. Michael S. Sanders, 4 vols (London and Bristol: Routledge/Thoemmes Press, 2001), 1:32.
8. Mary Robinson, *Memoirs of the Late Mrs Robinson, Written by Herself*, 2 vols (London: Richard Phillips, 1803), 2:10. See also Sharon M. Setzer, 'The Gothic Structure of Mary Robinson's *Memoirs*', in *Romantic Autobiography in England*, ed. Eugene Stelzig (Farnham: Ashgate, 2009), 31-48.
9. Mary Robinson, *Walsingham; or, The Pupil of Nature*, 4 vols (London: T.N. Longman, 1797), 3:200, 202.
10. Robinson, *Memoirs*, 2:154.
11. See McInnes, 'Wollstonecraft's Legion', 487.
12. Mary Hays, *Appeal to the Men of Great Britain in* [sic] *Behalf of Women* (London: J. Johnson and J. Bell, 1798), [125], 127. See also *The Radicals*, eds Mulvey-Roberts and Mizuta.
13. *The English Review; or, an Abstract of English and Foreign Literature* (1793), 22:253, 256. These passages refer to Hays's *Letters and Essays, Moral and Miscellaneous* (1793), in which she makes use of Wollstonecraft's technique of combining sentimental and rational discourse in arguing for women's intellectual and moral worth; see Mary Hays, *The Victim of Prejudice*, ed. Eleanor Ty (Peterborough: Broadview Press, 1998), xii. The reviewer's identity is revealed in Richard Polwhele, *Biographical Sketches in Cornwall*, 3 vols in 1 (London: J.B. Nichols and Son, Longman and Co., Simpkin and Marshall, and G.B. Whittaker and Co., 1831), 3:60.
14. *The Idea of Being Free: A Mary Hays Reader*, ed. Gina Luria Walker (Peterborough: Broadview Press, 2006), 288.
15. Quoted by Martin Gorsky, *Patterns of Philanthropy: Charity and Society in Nineteenth-Century Bristol* (Woodbridge: Boydell & Brewer, 2011), 131.
16. Anonymous review of *The Brothers; or Consequences*, in the *Gentleman's Magazine*, September 1816, 251.
17. This tract was also known as *Savings Bank. Loc. cit.*, n.
18. *Ibid.*, 251.
19. *Ibid.*, 252, 251.

20. *State of the Prudent Man's Friend Society for the year 1814* (Bristol, 1814), Bristol Reference Library, 9810-1. Quoted by Gorsky, *Patterns of Philanthropy*, 131-2.
21. *Gentleman's Magazine*, September 1816, 252. William Button, who published *The Brothers*, also brought out a religious periodical in which Hays is admonished for repeatedly using a 'profane exclamation' in her otherwise 'well-told tale', which is praised for being moral, entertaining and religious; see anonymous review of *The Brothers* in the *Baptist Magazine*, 8 (1816), 80.
22. See Mary Robinson, *Selected Poems*, ed. Judith Pascoe (Peterborough: Broadview Press, 2000), 63.
23. For an indication of her attitudes, see Cato Marks, '"Let poor volk pass": Dialect and Writing the South-West Poor out of Metropolitan Political Life in Hannah More's *Village Politics* (1792)', *Romanticism*, 20,1 (2014), 43-59.
24. See Cathy Hartley, *Historical Dictionary of British Women* (London: Taylor & Francis, 2004), 211.
25. For a discussion of Yearsley and Bristol, see Kerri Andrews, 'In her Place: Ann Yearsley or "The Bristol Milkwoman"', in *Literary Bristol*, ed. Marie Mulvey-Roberts (Bristol: Redcliffe Press, 2015), 83-104. See also Mary Waldron, *Lactilla, Milkwoman of Clifton: The Life and Writings of Ann Yearsley, 1753–1806* (Athens and London: The University of Georgia Press, 1996).
26. *Letters of Anna Seward: Written between the Years 1784 and 1807*, 6 vols (Edinburgh: Constable; London: Longman, Hurst, Rees, Orme and Browne, 1811), 1:121.
27. Letter to Miss Barker, London, 1801 in *Selections from the Letters of Robert Southey*, ed. John Wood Warter, 4 vols (London: Longman, Brown, Green and Longmans, 1856), 1:180.
28. *The Poetical Works of Robert Southey, Collected by Himself*, 10 vols (London: Longman, Orme, Brown, Green and Longmans, 1837–8), 2:3.
29. Letter to John Cam Hobhouse, Venice, 11 November 1818 in *Byron's Letters and Journals: A New Selection*, ed. Richard Lansdown (Oxford: Oxford University Press, 2015), 304.
30. *Ibid.*, 303. See Peter Cochran, *Byron and Bob: Lord Byron's Relationship with Robert Southey* (Newcastle-upon-Tyne: Cambridge Scholars, 2010), 68-108.
31. Letter 39, to William Taylor, Keswick, 1 July 1804 in *A Memoir of the Life and Writings of the Late William Taylor of Norwich*, ed. J.W. Robberds, 2 vols (London: J. Murray, 1843), 1:507.
32. Quoted by David Hussey, 'Leisure and Commerce: The Hotwell and thc Port of Bristol, 1750–1850', in *A City Built upon the Water: Maritime Bristol 1750–1900*, ed. Steve Poole (Bristol: Redcliffe Press, 2013), 31–50, 47.

33. See Janet Todd, *Rebel Daughters: Ireland in Conflict 1798* (London: Penguin, 2004), 105-6.
34. Quoted by Janet Todd, *Mary Wollstonecraft: A Revolutionary Life* (London: Weidenfeld & Nicolson, 2000), 110.
35. See William Godwin, *Memoirs of the Author of A Vindication of the Rights of Woman*, 2nd ed. (London: J. Johnson, 1798), 60.
36. See Hussey, 'Leisure and Commerce', 45.
37. See *The Cambridge Companion to Mary Wollstonecraft*, ed. Claudia L. Johnson (Cambridge: Cambridge University Press, 2002), xvi.
38. Many years later, Wollstonecraft would attempt suicide by throwing herself off Putney Bridge into the River Thames. See Claire Tomalin, *The Life and Death of Mary Wollstonecraft* (New York and London: Harcourt, Brace, Jovanovich, 1974), 186-7.
39. See *ibid.*, 60.
40. See Mary Wollstonecraft, *Mary* and *Maria*, Mary Shelley, *Matilda*, ed. Janet Todd (Harmondsworth: Penguin, 1992), xviii.
41. Mary Wollstonecraft, 'The Cave of Fancy', in *The Works of Mary Wollstonecraft*, eds Janet Todd and Marilyn Butler, 7 vols (London: Pickering and Chatto, 1989), 1:191, 192.
42. *Ibid.*, 1:191-2.
43. See J.M.W. Turner, *The Avon Gorge at Bristol with the Old Hot Wells House* (c.1792).
44. See Edmund Burke, *A Philosophical Enquiry into the Origin of our Ideas of the Sublime and Beautiful* (London: R. and J. Dodsley, 1757), 52.
45. Wollstonecraft, 'The Cave of Fancy', 1:192.
46. Isambard Kingdom Brunel (1806–59) would use these cliffs to support his famous Clifton Suspension Bridge.
47. The old Hotwell House was demolished in 1822 and four years later was replaced by a new building, which no longer remains today.
48. Hussey, 'Leisure and Commerce', 33.
49. Wollstonecraft, 'The Cave of Fancy', 1:192.
50. Hussey, 'Leisure and Commerce', 44.
51. See Anon., *The Hand Book for Visitors to the Bristol & Clifton Hotwells* (Bristol: R.W. Smith, undated), 39-43. It was written during the reign of Queen Victoria. There are plants unique to the Avon Gorge.
52. Wollstonecraft, 'The Cave of Fancy', 1:195.
53. See Todd, *Rebel Daughters*, 325-6.
54. See Mary Wollstonecraft, *Thoughts on the Education of Daughters*, ed. Janet Todd (Bristol: Thoemmes Press, 1995), 16, 18.

55. See Marie Mulvey-Roberts, 'Gothic Bristol: A City of Darkness and Light', in *Literary Bristol: Writers and the City*, ed. Mulvey-Roberts, 29-58, 51-6 and *Dangerous Bodies: Historicising the Gothic Corporeal* (Manchester: Manchester University Press, 2016), 61-2.
56. Another Mary linked to Bristol was the poet Mary Bryan (1780–1838), who married a Bristol printer and bookseller and ran the business from 52 Corn Street. She published *Sonnets and Metrical Tales* in 1815, the year in which Mary Shelley visited the city. See Dresser, ed. *Women and the City*, 78-9.

Chapter Seven: A Quest for Female Sexual Agency in the Eighteenth-Century Novel

1. The term 'long eighteenth century' is used by historians to refer to a more natural historical period which extends beyond the arbitrary dates of the standard calendar definition (1700–1799). Various date ranges are applied to the term, but here it refers to the period from 1660 to 1832.
2. Mrs A. Behn, *The Fair Jilt: or, the History of Prince Tarquin and Miranda* (London: Will. Canning, 1688), 49.
3. Eliza Haywood, 'Fantomina: Or, Love in a Maze', in *Secret Histories, Novels, and Poems*, 2nd ed., 4 vols (London: Dan. Browne and S. Chapman, 1725), 3:287-8.
4. Mary Davys, *The Reform'd Coquet; or, Memoirs of Amoranda. A Surprising Novel* (Dublin: R. Gunne, 1735), 94.
5. Letter 73, Mr Belford to Robert Lovelace, Esq., [London], n.d., in Samuel Richardson, *Clarissa. Or, the History of a Young Lady*, 7 vols (London: A. Millar, J. and J. Rivington, John Osborn, 1748), 6:260.
6. Anna Clark, *Women's Silence, Men's Violence: Sexual Assault in England 1770–1845* (London and New York: Pandora, 1987), 30. The reference is PRO Assi. 45/35/3/27, 11 March 1786. See also Misty Krueger, 'The Rhetoric of Rape: William Blake's *Visions of the Daughters of Albion* as Eighteenth-Century Rape Trial', in *Interpreting Sexual Violence, 1660–1800*, ed. Anne Greenfield (London: Pickering & Chatto, 2013), 149-62.
7. William Blackstone, *Commentaries on the Laws of England*, 4th ed., 4 vols (Oxford: Clarendon, 1770), 4:210, and see *ibid.*, 4:215.
8. Penelope Aubin, *The Strange Adventures of the Count de Vinevil and his Family* (London: E. Bell et al., 1721), 27-8. Penelope Aubin was an English novelist, poet and translator (from the French) who wrote seven novels between 1721 and 1728.
9. *Ibid.*, 28.
10. Samuel Richardson, *Pamela: Or, Virtue Rewarded*, 4th ed., 2 vols (London: C. Rivington and J. Osborn, 1741), 1:162.

11. Eliza Haywood, *Love in Excess: or, The Fatal Enquiry, A Novel*, 6th ed. (London: D. Browne, jun. and S. Chapman, 1725), 26.
12. *Ibid.*, 94.
13. *Ibid.*, 95.
14. Eliza Haywood, *The History of Miss Betsy Thoughtless*, 2nd ed., 4 vols (London: T. Gardner, 1751), 3:209-10.
15. See Mary Wollstonecraft, *A Vindication of the Rights of Woman* (London: J. Johnson, 1792), 99-100, n.
16. Blackstone, *Commentaries*, 1:442.
17. *Loc. cit.* See also Janelle Greenberg, 'The Legal Status of the English Woman in Early Eighteenth-century Common Law and Equity', *Studies in Eighteenth-Century Culture* (1975), 4:171-81, especially 172.
18. Mary Wollstonecraft, *Maria: or, The Wrongs of Woman. A Posthumous Fragment* (Philadelphia: James Carey, 1799), 148.
19. *Ibid.*, xi.
20. See *ibid.*, 160-3.
21. *Ibid.*, 225.
22. *Ibid.*, 226.
23. See Gina Luria Walker, *Mary Hays (1759–1843): The Growth of a Woman's Mind* (Aldershot: Ashgate, 2006), 48-53.
24. See *ibid.*, 134-5.
25. The mathematician William Frend was banished from Cambridge after a trial for blasphemy and sedition. They met when Frend responded to Hays's first independent publication: a pamphlet (which appeared under the pseudonym 'Eusebia') entitled *Cursory Remarks on an Enquiry into the Expediency and Propriety of Public or Social Worship* (1791). Like Frend, Hays declared herself a Unitarian in 1791.
26. Mary Hays, *The Memoirs of Emma Courtney*, 2 vols (London: G.G. and J. Robinson, 1796), 2:68.
27. *Ibid.*, 2:189.
28. *Ibid.*, 2:190.
29. Mary Hays, *The Victim of Prejudice*, 2 vols (London: J. Johnson, 1799), 1:162.
30. *Ibid.*, 1:167-8.
31. *Ibid.*, 2:83.
32. *Ibid.*, 2:81-2.
33. Julia Prewitt Brown, *Jane Austen's Novels: Social Change and Literary Form* (Cambridge, MA.: Harvard University Press, 1979), 156.
34. Ashley Tauchert, *Romancing Jane Austen* (Palgrave: Basingstoke, 2005), xiii.

35. Jane Austen, *Sense and Sensibility* (Oxford: Oxford University Press, 2004), 'Introduction' by Margaret Ann Doody, vii-xxxix (xv).
36. *Ibid.*, 33.
37. *Ibid.*, 156.
38. *Ibid.*, 39.
39. *Ibid.*, 288.
40. Jane Austen, *Mansfield Park* (New York: Derby & Jackson, 1860), Chapter 47, 427.

Chapter Eight: Scold, Punish, Pity or Seduce? The Confused Rhetoric of *Advice to Unmarried Women* (1791)

1. John Gregory, *A Father's Legacy to his Daughters*, 2nd ed. (London: W. Strahan, T. Cadell; Edinburgh: W. Creech, 1774), 31-2.
2. Jane Austen, *Northanger Abbey*, ed. Claire Grogan (Peterborough, Ontario: Broadview Press, 1996), 124.
3. [Richard Brinsley Sheridan], *The Rivals, A Comedy* (London: John Wilkie, 1775), 10.
4. Gregory, *Father's Legacy*, 34.
5. See *Advice to Unmarried Women: To Recover and Reclaim the Fallen; and to Prevent the Fall of Others, into the Snares and Consequences of Seduction* (London: J.F. and C. Rivington, 1791), iv. Two candidates for authorship are Jelinger Symons (1748–1810) and Benjamin Choyce Sowden (d. 1796), both of whom ministered in Hackney and published pamphlets and sermons. I am indebted to Carolyn D. Williams for this information.
6. *Ibid.*, iii.
7. *Ibid.*, iv.
8. *Ibid.*, 12.
9. *Ibid.*, 11, 12.
10. *Ibid.*, 11.
11. *Ibid.*, 14.
12. *Loc. cit.*
13. *Ibid.*, 18.
14. Martin Madan, *Thelyphthora*, 2 vols (London: J. Dodsley, 1780), 1:12-3. Further discussion of this work can be found in the Introduction; for the full title, see my Further Reading list. I am grateful to Carolyn D. Williams for bringing this publication and its author to my attention.
15. *Advice*, 20.
16. *Love Given O're: or, a Satyr against the Pride, Lust, and Inconstancy, &c. of Woman* (London: Andrew Green, 1682), 2. For a study of extreme early modern misogyny, see Felicity Nussbaum, *The Brink of All We Hate: English Satires on Women, 1660–1750* (Lexington: University of Kentucky Press, 1984).

17. *Advice*, 27.
18. The real-life story of Peg Plunkett, explored in Chapter 9, underlines the difficulties faced by a fallen woman seeking employment: 'Who would have taken a servant without a character? and who had I to give me one?' *Memoirs of Mrs. Margaret Leeson*, 3 vols (Dublin: Printed for the Authoress, and Sold by the Principal Booksellers, 1795–97), 1(1795):113-4.
19. *Advice*, 31.
20. It is worth noting that the pamphlet never addresses the possibility that a fallen woman did not come to that state by choice, but was raped. Passages such as these, which warn young women against the dangers of mundane pleasantries, invite speculation about but provide no answers for how often 'seduction' included violent coercion; it is highly likely that the victim was held responsible regardless of the circumstances.
21. *Ibid.*, 32.
22. *Loc. cit.*
23. *Ibid.*, 33.
24. *Ibid.*, 34.
25. 'Honoria', *The Female Mentor: or, Select Conversations*, 2 vols (London: T. Cadell, 1793), 1:117.
26. *Advice*, 35.
27. *Ibid.*, 36-7.
28. *Ibid.*, 44.

Chapter Nine: Friendships: Commonalities across the Centuries

1. Letter 3, Mary Astell to John Norris, 31 October 1693, in [Mary Astell] and John Norris, *Letters Concerning the Love of God, Between the Author of the Proposal to the Ladies and Mr. John Norris* (London: Samuel Manship and Richard Wilkin, 1695), 48-9.
2. See Julie Peakman, '"The best freind in the world": The Relationship between Emma Hamilton and Queen Maria Carolina of Naples', in *Woman to Woman: Female Negotiations During the Long Eighteenth Century*, eds Carolyn D. Williams, Angela Escott, and Louise Duckling (Newark: University of Delaware Press, 2010), 173-89.
3. For more information concerning Peg's relationship with Mr Leeson, see *Memoirs of Mrs. Margaret Leeson. Written by Herself; and Interspersed with Several Interesting and Amusing Anecdotes, of Some of the most Striking Characters of Great-Britain and Ireland*, 3 vols (Dublin: Sold by the Principal Booksellers, 1795–7), 1:127-9. The first and second volumes, published in 1795, were 'Printed for the Authoress'; these words are omitted from the

title page of the third volume, published posthumously in 1797. For more information on Peg in general, see also *Whore Biographies 1700–1825*, ed. Julie Peakman, 8 vols (London: Pickering & Chatto, 2006–2007), 6 (2007) and Julie Peakman, *Peg Plunkett: Memoirs of a Whore* (London: Quercus, 2015).

4. Leeson, *Memoirs*, 1:114.
5. *Ibid.*, 1:115.
6. See *ibid.*, 1:195-204.
7. *Ibid.*, 3:2.
8. *Ibid.*, 3:26.
9. *Ibid.*, 2:133.
10. *Ibid.*, 2:52.
11. *Ibid.*, 1:242.
12. *Ibid.*, 2:62.
13. *Ibid.*, 2:55.
14. *Ibid.*, 2:56-7.
15. *Ibid.*, 2:57.
16. *Ibid.*, 2:58.
17. *Ibid.*, 2:63.
18. *Ibid.*, 3:[1].
19. *Ibid.*, 2:116.
20. *Ibid.*, 2:133.
21. *Ibid.*, 2:29.
22. *Ibid.*, 3:91.
23. *The Life of Mrs. Margaret Leeson alias Peg Plunket. Written by Herself: In which are given Anecdotes and Sketches of the Lives and Bon Mots of some of the most Celebrated Characters in Great-Britain and Ireland, Particularly of all the Filles des Joys and Men of Pleasure and Gallantry, Who usually frequented her Citherean Temple for this Thirty Years past. Three Volumes Complete in One* (Dublin: Printed and Sold by the Principal Booksellers, 1798), 81.
24. Leeson, *Memoirs*, 3:7.
25. *Ibid.*, 3:170.
26. *Loc. cit.*
27. *Ibid.*, 3:172.
28. *Ibid.*, 3:127.
29. See *ibid.*, 3:48-9.
30. *Ibid.*, 3:106.
31. *Ibid.*, 3:111.
32. *Ibid.*, 3:100, 101.
33. *Ibid.*, 3:104, 105.

34. *Ibid.*, 3:102.
35. *Ibid.*, 3:103.
36. *Ibid.*, 3:34.
37. *Ibid.*, 3:35.
38. *Ibid.*, 3:151-2.
39. *Ibid.*, 3:260.
40. *Ibid.*, 2:230.
41. *Ibid.*, 3:299; see also *ibid.*, 3:2-3.
42. *Ibid.*, 3:331; see also Peakman, *Peg Plunkett*, 186.
43. See Leeson, *Memoirs*, 1:113.
44. *Ibid.*, 2:52-3.
45. [Francis Grose], *A Classical Dictionary of the Vulgar Tongue* (London: S. Hooper, 1785), F2r.
46. [Edward Ward], *The Secret History of Clubs* (London: Printed and Sold by the Booksellers, 1709), 301.
47. *Ibid.*, 304.
48. *Ibid.*, 301.
49. *Ibid.*, 302.
50. *Ibid.*, 302, 303.
51. *Ibid.*, 304.
52. Anon., *Memoirs of the Celebrated Miss Fanny Murray. Interspersed with the Intrigues and Amours of Several Eminent Personages. Founded on* Real Facts, 2 vols (Dublin: Faulkner, 1759), 1:60.
53. *Ibid.*, 1:61.
54. Peakman, *Peg Plunkett*, 143-4.
55. *Memoirs of the Celebrated Miss Fanny Murray*, 1:62.

Chapter Ten: Rivalry, Camaraderie and the Prima Donnas: Elizabeth Billington and Gertrude Mara

1. Suzanne Aspden, *The Rival Sirens: Performance and Identity on Handel's Operatic Stage* (Cambridge: Cambridge University Press, 2013), 1.
2. See Felicity Nussbaum, *Rival Queens: Actresses, Performance, and the Eighteenth-Century British Theater* (Philadelphia: University of Pennsylvania Press, 2010), 11-14.
3. Dan H. Marek, *Alto: the Voice of Bel Canto* (Lanham: Rowman & Littlefield, 2016), 52.
4. See Aspden, *Rival Sirens*, 4.
5. Pier Francesco Tosi, *Observations on the Florid Song; Or, Sentiments on the Ancient and Modern Singers*, trans. by John Ernest Galliard (London: J. Wilcox, 1742), 155.

6. See *ibid.*, 170.
7. Simon McVeigh, *Concert Life in London from Mozart to Haydn* (Cambridge: Cambridge University Press, 2006), 144.
8. J. Potter, 'The tenor-castrato connection, 1760–1860', *Early Music* 35 (2007), 97-110, 97.
9. Farinelli is said to have performed an aria with trumpet obbligato, which developed into a contest between singer and trumpeter. The castrato demonstrated such excellent technique and ornamentation that he surpassed the trumpet-player, stirring the audience into thunderous shouts of acclaim and applause. Unfortunately, no surviving work performed by Farinelli includes a trumpet obbligato, so the story is no more than a frequently-repeated anecdote. Despite this, scholars such as Nicholas Clapton have theorized about how Farinelli achieved such rapidity of execution, stating that he deliberately cultivated this skill by attending lessons with the castrato Antonio Bernacchi (1685–1756), a former singing star whose talent for rapid execution was exceptional. See Clapton, 'Carlo Broschi Farinelli: Aspects of his Technique and Performance', *Journal for Eighteenth-Century Studies*, 28 (2005), 323-38, 325.
10. Potter, 'The tenor-castrato connection', 97. See also John Potter and Neil Sorrell, *A History of Singing* (Cambridge: Cambridge University Press, 2012), 119.
11. 'To the Printer of the Morning Chronicle', *Morning Chronicle and London Advertiser*, 21 February 1785, 4.
12. 'Operatical Intelligence', *Morning Herald*, 8 May 1786, 3.
13. 'Covent Garden. By command of Their Majesties', *Public Advertiser*, 13 February 1786, 1.
14. 'Theatrical Intelligence', *Morning Herald*, 14 February 1786, 3; 'Theatre. Covent-Garden', the *General Advertiser*, 8 March 1786, 3.
15. Mortellari was an Italian composer who studied under Niccolò Piccinni (1728–1800). He settled in London in 1785. See John S. Sainsbury and Alexandre Choron, *A Dictionary of Musicians: from the Earliest Ages to the Present Time*, 2nd ed., 2 vols (London: Sainsbury and Co., 1827), 2:152-3; *Morning Chronicle and London Advertiser*, 26 April 1786, 3.
16. 'The Theatre', *Morning Post and Daily Advertiser*, 8 March 1786, 3.
17. See Dorothea Link, ed., *Arias for Nancy Storace: Mozart's first Susanna* (London: A-R Editions, 2002).
18. Letter 31, from Anna Seward to Mrs Martin, Lichfield, 5 June 1786, in *Letters of Anna Seward: Written Between the Years 1784 and 1807*, ed. A. Constable, 6 vols (Edinburgh: Archibald Constable and Company; London: Longman, Hurst, Rees, Orme and Brown, William Miller and John Murray, 1811), 1:153.

19. For her opinion of Mara, see Letter 20, from Anna Seward to Mrs. Cotton, Lichfield, 27 October 1785, in *ibid.*, 1:89.
20. Charles Burney, *A General History of Music, From the Earliest Ages to the Present Period*, 4 vols (London: Printed for the author: sold by Payne and Son; Robson and Clark; and G.G.J. and J. Robinson, 1776–1789), 4:681.
21. 'Mrs. Billington', *World*, 25 October 1788, 3.
22. 'Covent Garden Theatre', *Morning Chronicle and London Advertiser*, 3 November 1788, 3.
23. 'To the Editor of the Morning Post', *Morning Post and Daily Advertiser*, 2 December 1791, 3.
24. 'Theatres', *Gazetteer and New Daily Advertiser*, 21 November 1791, 2.
25. 'Haymarket Theatre', *Morning Chronicle*, 18 November 1791, 3.
26. 'Theatre', *The Times*, 28 November 1791, 2.
27. 'Theatres', *Star*, 21 November 1791, 3.
28. 'Theatre', *London Chronicle*, 19 November 1791-22 November 1791, 3.
29. See 'Mara, Mme Giovanni Battista, Gertrud Elisabeth, née Schmeling' in *A Biographical Dictionary of Actors, Actresses, Musicians, Dancers, Managers and Other Stage Personnel in London, 1660–1800*, eds Philip H. Highfill, Jr, Kalman A. Burnim and Edward A. Langhans, 20 vols (Carbondale and Edwardsville: Southern Illinois University Press, 1973–1993), 10:83.
30. *Ah che nel petto io sento*. [Song, adapted to G. Paisiello's *Nel cor più.*] Sung by Madam Mara in the opera of *Idalide*, and with English words as sung by Mrs Billington (Dublin: Edmund Lee, 1795); Thomas Augustine Arne, *The soldier tir'd of war's alarms: sung by Mrs. Billington and by Madme. Mara in Artaxerxes composed by Dr. Arne* (London: s.n., 1798).
31. See 'Antient Musick', *Morning Chronicle and London Advertiser*, 11 May 1787, 3; 'Grand Musical Festival, Westminster Abbey', *Bath Chronicle*, 31 May 1787, 3.
32. *World*, 19 December 1787, 3.
33. *The New Monthly Magazine and Humorist* (1838), 54:219.
34. 'Madame Mara's Concert and Last Performance in this Country', *Morning Chronicle*, 1 June 1802, 1.
35. Michael Kelly and Theodore Edward Hook, *Reminiscences of Michael Kelly of the King's Theatre, and Theatre Royal Drury Lane, including a period of nearly half a century with original anecdotes of many distinguished literary persons, political, literary, and musical*, 2nd ed., 2 vols (London: H. Colburn 1826), 2:107.
36. Mara left her husband in 1794 and ran off with Florio. They travelled the continent together, but eventually separated sometime after 1803.
37. Thomas Green, 'Diary of a Lover of Literature', 3 June 1802, *Gentleman's Magazine*, March 1834, 246-7.

38. John Rowe Parker, *A Musical Biography: or Sketches of the lives and writings of eminent musical characters. Interspersed with an epitome of interesting musical matter* (Boston: Stone & Fovell, 1825), 146.

Chapter Eleven: Eliza O'Neill and the Art of Acting

My sincere thanks to Carolyn D. Williams for her editorial assistance.

1. See Charles Inigo Jones, *Memoirs of Miss O'Neill* (London: D. Cox, 1816), 10.
2. See James Boaden, *The Life of Mrs. Jordan*, 2 vols (London: Edward Bull, 1831), 2:289; Jones, 8; William Oxberry, *Dramatic Biography and Histrionic Anecdotes*, 6 vols in 3 (London: G. Virtue, 1825–27), 1:192-4; <https://austenonly.com/2010/06/08/eliza-oneil> (accessed October 2016).
3. See Jones, *Memoirs*, 99. Worth, respectively £19,260 and £385,200 at today's values. *Purchasing Power of British Pounds from 1270 to Present, Measuring Worth, 2018*. <https://www.measuringworth.com/ppoweruk/> (accessed April 2018). For confirmation that the carriage was a gift, see Oxberry, *Dramatic Biography*, 1:195.
4. For details of the Covent Garden theatre, see the *Illustrated London News*, 12 December 1846, 4–5; for O'Neill's ability to attract audiences, see Oxberry, *Dramatic Biography*, 1:195.
5. See Henry Saxe Wyndham, *The Annals of Covent Garden Theatre*, 2 vols (London: Chatto & Windus, 1906), 1:382; <http://www.historyofparliamentonline.org/volume/1820-1832/member/wrixon-becher-william-1780-1850> (accessed May 2018).
6. See James Boaden, *Memoirs of Mrs. Siddons*, 2 vols (London: Henry Colburn, 1827), 1:327.
7. See <https://www.npg.org.uk/collections/search/person/mp04109/sarah-siddons-nee-kemble> (accessed May 2018).
8. See Felicity Nussbaum, *Rival Queens: Actresses, Performance, and the Eighteenth-Century British Theater* (Philadelphia: University of Pennsylvania Press, 2010), 278-84.
9. For details of O'Neill's Covent Garden seasons, see John Genest, *Some Account of the English Stage*, 10 vols (Bath: H.E. Carrington, 1832), 9:8.
10. *La Belle Assemblée; Being Bell's Court and Fashionable Magazine*, January 1816, 135.
11. For a list of Siddons' roles, see Genest, *English Stage*, 8:308-12. For the roles created by O'Neill, see notes 73 and 74.
12. Following the Restoration in 1660, Charles ordered the reopening of public theatre. Influenced by his experience of theatre on the Continent, his patent of January 1663 (PRO, C66/3009, no. 3) to William Davenant explicitly directed 'we do likewise permit and give leave that all the women's parts to be acted in

either of the said two companies from this time to come may be performed by women', permitting women to perform as actresses on the public stage legitimately for the first time. See P. H. Fitzgerald, *A New History of the English Stage*, 2 vols (London: Tinsley Brothers, 1882), 1:77.

13. Jones, *Memoirs*, 73, 94.
14. See, e.g., *Shakespeare Made Fit: Restoration Adaptations of Shakespeare*, ed. Sandra Clark (London: J.M. Dent, 1997).
15. See Jones, *Memoirs*, 19-22.
16. *Ibid.*, 61.
17. *Ibid.*, 49.
18. *Ibid.*, 63, 52, 52, 52-3.
19. William Charles Macready, *Macready's Reminiscences, and Selections from his Diaries and Letters*, ed. Sir Frederick Pollock, 2 vols (London: Macmillan & Co., 1875), 1:97-8.
20. *The Life and Times of Frederick Reynolds. Written by Himself*, 2 vols in 1 (Philadelphia: H.C. Carey and I. Lea, 1826), 2:219.
21. William Hazlitt, *A View of the English Stage; or, A Series of Dramatic Criticisms* (London: Robert Stodart; Anderson and Chase, 1818), 20.
22. 'Timothy Crusty, Esq. M.A. and F.P.S.', 'Desultory Reminiscences of Miss O'Neill', *Blackwood's Edinburgh Magazine*, 27, 1830, 47-58, 53-4.
23. Anon., 'Miss O'Neill', *La Belle Assemblée*, January 1816, 3-5, 5.
24. [Roger Pickering], *Reflections upon Theatrical Expression in Tragedy* (London: W. Johnston, 1755), 31.
25. *Ibid.*, 3. For the importance of feeling to eighteenth-century acting theory, see Earl R. Wasserman, 'Sympathetic Imagination in Eighteenth-Century Theories of Acting', *Journal of English and Germanic Philology*, 46, 3 (1947), 264-72.
26. James Henry Leigh Hunt, *Critical Essays on the Performers of the London Theatres, Including General Observations on the Practise and Genius of the Stage* (London: John Hunt, 1807), 17.
27. *Ibid.*, 16.
28. *Ibid.*, 20.
29. *Ibid.*, 18.
30. Gilbert Austin, *Chironomia* (London: T. Cadell and W. Davies, 1806); Henry Siddons, *Practical Illustrations of Rhetorical Gesture and Action* (London: Richard Phillips, 1807).
31. Hunt, *Critical Essays*, 20.
32. *Ibid.*, 20-21.
33. 'Timothy Crusty', 'Desultory Reminiscences', 53.
34. Hunt, *Critical Essays*, Appendix, 2.

35. Oxberry, *Dramatic Biography*, 1:201.
36. *Ibid.*, 1:200.
37. Genest, *English Stage*, 8:604.
38. See Hunt, *Critical Essays*, 164, 74.
39. Jones, *Memoirs*, 53.
40. *Ibid.*, 57, 58.
41. *Ibid.*, 54.
42. *Diary, Reminiscences, and Correspondence of Henry Crabb Robinson*, selected and edited by Thomas Sadler, 3rd ed., 2 vols (London and New York: Macmillan and Co., 1872), 1:248.
43. Anon., *A descriptive portrait of Miss O'Neill in a critique on her exhibition of the characters of Mrs. Haller and Jane Shore* (London: printed for E. Williams, 1815), 5.
44. Jones, *Memoirs*, 89, 33.
45. *Ibid.*, 89.
46. 'Timothy Crusty', 'Desultory Reminiscences', 58.
47. Lady Pollock, *Macready as I Knew Him* (London: Remington and Co., 1884), 34.
48. Leigh Hunt, 'Theatrical Examiner No. 320, 26 April 1818', in *The Examiner, A Sunday Paper: Issues 523-574* (London: John Hunt, 1818), 268.
49. Hazlitt, *English Stage*, 72.
50. *Ibid.*, 72-3.
51. Jones, *Memoirs*, 40.
52. *Ibid.*, 78.
53. *Ibid.*, 47.
54. *Ibid.*, 49.
55. James Boaden, *Memoirs of John Philip Kemble*, 2 vols (London: Longman, 1825), 2:556-7.
56. Pollock, *Macready*, 29.
57. See entries for 23 December 1814 and 4 March 1815 in Eluned Brown, ed., *The London Theatre 1811–1866: Selections from the Diary of Henry Crabb Robinson* (London: The Society for Theatre Research, 1966), 59, 62.
58. 23 December 1814, in *ibid.*, 60.
59. 22 June 1818, in *ibid.*, 85.
60. See 3 December 1834, 23 October 1848 and 8 July 1857 in *ibid.*, 145, 186, 203.
61. *Macready's Reminiscences*, 1:174, and see 423.
62. Boaden, *Kemble*, 2:556.
63. Oxberry, *Dramatic Biography*, 1:201.
64. Jones, *Memoirs*, 33.

65. 'Timothy Crusty', 'Desultory Reminiscences', 56.
66. Dr Samuel Johnson, *Dictionary of the English Language*, 8th ed., 2 vols (London: J.F. and C. Rivington, et al., 1786), 1: sub 'GENIUS'.
67. 'Timothy Crusty', 'Desultory Reminiscences', 52.
68. *Ibid.*, 56.
69. *Ibid.*, 57.
70. *Loc. cit.*
71. Oxberry, *Dramatic Biography*, 1:202.
72. *Ibid.*, 1:198.
73. *Loc. cit.*
74. See *The Letters of Percy Bysshe Shelley*, ed. F.L. Jones, 2 vols (Oxford: Clarendon Press, 1964), 2:102.
75. See Jacqueline Mulhallen, *The Theatre of Shelley* (Cambridge: Open Book Publishers, 2010), 98; *The Letters of Mary Wollstonecraft Shelley*, ed. Betty T. Bennett, 3 vols (Baltimore and London: Johns Hopkins University Press, 1980–1988), 1:127.
76. *Bell's Life in Sydney and Sporting Reviewer*, NSW, Saturday, 17 November 1855, 1.
77. *Boston Post Supplement*, Monday, 18 November 1872, 5.

Chapter Twelve: Better than the Men: The Uses and Abuses of Women's Strength, Speed, Skill and Endurance in the Long Eighteenth Century

1. An earlier version of this paper was presented at a Women's Studies Group seminar, January 2013. I have also discussed this topic in 'Women as athletes in Early Modern Britain', *Early Modern Women: an Interdisciplinary Journal* 10, 2 (2016), 42-64.
2. The *Kentish Gazette*, 18-22 May 1776; the *Kentish Gazette*, 28 June-2 July 1783, the *Kentish Gazette*, 24 May 1796.
3. The *Reading Mercury and Oxford Gazette*, 27 June 1774; the *Reading Mercury and Oxford Gazette*, 11 July 1774; the *Reading Mercury and Oxford Gazette*, 20 June 1796.
4. The original handbill is in the author's collection and is included in the plates section of this book.
5. W. Hylton Dyer Longstaffe, *The History and Antiquities of the Parish of Darlington in the Bishoprick* (London: J. Henry Parker, 1854), 310.
6. The *Kentish Gazette*, 2-6 July 1768; 6-9 July 1768; 9-13 July 1768.
7. *Ibid.*, 23-27 July 1768.
8. *Ibid.*, 2-6 July 1768.

9. *Ibid.*, 16-20 July 1768; 20-23 July 1768; 23-27 July 1768; 27-30 July 1768.
10. *Mist's Weekly Journal*, 23 October 1725.
11. *Ipswich Journal*, 16 July 1726.
12. *Read's Weekly Journal, or British Gazetteer*, 2 August 1735.
13. The *Sussex Weekly Advertiser, or Lewes Journal*, 6 September 1762.
14. The *Edinburgh Evening Courant*, 12 June 1786.
15. Oliver Heywood, *The Rev. Oliver Heywood, B.A. 1630–1702; His Autobiography, Diaries, Anecdote and Event Books*, 3 vols (Brighouse: A.B. Bayes, 1881), 2:284.
16. The *Kentish Gazette*, Friday, 5 August 1791.
17. The *Kentish Gazette*, 25-28 July 1772.
18. *Drewry's Derby Mercury*, 3 July 1772.
19. Oliver Goldsmith, *The Vicar of Wakefield*, 3rd ed., 2 vols (London: F. Newbery, 1766), 1:95. On interactions of class and gender, see Betty Rizzo, 'Equivocations of Gender and Rank: Eighteenth-Century Sporting Women', *Eighteenth-Century Life*, 26, 1, 70-93.
20. This system of racing was based on the Articles for the *Newmarket Town Plate* of 1664. See *Articles ordered by his Majestie to be observed by all persons that put in horses to run for the Plate, the new Round-heate at Newmarkett, set out the [Thu] 16th day of October [1664], in the 17th year of our Soveraign Lord King Charles II. Which Plate is to be rid for yearly, the seconde Thursday in October, for ever*, in J.P. Hore, *The History of Newmarket: and the Annals of the Turf: with Memoirs and Biographical Notices of the Habitués of Newmarket, and the Notable Turfites, from the Earliest Times to the End of the Seventeenth Century*, 3 vols (London: A.H. Baily & Co., 1886), 2:246-9.
21. The *Ipswich Journal*, 25 July 1795; *The Sporting Magazine; or Monthly Calendar, of Transactions of the Turf, the Chase, And every other Diversion interesting to the Man of Pleasure, Enterprize, and Spirit*, 18 (August 1801), 247.
22. *Purchasing Power of British Pounds from 1270 to Present, Measuring Worth, 2018.* <https://www.measuringworth.com/ppoweruk/> (accessed April 2018).
23. Andrew Huxtable, ed., *A Statistical History of UK Track and Field Athletics* (London; National Union of Track and Field Statisticians, 1990), 52. Eric L. Cowe, *Early Women's Athletics: Statistics and History*, Vol. 1 (Keighley, W. Yorks: Eric L. Cowe, 1999).
24. P.F. Radford and A.J. Ward-Smith, 'British Running Performances in the Eighteenth Century', *Journal of Sports Sciences*, 21 (2003), 429-38.
25. For stoolball, see David Block, *Baseball before we knew it: A Search for the Roots of the Game* (Lincoln and London: University of Nebraska Press, 2005), 111-9. For football, see Auslan Cramb, 'Church records reveal women's football in

1628', the *Telegraph*, 4 October 2003. For the other pastimes mentioned, see Peter Radford, 'Women as Athletes in Early Modern Britain'.

26. In January 2014, at the invitation of the Women's Studies Group, I was able to be part of their panel at the British Society for Eighteenth-Century Studies Conference at Oxford. The theme was 'Women and Power Play', and I was able to turn my attention to the question of just how good some eighteenth-century sportswomen were. For an extended version of this paper, see Peter Radford, 'Was the Long Eighteenth Century a Golden Age for Women in Sport? The Cases of Mme Bunel and Alicia Thornton', *Early Modern Women: An Interdisciplinary Journal*, 12 (2017), 183-94.
27. Anon., *Cricket. An Heroic Poem: Illustrated with Critical Observations of Scriblerus Maximus* (London: W. Bickerton, [1744]), 2, 14. (The book was mentioned in the 'New Books' section of the *Scots Magazine* for July 1744, published 1 July 1744, 348.) A later edition appears as James Love, *Cricket. An Heroic Poem: Illustrated with Critical Observations of Scriblerus Maximus* (London: Printed for the Author, 1770).
28. *Ibid.*, 11, 12.
29. H.T. Waghorn, *The Dawn of Cricket* (London: The Marylebone Cricket Club, 1906), 14-15.
30. *St James's Evening Post*, 8-10 August 1745; *Penny London Post or Morning Advertiser*, 9-12 August 1745; the *Derby Mercury*, 9-16 August 1745.
31. *London Evening Post*, 8-10 August 1745; the *Newcastle Courant*, 10-17 August 1745.
32. *Jackson's Oxford Journal*, Saturday, 27 February 1768; the *Caledonian Mercury*, 2 March 1768.
33. The *Hull Packet*, Tuesday, 27 August 1805.
34. The *Caledonian Mercury*, Saturday, 12 March 1768.
35. The *Gazetteer and New Daily Advertiser*, 14 March 1767.
36. *The Sporting Magazine*, 24 September 1804, 228-9, 284.
37. The *Manchester Mercury and Harrop's General Advertiser*, 23 June 1767. All quotations referring to the 1767 competition are taken from this source.
38. Patricia Baines, *Spinning Wheels, Spinners & Spinning* (London: Batsford Limited, 1977), 54. This stick was sometimes called a wheel boy, a wheel dolly or a wheel finger.
39. John Styles, Research Professor in History, University of Hertfordshire, Honorary Senior Research Fellow, Victoria and Albert Museum (personal communication, 29 November 2016).
40. The *Leeds Intelligencer*, 9 August 1785.
41. Baines, *Spinning Wheels, Spinners & Spinning*, 61.
42. Colonel [William] Fullarton, *General View of the Agriculture of Ayr, with Observations on the Means of Its Improvement* (Edinburgh: John Paterson, 1793), 78.

43. The *Edinburgh Advertiser*, 29 October 1817.
44. *The Globe*, 11 December 1815.
45. *Annals of Sporting*, 4 (1823): 123, 207, 277; *Morning Advertiser*, 27 August 1823.
46. *Annals of Sporting*, 10 (1826): 305, 306; 11 (1827): 45, 49; *Bell's Life in London and Sporting Chronicle*, 20 May 1827; The *London Packet*, 5-7 November 1827.
47. *Annals of Sporting*, 10 (1826): 306.
48. *Annals of Sporting*, 11 (1827): 49.
49. *The Patriot, or Carlisle and Cumberland Advertiser*, 29 November 1817.
50. The *London Packet*, 21 August 1833.
51. Robert Bald, *A General View of the Coal Trade of Scotland, Chiefly that of the River Forth and Mid-Lothian. To Which is Added, an Inquiry into the Condition of the Women Who Carry Coals Under Ground in Scotland, Known by the Name of Bearers* (Edinburgh: Oliphant, Waugh, and Innes, 1812), 135-6.
52. *Ibid.*, 132.
53. *Ibid.*, 134, 135.
54. See Risca, South Wales, Commissioners for Inquiring into the Employment and Condition of Children in Mines and Manufactories. *First Report of the Commissioners. Mines* (London: Her Majesty's Stationery Office, 1842), 102.
55. See Susan Greaney, 'Going Underground; the Secrets of Neolithic Mining', *Current Archaeology*, no. 327 (May 2017), 50-3.
56. *First Report*, 90-1.
57. Peter McNeill, *Tranent and its Surroundings: Historical, Ecclesiastical & Traditional*, 2nd ed. (Edinburgh: John Menzies and Company, 1884), 31.
58. *First Report*, 93-4.
59. See McNeill, *Tranent and its Surroundings*, 34-5.
60. *First Report*, 93.
61. McNeill, *Tranent and its Surroundings*, 31.
62. See, e.g., R.H. Horne, 'Children's Employment Commission', *The Illuminated Magazine*, 1 (May 1843), 45-53.
63. *First Report*, 91-2.
64. *Ibid.*, 92.
65. *Loc. cit.*
66. *Loc. cit.*
67. *Ibid.*, 91.
68. R.H. Horne, 'Children's Employment Commission', 46.
69. *Ibid.*, 45.
70. *Loc. cit.*

71. Dr Alexander Carlyle, 'The Parish of Inveresk', in Sir John Sinclair, *The Statistical Account of Scotland*, 21 vols (Edinburgh: William Creech, 1791–1799), 16 (1795):19, 17.
72. *Ibid.*, 16:18, note.
73. *Ibid.*, 16:19.

Chapter Thirteen: 'Merely butterflies of a season'? The Halls, Ideology and Control in the Early Nineteenth-Century Annuals

1. [S.C. Hall], preface to *The Amulet. A Christian and Literary Remembrancer*, ed. S.C. Hall (London: Frederick Westley and A.H. Davis, 1832), iii.
2. [S.C. Hall], preface to *The Amulet; or, Christian and Literary Remembrancer*, ed. S.C. Hall (London: W. Baynes & Son, 1826), vi-vii.
3. *Ibid.*, vii.
4. Anne Renier, *Friendship's Offering: An Essay on the Annuals and Gift Books of the Nineteenth Century* (London: Private Libraries Association, 1964), 7.
5. S.C. Hall, *Retrospect of a Long Life from 1815 to 1883*, 2 vols (London: Bentley & Son, 1883), 1:309. Worth £16,080 at today's values. *Purchasing Power of British Pounds from 1270 to Present, Measuring Worth, 2018.* <https://www.measuringworth.com/ppoweruk> (Accessed May, 2018).
6. William Makepeace Thackeray, *The History of Pendennis* (London: Smith, Elder & Co., 1898), Chapter 31, 307.
7. Katherine D. Harris, *Forget Me Not: The Rise of the British Literary Annual, 1823–1835* (Athens: Ohio University Press, 2015), 251.
8. Barbara Onslow, *Women of the Press in Nineteenth-Century Britain* (Basingstoke: Macmillan, 2000), 18.
9. C.J. Hamilton, *Notable Irishwomen* (Dublin: Sealy, Bryers & Walker [1900]), 129.
10. Kathryn Ledbetter, *Victorian Periodicals: Commodities in Context* (Abingdon: Routledge, 2007), 14.
11. George Eliot, *Middlemarch*, 2 vols (New York: The Century Co., 1910), 1:389.
12. *Ibid.*, 1:391.
13. Chas T. Tallent-Bateman, 'The "Forget-Me-Not"', *Papers of the Manchester Literary Club* (1902), 28:78-98, 97.
14. Letter to William Henry Brookfield, Somersby, 3 August [1831] in *The Letters of Alfred Lord Tennyson*, eds Cecil Y. Land and Edgar F. Shannon, Jr, 3 vols (Cambridge, MA: Harvard University Press, 1981–1990), 1:63.
15. Letter to Allan Cunningham, Keswick, 21 December 1828 in *The Life and Correspondence of Robert Southey*, ed. the Rev. Charles Cuthbert Southey, 6 vols (London: Longman, Brown, Green & Longmans, 1849–1850), 5:339.

16. Letter to Bernard Barton, Holborn, 30 August 1830 in *The Works of Charles Lamb*, ed. Sir Thomas Noon Talfourd, 5 vols (New York: A.C. Armstrong and Son, 1886), 2:314.
17. *The Spirit and Manners of the Age* [ed. S.C. Hall] (London: Frederick Westley and A.H. Davis, 1826), 1 [January to June]:[iii].
18. *Ibid.*, preface, [v].
19. *The Spirit and Manners of the Age* [ed. S.C. Hall] (London: Frederick Westley & A.H. Davis, 1826), 2 [July to December]:[iii].
20. Elizabeth Eger and Lucy Pelz, *Brilliant Women: 18th-Century Bluestockings* (London: National Portrait Gallery Publications, 2008), 115. See, e.g., her letter to Sir W.W. Pepys, Barley Wood, 23 December 1820 in William Roberts, ed., *Memoirs of the Life and Correspondence of Mrs Hannah More*, 3rd ed., 4 vols (London: R.B. Seeley and W. Burnside, 1835), 4:159-60.
21. [S.C. Hall], preface to *The Spirit and Manners of the Age* (1826), 2:v.
22. See *The Spirit and Manners of the Age* (1829), 35-41, 119-23, 180-3.
23. *The Spirit and Manners of the Age* (1826), 2:78-9, 79.
24. See Seamus Deane, *A Short History of Irish Literature* (London: Hutchinson, 1986), 95-6.
25. Joep Leerssen, *Critical Conditions: Field Day Essays & Monographs. Remembrance and Imagination: Patterns in the Historical and Literary Representation of Ireland in the Nineteenth Century* (Cork: Cork University Press, 1996), 170.
26. Mr and Mrs S.C. Hall, *A Week at Killarney* (London: J.S. Virtue, 1858), [1].
27. Terry Eagleton, *Heathcliff and the Great Hunger: Studies in Irish Culture* (London: Verso, 1996), 127.
28. S.C. Hall, *Retrospect of a Long Life*, 2:484.
29. William Makepeace Thackeray, *The Irish Sketch Book of 1842* (New York: Charles Scribner's Sons, 1911), 7.
30. Mrs S.C. Hall, 'Luke O'Brian', *The Iris: A Literary and Religious Offering*, ed. the Revd Thomas Dale (London: Sampson Low; Hurst, Chance & Co., 1830), 112-125, 123.
31. Thomas Pringle, 'The Slave Dealer', *ibid.*, 129-31, 129.
32. 'M.G.T', 'The Convert of the Harem', *The Iris* (London: Sampson Low; Hurst, Chance & Co., 1831), 133-40, 140.
33. *Ibid.*, 134.
34. *Ibid.*, 139, 140.
35. Mrs S.C. Hall, 'The Curse of Property. A Sketch of Irish Mismanagement', *ibid.*, 225-65, 226, 265.
36. Joseph Lennon, *Irish Orientalism: A Literary and Intellectual History* (Syracuse NY: Syracuse University Press, 2004), 142.

37. See [William Makepeace Thackeray], 'A Word on the Annuals', *Fraser's Magazine for Town and Country* [ed. William Maginn, alias 'Oliver Yorke'], 16 (July to December 1837), 759. See also 'My Turkish Visit', *The Keepsake for 1838* [ed. Frederick Mansell Reynolds], (London: Longman, Orme, Brown, Green and Longmans, 1837), 23-44.
38. Anon., 'The African', *Friendship's Offering: A Literary Album, and Christmas and New Year's Present* [ed. Thomas Pringle], (London: Smith, Elder and Co., 1830), 177-80, 179.
39. *Ibid.*, 97-8, 98.
40. Mrs S.C. Hall, 'Larry Moore. An Irish Sketch', *ibid.*, 299-309, 299.
41. *Ibid.*, 308.
42. *Ibid.*, 307.
43. *Ibid.*, 299.
44. Marion Durnin, introduction to Mrs S.C. Hall, *Sketches of Irish Character*, ed. Marion Durnin (London and New York: Routledge, 2016), xvi.
45. Mary Jean Corbett, *Allegories of Union in Irish and English Writing, 1790–1870: Politics, History, and the Family from Edgeworth to Arnold* (Cambridge: Cambridge University Press, 2000), 16.
46. Mrs S.C. Hall, 'Annie Leslie', *The Amulet; A Christian and Literary Remembrancer*, ed. S.C. Hall (London: Frederick Westley and A.H. Davis, 1830) 103-44, 111.
47. Mrs S.C. Hall, 'The Mosspits', *The Amulet* (1832), 91-146, 105.
48. Lynne Vallone, *Becoming Victoria* (New Haven, CT: Yale University Press, 2001), 97.
49. *The Amulet* (1832), 212-50, 212.
50. *Ibid.*, 229.
51. Mrs S.C. Hall, introduction to Mrs S.C. Hall, *Sketches of Irish Character*, 3rd ed. (London: How and Parsons, 1842), [v]; *The Amulet* (1832), 229.
52. *The Amulet* (1832), 232.
53. Mrs S.C. Hall, introduction to *Sketches of Irish Character (*1842), [v].
54. *Ibid.*, [v], vi.
55. Mr and Mrs S.C. Hall, *Ireland: its Scenery, Character, &c.*, 3 vols (London: How and Parsons, 1841–43), 2:161.
56. S.C. Hall, *Retrospect of a Long Life*, 1:306.
57. See *ibid.*, 1:307. *Purchasing Power of British Pounds from 1270 to Present, Measuring Worth, 2018.* <https://www.measuringworth.com/ppoweruk> (accessed April 2018). For further details of production costs and income, see Katherine Harris, *Forget Me Not*, 188-93.
58. S.C. Hall, *Retrospect of a Long Life*, 1:310, 311.

Conclusion: *Queens of Literature*: Royals, Role Models and the Construction of Women's History

My sincere thanks to Carolyn D. Williams for sharing her expertise and additional material on Lady Jane Grey.

1. Eva Hope, *Queens of Literature of the Victorian Era* (London: Walter Scott, 1886), 1, 259. Born Mary Anne Hearn, Hope also published religious works under the name of Marianne Farningham.
2. *The Angel in the House* (1854) is a narrative poem by Coventry Patmore (1823–96), which idealized women as paragons of domesticity.
3. For a select bibliography of works dealing exclusively or substantially with women, see *The Oxford Guide to British Women Writers*, ed. Joanne Shattock (Oxford: Oxford University Press, 1993), 483-4.
4. Alison Chapman, 'Achieving fame and canonicity', in *The Cambridge Companion to Victorian Women's Writing*, ed. Linda H. Peterson (Cambridge: Cambridge University Press, 2015), 73-86, 80.
5. Queen Victoria's journals are available online at <http://www.queenvictoriasjournals.org> (accessed May 2018).
6. *Leaves from the Journal of our life in the Highlands, from 1848–1861*, ed. Arthur Helps (London: Smith, Elder and Co., 1868), vi, vii.
7. *Ibid.*, x.
8. See Introduction, Michael Dobson and Nicola J. Watson, *England's Elizabeth: An Afterlife in Fame and Fantasy* (Oxford: Oxford University Press, 2002), 1-31, 4.
9. *Notes of Ben Jonson's Conversations with William Drummond of Hawthornden* (London: Printed for the Shakespeare Society, 1842), 23.
10. See 'Scandal', in Dobson and Watson, *England's Elizabeth*, 79-83.
11. See Carolyn D. William's introduction to this volume for valuable context on the reproductive capacity of queens in this period and the role of women in maintaining the succession.
12. Agnes Strickland, *Lives of the Queens of England, from the Norman Conquest*, 12 vols (London: Henry Colburn, 1840–8), 12:120, 119.
13. *Ibid.*, 12:120.
14. Douglas Jerrold, 'Elizabeth and Victoria', *The Illuminated Magazine*, 1 (May 1843), 3-8, 8.
15. See *Elizabeth I Collected Works*, eds Leah S. Marcus, Janel Mueller and Mary Beth Rose (Chicago: The University of Chicago Press, 2000), xii-xiii.
16. *Ibid.*, 133-4.
17. George Puttenham, *The Arte of English Poesie* (London: Richard Field, 1589), 207.
18. *Ibid.*, 206.

19. 'Queen Elizabeth' in Alexander Dyce, *Specimens of British Poetesses* (London: T. Rodd and S. Prowett, 1825), 15-23, 15.
20. *Ibid.*, iv.
21. Letter 513 to Alexander Dyce, Rydal Mount, Kendal, 10 May 1830, *Letters of the Wordsworth Family from 1787 to 1855*, ed. William Knight, 3 vols (Boston: Ginn, 1907), 2:427.
22. See 'Anne, Countess of Winchelsea [*sic*]', in *Specimens*, 134-46.
23. *Ibid.*, 18.
24. George Bethune, *The British Female Poets* (Philadelphia: Lindsay & Blakiston, 1848), 20.
25. *Ibid.*, 22.
26. Mrs Jameson, *Memoirs of Celebrated Female Sovereigns*, 2 vols (London: Henry Colburn, 1831), 1: 305, 306.
27. Marcus et al., eds, *Elizabeth I*, xii.
28. Speech 3, Version 2. 1559. 'Her answer to [the Commons'] petition that she marry' in *ibid.*, 58-60, 59.
29. Jameson, *Celebrated Female Sovereigns*, 322, 319.
30. Preface, H.G. Adams, ed., *A Cyclopaedia of Female Biography, consisting of sketches of all women who have been distinguished by great talents, strength of character, piety, benevolence, or moral virtue of any kind, forming a complete record of womanly excellence or ability* (Glasgow: Robert Forrester, 1866), iii. *Female Biography* is a heavily-edited version of Sarah Josepha Hale, *Woman's Record: or, Sketches of all Distinguished Women* (New York: Harper & Brothers, 1853).
31. Adams, *Female Biography*, 753.
32. *Ibid.*, 755, 757.
33. *Ibid.*, 378; Hope, *Queens of Literature*, 259.
34. Adams, *Female Biography*, 346.
35. *Ibid.*, 347.
36. See Roger Ascham, *The Scholemaster* (London: John Daye, 1570), 11v-12r.
37. Adams, *Female Biography*, 347. Extracts from an early published version of the letter are included in Chapter 1.
38. David Hume, *The History of England, from the Invasion of Julius Caesar to the Revolution in 1688*, 8 vols (London: A. Millar, 1763), 4:420. Michelangelo Florio calls the document a '*Lettera … scritta nel fine d'un suo testamento nuovo Greco*' ('Letter … written at the end of her Greek New Testament'), where *Greco* agrees with the masculine *testamento*; if he had thought the letter was in Greek the word would have been *Greca*. See *Historia de la vita e de la morte de l'Illustrissima Signora Giovanna Graia* ([Middelburg]:

Richardo Pittore, 1607), 117. I am grateful to Carolyn D. Williams for providing this material.

39. Adams, *Female Biography*, 347.
40. *Religious Magazine: Or, Spirit of the Foreign Theological Journals*, March 1829, 193. This is an accurate reflection of an early account given in Florio, *Historia de la vita*, 135.
41. Nicholas Harris Nicolas, *The Literary Remains of Lady Jane Grey: With a Memoir of Her Life* (London: Harding, Triphook and Lepard, 1825), Preface, xcv.
42. Jane Austen, *Juvenilia*, ed. Peter Sabor (Cambridge: Cambridge University Press, 2006), 182-3.
43. Letter 155 to Fanny Knight, 23 March 1817, *Jane Austen's Letters*, ed. Deirdre Le Faye (Oxford: Oxford University Press, 2011), 350.
44. Adams, *Female Biography*, 268.
45. *Ibid.*,108.
46. See *Female Biography; or, Memoirs of Illustrious and Celebrated Women, of all Ages and Countries* (London: R. Phillips, 1803) and *Memoirs of Queens* (London: Allman, 1821).
47. Eva Hope, *Queens of Literature*, 3.
48. Mrs Jameson, *Characteristics of Woman*, 2 vols (London: Saunders and Otley, 1832), 1:xvii.

Further Reading

Databases and Online Resources

Early English Books Online (EEBO) <http://eebo.chadwyck.com>
Eighteenth-century Collections (ECCO) <https://www.gale.com/uk>
'Purchasing Power of British Pounds from 1270 to Present Measuring Worth' <https://www.measuringworth.com/ppoweruk>
Queen Victoria's Journals <http://www.queenvictoriasjournals.org>
'The *Gentleman's Magazine*, 1731–1907' <onlinebooks.library.upenn.edu/webbin/serial?id+gentlemans>
The Oxford Dictionary of National Biography < http://www.oxforddnb.com>

Preface

Louise Duckling, Angela Escott, Daniel J.R. Grey, Victoria Joule, Sarah Oliver and Carolyn D. Williams, eds, *Women's Writing* Special Issue 'Women Out Loud', 17.1 (2010)
Carolyn D. Williams, Angela Escott and Louise Duckling, eds, *Woman to Woman: Female Negotiations During the Long Eighteenth Century* (Newark: University of Delaware Press, 2010)

Chapter One: Michelangelo Florio and Lady Jane Grey: A Case Study of a Book Dedication to a Royal Tudor Lady

de Lisle, Leanda, *The Sisters who would be Queen: The Tragedy of Mary, Katherine & Lady Jane Grey* (London: HarperPress, 2009)
Hull, Suzanne W., *Chaste, Silent & Obedient: English Books for Women, 1475–1640* (San Marino: Huntington Library, 1982)
Ives, Eric, *Lady Jane Grey: A Tudor Mystery* (Oxford: Wiley-Blackwell, 2011)
Schutte, Valerie, *Mary I and the Art of Book Dedications: Royal Women, Power, and Persuasion* (New York: Palgrave Macmillan, 2015)

Chapter Two: '*The* Wine *much better then the* Bush': Thomas Lodge's Address to the Reader in *The Countesse of Lincolnes Nurserie*

Brown, Silvia, ed., *Women's Writing in Stuart England: The Mothers' Legacies of Dorothy Leigh, Elizabeth Joscelin and Elizabeth Richardson* (Stroud: Sutton Publishing, 1999)

Clinton, Elizabeth, 'The Countesse of Lincolnes Nurserie' in *Flesh and Spirit: An Anthology of Seventeenth-century Women's Writing*, ed. by Rachel Adcock, Sara Read and Anna Ziomek (Manchester: Manchester University Press, 2014)

Tenney, Edward Andrews, *Thomas Lodge* (Ithaca: Cornell University Press, 1935)

Chapter Three: God-Given Pleasure: Aphrodisiacs, Fertility and Sexual Pleasure in Early Modern England

Crawford, Patricia, *Blood, Bodies and Families in Early Modern England* (Abingdon: Routledge, 2014)

Evans, Jennifer, *Aphrodisiacs, Fertility and Medicine in Early Modern England* (Woodbridge: The Boydell Press, 2014)

Fairchilds, Cissie C., *Women in Early Modern Europe, 1500–1700* (Harlow: Pearson Longman, 2007)

Macfarlane, Alan, *Marriage and Love in England: Modes of Reproduction, 1300–1840* (Oxford: Basil Blackwell, 1986)

Chapter Four: Tweaking the Biography of Anne Finch

Backscheider, Paula R., *Eighteenth-Century Women Poets and Their Poetry: Inventing Agency, Inventing Genre* (Baltimore: The Johns Hopkins University Press, 2005)

Finch, Anne, *The Poems of Anne Countess of Winchilsea from the original edition of 1713 and from unpublished manuscripts*, ed. Myra Reynolds (Chicago: The University of Chicago Press, 1903).

Kennedy, Deborah, *Poetic Sisters: Early Eighteenth-Century Women Poets* (Lewisburg: Bucknell University Press, 2013)

McGovern, Barbara and Charles H. Hinnant, *The Anne Finch Wellesley Manuscript Poems: A Critical Edition* (Athens and London: The University of Georgia Press, 1998)

Staves, Susan, *A Literary History of Women's Writing in Britain, 1660–1789* (Cambridge: Cambridge University Press, 2006)

Chapter Five: 'For ever shaded by oblivion's veil': Obituarizing Women in the Eighteenth-Century *Gentleman's Magazine*

Barker, Hannah and Chalus, Elaine, eds, *Gender in Eighteenth-Century England: Roles, Representations and Responsibilities* (Harlow: Longman, 1997)

Batchelor, Jennie and Powell, Manushag, eds, *Women's Periodicals and Print Culture in Britain, 1690–1820s: The Long Eighteenth Century* (Edinburgh: Edinburgh University Press, 2018)

Gleadle, Kathryn, *Borderline Citizens: Women, Gender, and Political Culture in Britain, 1815–67* (Oxford: Oxford University Press, 2009)

Hill, Bridget, *Women, Work, and Sexual Politics in Eighteenth-Century England* (Oxford: Basil Blackwell, 1989)

Chapter Six: Female Radicals in Bristol: The Three Marys and Mary Wollstonecraft's 'The Cave of Fancy'

Dresser, Madge, ed., *Women and the City: Bristol 1373–2000* (Bristol: Redcliffe Press, 2016)

Duffus, Jane, *The Women Who Built Bristol 1184–2018* (Bristol: Tangent Press, 2018)

Hays, Mary, *The Victim of Prejudice*, ed. Eleanor Ty (Peterborough: Broadview Press, 1998)

Mulvey-Roberts, Marie, ed. *Literary Bristol* (Bristol: Redcliffe Press, 2015)

______ and Mizuta, Tamae, eds, *The Radicals: Revolutionary Women* (London and Bristol: Routledge/Thoemmes Press, 1994)

Polewhele [*sic*], Richard, *The Unsex'd Females* (New York: Wm. Cobbett, 1800)

Robinson, Mary, *Memoirs of the Late Mrs Robinson, Written by Herself*, 2 vols (London: Richard Phillips, 1803)

Todd, Janet, *Mary Wollstonecraft: A Revolutionary Life* (London: Weidenfeld & Nicolson, 2000)

Walker, Gina Luria, ed., *The Idea of Being Free: A Mary Hays Reader* (Peterborough: Broadview Press, 2006)

Chapter Seven: A Quest for Female Sexual Agency in the Eighteenth-Century Novel

Clark, Anna, *Women's Silence, Men's Violence: Sexual Assault in England 1770–1845* (London and New York: Pandora, 1987)

Hays, Mary, *The Memoirs of Emma Courtney*, 2 vols (London: G.G. and J. Robinson, 1796)

______, *The Victim of Prejudice*, 2 vols (London: J. Johnson, 1799)

Walker, Gina Luria, *Mary Hays (1759–1843): The Growth of a Woman's Mind* (Aldershot: Ashgate, 2006)

Wollstonecraft, Mary, *A Vindication of the Rights of Woman* (London: J. Johnson, 1792)

______, *Maria: or, The Wrongs of Woman. A Posthumous Fragment* (Philadelphia: James Carey, 1799)

Chapter Eight: Scold, Punish, Pity or Seduce? The Confused Rhetoric of *Advice to Unmarried Women* (1791)

Anon., *Advice to Unmarried Women: To Recover and Reclaim the Fallen; and to Prevent the Fall of Others, into the Snares and Consequences of Seduction* (London: J.F. and C. Rivington, 1791)

Gregory, John, *A Father's Legacy to his Daughters*, 2nd ed. (London: W. Strahan, T. Cadell; Edinburgh: W. Creech, 1774)

Madan, Martin, *Thelyphthora; or, A Treatise on Female Ruin, in its Causes, Effects, Consequences, Prevention, and Remedy; Considered on the Basis of the Divine Law: Under the Following Heads, viz. Marriage, Whoredom, and Fornication, Adultery, Polygamy, Divorce; With Many Other Incidental Matters; Particularly Including An Examination of the Principles and Tendency of Stat. 26 Geo. II c. 33. Commonly Called the Marriage Act*, 2 vols (London: J. Dodsley, 1780)

Nussbaum, Felicity, *The Brink of All We Hate: English Satires on Women, 1660–1750* (Lexington: University of Kentucky Press, 1984)

Chapter Nine: Friendships: Commonalities across the Centuries

Julie Peakman, '"The best freind in the world": The Relationship between Emma Hamilton and Queen Maria Carolina of Naples', in *Woman to Woman: Female Negotiations During the Long Eighteenth Century*, eds Carolyn D. Williams, Angela Escott and Louise Duckling (Newark: University of Delaware Press, 2010), 173-89.

______, ed., *Whore Biographies 1700–1825*, 8 vols (London: Pickering & Chatto, 2006–2007), 6 (2007).

______, *Peg Plunkett: Memoirs of a Whore* (London: Quercus, 2015)

Chapter Ten: Rivalry, Camaraderie and the Prima Donnas: Elizabeth Billington & Gertrude Mara

Aspden, Suzanne, *The Rival Sirens: Performance and Identity on Handel's Operatic Stage* (Cambridge & New York: Cambridge University Press, 2013)

Nussbaum, Felicity, *Rival Queens, Actresses, Performance, and the Eighteenth-Century British Theater* (Philadelphia: University of Pennsylvania Press, 2010)

Potter, John & Sorrell, Neil, *A History of Singing* (Cambridge: Cambridge University Press, 2012)

Chapter Eleven: Eliza O'Neill and the Art of Acting

Jones, Charles Inigo, *Memoirs of Miss O'Neill* (London: D. Cox, 1816)

Mulhallen, Jacqueline, *The Theatre of Shelley* (Cambridge: Open Book Publishers, 2010)

Chapter Twelve: Better than the Men: The Uses and Abuses of Women's Strength, Speed, Skill and Endurance in the Long Eighteenth Century

Baines, Patricia, *Spinning Wheels, Spinners & Spinning* (London: Batsford Limited, 1977)

Bald, Robert, *A General View of the Coal Trade of Scotland, Chiefly that of the River Forth and Mid-Lothian. To Which is Added an Inquiry into the Condition of the Women Who Carry Coals Under Ground in Scotland, Known by the Name of Bearers* (Edinburgh: Oliphant, Waugh and Innes, 1812)

Horne, R.H., 'Children's Employment Commission. First Report of the Commissioners, on Mines', *The Illuminated Magazine*, Vol. 1, 1843

Radford, P.F., and Ward-Smith, A.J., 'British Running Performances in the Eighteenth Century', *Journal of Sports Sciences*, 21 (2003), 429-38

Radford, Peter, 'Was the Long Eighteenth Century a Golden Age for Women in Sport? The Cases of Mme Bunel and Alicia Thornton', *Early Modern Women: An Interdisciplinary Journal*, 12 (2017), 183-94

Chapter Thirteen: 'Merely butterflies of a season'? The Halls, Ideology and Control in the Early Nineteenth-Century Annuals

Hall, S.C., *Retrospect of a Long Life from 1815 to 1883*, 2 vols (London: Bentley & Son, 1883)

Hall, S.C., Mrs, *Sketches of Irish Character*, ed. Marion Durnin (London and New York: Routledge, 2016)

Harris, Katherine D., *Forget Me Not: The Rise of the British Literary Annual, 1823–1835* (Athens: Ohio University Press, 2015)

Ledbetter, Kathryn, *Victorian Periodicals: Commodities in Context* (Abingdon: Routledge, 2007)

Onslow, Barbara, *Women of the Press in Nineteenth-Century Britain* (Basingstoke: Macmillan, 2000)

Conclusion: *Queens of Literature*: Royals, Role Models and the Construction of Women's History

Austen, Jane, *Juvenilia*, ed. Peter Sabor (Cambridge: Cambridge University Press, 2006)

Dobson, Michael and Watson, Nicola J., *England's Elizabeth: An Afterlife in Fame and Fantasy* (Oxford: Oxford University Press, 2002)

Hale, Sarah Josepha, *Woman's Record: or, Sketches of all Distinguished Women* (New York: Harper & Brothers, 1853)

Hope, Eva, *Queens of Literature of the Victorian Era* (London: Walter Scott, 1886)

Marcus, Leah S., Mueller, Janel and Rose, Mary Beth, *Elizabeth I Collected Works* (Chicago: The University of Chicago Press, 2000)

Strickland, Agnes, *Lives of the Queens of England, from the Norman Conquest*, 12 vols (London: Henry Colburn, 1840–8)

Index

'Exploring the Lives of Women, 1558-1837' is an engaging and lively collection of original, thought-provoking essays. Its route from Lady Jane Grey's nine-day reign to Queen Victoria's accession provides ample opportunities to examine complex interactions between gender, rank, and power. Yet the book's scope extends far beyond queens: its female cast includes servants, aristocrats, literary women, opera singers, actresses, fallen women, athletes and mine workers.

The collection explores themes relating to female power and physical strength; infertility, motherhood, sexuality and exploitation; creativity and celebrity; marriage and female friendship. It draws upon a wide range of primary materials to explore diverse representations of women: illuminating accounts of real women's lives appear alongside fictional portrayals and ideological constructions of femininity. In exploring women's negotiations with patriarchal control, this book demonstrates how the lived experience of women did not always correspond to prescribed social and gendered norms, revealing the rich complexity of their lives.

This volume has been published to commemorate the 30th anniversary of the Women's Studies Group 1558-1837. The group was formed to promote research into any aspect of women's lives as experienced or depicted within this period. The depth, range and creativity of the essays in this book reflect the myriad interests of its members.

AUTHORS ON THE STAIRS AT HARRIS & HARRIS BOOKS

THURSDAY 26TH SEPTEMBER

6:30PM: DRINKS RECEPTION

7:00PM: EVENT START

TICKETS ARE FREE FROM THE BOOKSHOP

CONTACT: 01787 277267

ISBN: **9781526751393** | PAPERBACK | **224** PAGES | **£12.99**

Pen & Sword Books, 47 Church St, Barnsley, S70 2AS. Tel: **01226 734222**
Website: **www.pen-and-sword.co.uk** Email: **enquiries@pen-and-sword.co.uk**

EXPLORING THE LIVES OF WOMEN

1558–1837

LOUISE DUCKLING · SARA READ
FELICITY ROBERTS · CAROLYN D. WILLIAMS